OREGON STATE GRANGE

OREGON STATE GRANGE

SERVING COMMUNITIES FOR 150 YEARS

MARILYN REIHER

Oregon State Grange: Serving Communities for 150 Years

For more information, email m_reiher@comcast.net.

ISBN: 979-8-89109-230-3 (paperback)
ISBN: 979-8-89109-360-7 (hardcover)
ISBN: 979-8-89109-231-0 (ebook)

PREFACE

The author won 2nd prize in the 5-8-year age group in the Declamatory contest and recited her monologue during the 1948 State Session in Astoria. It was the first time she had seen a microphone or spoken to 300 adults.

For the 50th anniversary of the Oregon State Grange, State Lecturer Minnie Bond wrote and read an essay entitled "A Short History of the Oregon State Grange from 1873 to 1923." F. M. Gill also wrote and read a "History of the Legislative Work of the Grange." Both were published in the *Journal of Proceedings* of the 1923 State Session.

A 20+ page article was published in the October 6, 1948 issue of the *Oregon State Grange Bulletin* documenting the first Granges in Oregon, the first Session, and the State Grange's accomplishments in its first 75 years.

Surprisingly, that paper published only a two-column original article for the 100th anniversary.

For the 125th anniversary the State Grange published a pamphlet that listed state officers. In addition, ten pages described the organization's Education, Grange Women's Activities, Junior, Legislative, and Youth programs.

State President Susan Noah wanted a more comprehensive history for the organization's 150th anniversary. She handed me a copy of a book that had been written for another State Grange's 150th celebration. As I thumbed through it, the organization appeared random. The information on each of their State Masters left me asking, "But what did he do?" The words, "I can do better than that." slipped out of my mouth before I realized what I was agreeing to.

I spent a year and a half reading the *Proceedings* of the Oregon State Grange from its organizing session in 1873 through 2022. I made notes on the number of delegates, resolutions, and candidates as well when policy stands were taken, the first Rosebud Drill, and the first Ag Tour. I have 227 pages of typed notes that are easy to search.

I also consulted Oregon Historic Newspapers to see what print media reported on each Session. Ballotpedia identified what ballot measures were passed and when. I often read issues of the *Grange Bulletin* for background information on specific topics.

I was born into the Grange. I joined North Bayside Juvenile Grange #99 the week of my fifth birthday. I had already attended lots of Grange meetings. My Dad John Reiher, his parents, four brothers, and two sisters joined North Bayside #691 in 1928. Dad served as Master and Secretary. He was Master of Coos County Pomona #30 in 1949 when the Session was held in Coos Bay.

My Mother Hilda Reiher joined Pine Forest #632 in 1930 when she was a teacher in Bend. She loved Central Oregon, but her sinuses preferred the coast, so she moved back home, demited to North Bayside, and was elected Master. I was surprised to read that she was a delegate in 1934 before my parents were married. While Mother was State Juvenile Superintendent (now Junior Director) in the 1940s, she and I visited lots of Granges.

I joined North Bayside #691 in 1958. While I was at a high school football game, members elected me Lecturer. I loved planning programs for two meetings per month. Average attendance was 50. I resigned when I moved away to college. After that I lived out of state for 40 years but retained my membership.

When I retired, I moved back to Oregon and immediately had a circle of Grange friends. My calendar was filled with more activities and meetings than I had time to attend. I was happy to give back to the organization in exchange for the benefits I received as a young member. Knowing how to conduct a meeting, write minutes, and the basics of parliamentary procedure helped me throughout my education and careers.

I'm not a "real historian." However, I earned a Master's degree in Rhetoric and Public Address from Temple University in Philadelphia. We studied famous speeches, the times in which they were delivered, and their effects. Classes covered lots of history. My thesis was an analysis of a U. S. Senate debate on the proposed Hells Canyon Dam on the Snake River. I picked that topic because my dad was a public power advocate who followed the issue and reported on it at our kitchen table, and not as my advisor claimed because I wanted to write "hell" and "dam" in the same sentence. That Senate debate was a perfect subject because it was timed with some Senators presenting the affirmative side and others the negative with a real back and forth exchange. Often a Senator speaks against a bill on a Tuesday afternoon and another in favor of it on Thursday morning. Neither hears what the other said. My analysis showed that what I had been teaching students at the University of Puget Sound matched what the U. S. Senate practiced.

Since my professors in Philadelphia knew little about hydroelectric dams or why this issue was important to Oregonians, I spent weekends in libraries in Seattle, Portland, and Boise reading local newspapers on microfiche. I found relevant documents in university libraries. This research more than fifty years ago was great preparation for writing this book.

My hope is that current members gain an appreciation of the sacrifices made by those who preceded us. Nearly everyone has relatives who struggled to make a living working the land. Many joined the Grange to learn from each other, support the organization's causes, buy from a cooperative or a mutual insurance company. This book records some of the many policies, events, ideas, and contests that have been tried. Maybe some should be recycled.

Thanks to the current Oregon State Grange President Jay Sexton and the office staff for their interest, support, and suggestions. Any omissions and misinterpretations are mine alone.

CONTENTS

1. Introduction 1
2. Why Has the Oregon State Grange Survived 150 years? 5
3. Why Did the Grange Catch on So Quickly? 22
4. Organizing Session of the Oregon State Grange 27
    Daniel Clark 30
5. One Step Forward, Two Back 33
    William Cyrus 36
    A. R. Shipley 39
    R. P. Boise 44
    H. E. Hayes 47
    Jacob Voorhees 52
    William M. Hilleary 55
6. Two Steps Forward, One Back 58
    B. G. Leedy 61
    Austin T. Buxton 64
    Charles E. Spence 69
    George A. Palmiter 74
7. A Stumble Before Marching Forward 77
    C. C. Hulet 81
    M. C. Glover 84
    Ray W. Gill 86
    Morton Tompkins 93
8. Marching to Success 96
    Elmer McClure 101
    Allen P. Wheeler 107
    Ted Sims 113
    W. C. Harris 116

9. Staying in Step.. 119
Morton V. Wolverton.. 122
Wayne Johnson.. 125
Dale W. Morris 132
Edward L. Luttrell 134
10. Meeting Challenges of a New Century 136
Mike Stewart 140
John Fine.. 143
Phyllis Wilson 146
Larry Rea.. 153
Mark Noah 155
Susan Noah 157
Jay Sexton 162
11. State Sessions and Delegates 165
12. Deputies 233
13. Membership.. 238
14. Juvenile and Junior Granges 246
15. Youth.. 257
16. County Councils and Pomona Granges.. 266
17. Oregon State Grange Bulletin.. 273
18. Standing Committees 279
Legislative Committee 280
Grange Workers' Activities Committee.. 285
Agriculture Committee 293
Education Committee.. 296
Public Power, Utilities, Energy Committee.. 298
Deaf Awareness and Family Health Committee.. 299
Community Service Committee 301
Veterans Committee 304
19. Interim Committees 306
Oregon Agricultural College 306
20. Cooperatives and Affiliate Companies.. 310

Epilogue.. 319
Appendix: Subordinate/Community Granges.. 321
About the Author 359

INTRODUCTION

Summarizing 150 years in a few pages is a huge task. During that time the Oregon State Grange has achieved many successes. Most were not completed in a single year or even decade. A resolution was passed, a bill written, petitions circulated, citizens voted sometimes more than once, and finally the objective was achieved. Major achievements of the Oregon State Grange include:

- **Initiative and Referendum:** Passage established in 1902 the "Oregon System" that allows voters to propose legislation or repeal laws passed by the legislature.
- **Direct Election of U.S. Senators:** Fought for voters, not the legislature, to choose Oregon's Senators in 1904. Beginning in 1914, the 17th Amendment to the U. S. Constitution ensured that U.S. Senators are directly elected by popular vote.
- **Recall:** Secured passage of a law in 1908 that lets voters remove an elected official from office.
- **Water rights:** Got the Water Code Law passed in 1909 ensuring that surface water belongs to the people of Oregon.
- **Women's Suffrage:** Took the lead in giving Oregon women the right to vote in 1912, eight years before it was granted nationally.
- **Hydroelectric Power:** Ensured in 1932 that Oregon could develop and distribute energy at low cost.

- **Sales tax:** Led defeat of this regressive tax nine times: 1933, 1934, 1936, 1944, 1947, 1969, 1985, 1986, and 1993.
- **Newborn Hearing Screening:** Got the law passed and signed by the Governor in 2000 that makes testing mandatory.
- **Grange Cooperatives:** Sold gasoline, supplies, and equipment at 35 local stores; insured members for fire, life, health, and auto; shared profits as dividends from 1885 to 2003.
- **20,000 to 30,000 Members:** Influenced the legislature between 1931 and 2000 due to our membership size.

The next chapter asks, "Why has the Oregon State Grange survived 150 years?" when many other organizations have not.

Chapter 2 asks "Why has the Oregon State Grange survived 150 years?" Many other organizations have not. Ten possible reasons are given.

Chapters 3 through 10 are chronological, focusing on two or three decades each, recounting the ups and downs in membership, finances, and influence. Personal profiles of the twenty-eight Brothers and two Sisters who served as State Masters/Presidents are integrated.

Chapter 11 describes State Sessions: When and where were annual meetings held, how many delegates, resolutions, and candidates were there, who were the officers, guests, and what fun did they have.

Chapter 12 shares first-person stories of Deputies who traveled throughout the state to organize, reorganize, and reactivate Granges.

Chapter 13 reports membership statistics and the work of the State Membership Committee, which since 1968 has provided incentives and assistance.

Chapter 14 documents the history of Juvenile and Junior Granges. Between 1904 and 2009, 358 were organized in Oregon. Today 1+ Juniors are members of 41 Granges in 19 counties. Because Oregon's Session is in June, Juniors have held their own Session since 1931. Former Juniors fondly remember summer camp, contests, tours, and fun.

Chapter 15 discusses Youth programs including state youth officers, community service projects, contests, and fundraising to finance trips to regional conferences and the National Session.

Chapter 16 traces the transition from County Councils to Pomonas Granges and tells the story of 200 members attending quarterly meetings that started mid-morning and lasted until late evening.

Chapter 17 focuses on the *Oregon State Grange Bulletin* that has kept members informed since 1907. Three Editors served for 17 or more years, and an Advertising Manager paid the bills for 50 years.

Chapter 18 describes how Standing Committees have done their jobs: how the Legislative Committee achieved success in Oregon's Legislature; Grange Workers Activities has preserved traditional homemaking skills; the Agriculture Committee has told the story of agricultures' importance; the Education and Energy committees have kept members informed; Deaf Awareness and Family Health has helped those with hearing loss; Community Service has collected data on the local contributions of Community Granges; the Veterans committee has honored members who have served.

Chapter 19 gives examples of Interim Committees with details on the Oregon Agricultural College committee that first reported to delegates on their campus visit in 1880.

Chapter 20 discusses Cooperatives and Affiliate Companies that have engaged in buying and selling and insured members for fire, liability, auto, life, and health.

The Epilogue answers a question often asked, "What will happen to the Community Grange when a certain member is no longer with us?" Frequently, someone steps up to take that member's place. It may be a family member, another Grange member, or someone from the community who realizes what the community would miss if the Grange closed.

WHY HAS THE OREGON STATE GRANGE SURVIVED 150 YEARS?

The Order of Patrons of Husbandry was founded on December 4, 1867 in Washington, D. C. It is the oldest agricultural advocacy organization in the United States. Initially members had to be farmers, their wives, and children. Members met once or twice a month, not just to socialize, but to share what they had read or learned from their own experimentation on what crops to grow and how to grow them. They also discussed lowering freight rates, improving market roads, and cooperative buying and selling.

The Grange Declaration of Purposes states, "We propose meeting together, talking together, working together, and in general, acting together for our mutual protection and advancement. We shall constantly strive to secure harmony, good will, and brotherhood, and to make our Order perpetual."

OREGON STATE GRANGE

When a state had six Granges, a State Grange could be organized. A State Grange was composed of Masters of Subordinate Granges and their wives who were Matrons (Grange members).

According to the current National Grange Digest of Laws, a State Grange is a Delegate body composed of two classes of members, namely:

(A) Voting Members (Delegates) – Masters/Presidents or elected alternates, who represent active Community and Pomona Granges within the jurisdiction of the State Grange, have the right to vote at its Annual Meeting.
(B) Non-Voting Members - All Fourth Degree members in good standing of active Community Granges within the jurisdiction of the State Grange who have received the Sixth Degree shall be non-voting members of such State Grange.

1873 was not a good time to launch a new organization. The Panic of 1873 was called the Great Depression until 1929. It was caused by the over expansion of railroads. At that time railroads were the largest employer in the U. S. other than agriculture. A large infusion of cash from speculators led to the construction of miles of tracks, docks, and factories without the assurance of customers. Jay Cooke & Company, a Philadelphia bank with branches in New York and Washington, D. C., was unable to sell several million dollars' worth of Northern Pacific Railway bonds. On September 18, 1873, the firm declared bankruptcy. It was fortunate that Oregon Grange members were 3,000 miles away and did not know how serious this event was. The depression lasted until 1879. The unemployment rate ranged from 8% to 14%.

Despite the bad timing, the Oregon State Grange got off to a strong start. However, early successes were mixed with major setbacks. At its peak 377 Granges were active. Total membership reached 32,000. Today there are 163 Granges with a membership of 4,600.

THE DECLINE OF ORGANIZATIONS

In his book *Bowling Alone* published in 2000, Robert D. Putnam reported that membership organizations declined by 58% between 1975 and 2000.

They included civic, religious, veterans, labor, volunteer, and fraternal organizations. Putnam used bowling as an illustration. Although the number of people who bowled increased, the number of people who bowled in leagues decreased. If people bowled alone, they did not participate in the social interaction and civic discussions that usually occurred in a league environment.

This decline in fraternal and civic organizations membership continued into the 2000s.

- Lions Clubs International dropped 12% between 1983 and 2012.
- Elks Lodges lost 18% between 1979 and 2012.
- Shriners International declined 27% between 1979 and 2012.
- Masonic Lodges were down 39% between 1959 and 2012.
- Jaycees (United States Junior Chamber of Commerce) dropped 44% between 1979 and 2012,
- Rotary International took in new members but did not retain them. They averaged 44,000 new members per year but lost an average of 51,000.

THE DECLINE OF FARMERS AND FARM ORGANIZATIONS

According to Bruce Sorte and Mallory Rahe of the Oregon State University Extension Service, principal operators of Oregon's farms and ranches make up less than one percent of the total population of Oregon. However, if paid and unpaid workers on farms and ranches are included, the total is approximately four percent of Oregon's population.

Although fewer Grange members are farmers, many current members grew up on farms, are avid gardeners, and/or care where their food comes from. Nationwide, Granges are active in 1,500 communities with 140,000 members.

In his 2012 Master's Address, Mark Noah claimed that "One of the reasons Grange continues to withstand the effects of time is the multi-faceted nature of our organization. There are so many reasons to belong and participate that we get tongue-tied when we try to explain it all."

These are ten reasons.

#1 FAMILY ORGANIZATION

From 1873, meetings and activities involved the entire family. Initially sixteen-year-olds and later fourteen-year-olds had an equal voice and vote with their parents and grandparents. At the State Grange level, youth could be delegates. In fact, in 2017 six of the sixteen state youth officers were delegates.

While other family members were meeting, children aged five to fourteen had their own Grange. They held meetings, elected officers, and voted to determine their activities and projects. Today children who are that age can participate in the adult organization as 1+ members. They can serve as a pro tem officer, help with community service projects, fundraisers, Lecturer's programs, fair booths, and any other activities the Grange sponsors.

Providing activities for everyone in the family eliminates the need for a babysitter. But also, it means that when children are old enough to become members, they know what the organization is, how it functions, and its cultural values. They know the names of the offices and understand officers' duties. They probably know key provisions of the By-Laws and appreciate the ritual. In other words, they become "Grangers" much quicker than many new members.

Being a family organization also ensured that the next generation carried on the tradition. The National Grange recognizes families who can trace five or more generations of membership. Eleven Oregon families have documented their Grange history and been recognized by the National Grange as Legacy Families.

#2 AN EQUAL VOICE AND VOTE FOR WOMEN

Caroline Hall, Oliver Hudson Kelley's niece, told him "Your organization will never be permanent if you leave the women out." Other fraternal organizations put women in auxiliaries. At one lodge, the women's restroom near the meeting room was very small, but there were additional stalls for women in the basement.

The Grange played an important role in Oregon's approving women's suffrage in November 1912. Granges allowed suffragettes to use their halls as meeting places for organizing the movement. In 1899 the Oregon State Grange passed a resolution written by Grange member Abigail Scott Duniway, who is remembered as Oregon's Mother of Equal Suffrage.

Governor Oswald West asked Abigail Scott Duniway to write and sign Oregon's Equal Suffrage Proclamation in 1912.

In 1960 the State Grange Home Economics Chairman estimated that Home Economics Clubs throughout Oregon raised more than $60,000 a year for their Grange treasuries. That money was used to fund hall maintenance, pay insurance, subsidize community service projects, and send delegates to State Session.

In the Grange a woman can be elected to any office. Four offices can be held only by women: The graces Ceres, Pomona, and Flora and the Lady Assistant Steward. The first women Master in Oregon was Lydia Carter who served as Master of Tualatin #111 (now Frogpond) in 1878. She is believed to have been the first in the nation. In 1889 the Women's Work Committee surveyed 11 counties and found three lady Masters, 18 Secretaries, 7 Lecturers, 8 Chaplains, and 11 Treasurers.

It took a surprisingly long time for the Oregon State Grange and the National Grange to elect women leaders. Phyllis Wilson was the first woman to be elected Oregon State Grange Master in 2006. Betsy Huber of Pennsylvania was elected the first woman Master of the National Grange in November 2015.

Yet over the years, women played pivotal roles in the organization. Clara Waldo was State Lecturer, *Grange Bulletin* Editor, and a State Deputy as well as on the Board of Regents of Oregon Agricultural College. Mary Howard served as State Secretary for 22 years, Bertha Beck for 32 years, and Mildred Norman for 22 years. These Sisters not only took minutes, but handled all administrative tasks of the organization.

Mary Howard, State Secretary, 1898-1920

Bertha Beck, State Secretary, 1920-1952

Mildred Norman, State Secretary, 1952-1974

At the 2022 State Session there were more women delegates (57) than men (45).

#3 GRASSROOTS ORGANIZATION

Grassroots movements are initiated by small groups of individuals to bring about changes in social policy or on political issues. Rather than being driven by money, the power of a grassroots movement comes from ordinary people sharing their sense of justice or their knowledge about a given issue and using their passion to influence policymakers. Grassroots movements are bottom-up, rather than top-down efforts, much the way grass grows.

Grange policies originate in Community Grange halls, not in Salem or on the tenth floor of an office building in Washington, D. C.

Any member can write a resolution that identifies a problem and proposes a solution on any topic. The format of a resolution is:

Whereas: This is true; and

Whereas: That is true. Therefore be it

Resolved: That (Grange name) asks/urges/supports...this action, solution, policy.

The author brings the resolution to a Community Grange meeting to be discussed by other members. They may have questions or suggestions for improvements. Their input may lead to amendments. When a Grange adopts a resolution, it becomes that Grange's policy. If the issue is local, the Grange Secretary should send copies of it to local officials and the press. If it is a county, state, or national issue, the Secretary will send a copy to other Granges, the Pomona Grange, and/or the State Grange.

What sounds like a great idea in one Grange hall may be strengthened by the input of others, more heads being better than one. Having other Granges endorse the idea also may increase its likelihood of being adopted by the Pomona. When adopted, the resolution becomes that Pomona's policy. The Pomona Secretary should send the resolution to the State Grange, government agencies or legislators, and other interested parties.

The State Grange assigns the resolution to a committee of delegates who will evaluate it to determine whether the subject is an appropriate policy for the State Grange to have and whether it should be adopted as presented. The committee may report favorable, unfavorable, favorable as amended, or no recommendation. The committee's report will be presented to the delegates at State Session to discuss and vote. If they adopt the committee's report, it becomes the State Grange's policy. If the issue is national, a copy will be sent to the National Grange for the consideration of delegates from other states.

Many Oregon policies from the initiative, referendum, and recall to newborn hearing screening have followed this path.

#4 NONPARTISAN

A dictionary definition of "nonpartisan" is "free from party affiliation, bias, designation." This means that the Grange as an organization neither supports nor opposes a party or a candidate for office.

Members are encouraged to support the party and candidates of their choice. According to the National Grange Digest:

> 2.5.3 We must always bear in mind that no one, by becoming a Patron of Husbandry, gives up that inalienable right and duty which belongs to every American citizen, to take a proper interest in the politics of one's country.
>
> 2.5.4 On the contrary, it is right for every member to do all in his or her power, legitimately, to influence for good the action of any political party to which he or she belongs. It is reserved by every Patron, as the right of a free citizen to affiliate with any party that will best carry out his or her principles.
>
> 10.1.4 No Grange of the various divisions of the Order shall use or allow to be used any name, insignia or mark

> of the Order in a manner which could indicate support, approval or opposition of any candidate for political office or any partisan political position."

Campaign signs must not be displayed on the Grange building or its grounds, even for non-partisan offices. The hall is not to be rented to a political party or campaign group because meeting notices would give the appearance that the Grange supports that party.

Discussions of candidates or parties are not allowed during Grange meetings. However, Granges are encouraged to hold a candidate forum, providing that they invite all candidates running for an office and give equal time to all who attend.

Being nonpartisan strengthens an organization's ability to advocate across partisan lines and have access to diverse community leaders and funding sources.

This does not mean that Granges avoid taking positions on issues. State Grange Legislative Director Mark Noah said, "As a non-partisan issue-oriented organization we are intensely interested in legislation that affects our members or will improve our lives. Rural high-speed internet connectivity is as important today as rural free delivery of mail was in times past." The State Grange has a part-time lobbyist in Salem and the National Grange has a full-time lobbyist in Washington, D. C.

#5 CIVIL DISCOURSE

In 150 years, Granges have sent more than 8,000 resolutions to the State Sessions to be discussed. Many led to vigorous debate. Some were decided by just a few votes.

The National Grange Digest states:

> 2.5.5 We acknowledge the broad principle that difference of opinion is no crime, and hold that "progress toward

> truth is made by differences of opinion," while "the fault lies in bitterness of controversy."

The Master/President has never allowed speakers to be interrupted. Meetings follow Roberts Rules of Order.

Former State Grange Attorney Nancy Murray put it this way, "The Grange allows diverse people to get together for a common purpose and in so doing build positive working relationships and even friendships with those they might never otherwise interact with. In so doing, the world becomes a little less divisive, the 'other' out there becomes a human being, and a relationship is formed that surpasses the loaded labels so much of our media promotes."

"Civility in discourse makes room for things to be accomplished together. The Grange motto is 'In essentials, unity; in non-essentials, liberty; in all things, charity.' These Grange values are important for our democracy to flourish."

In her 2017 Master's Address, State President Susan Noah stated, "We can take great pride in the fact that as Brothers and Sisters we debate issues and arrive at decisions through the use of civil discourse. We do not disparage one another for different beliefs; we talk to each other and try to understand the other's viewpoint. We do not always agree, but at the end of the day we are still a part of the Grange family."

#6 NONSECTARIAN

A dictionary definition of the term "nonsectarian" is "not affiliated with or restricted to a particular religious group." Most farmers were people of faith although they may not have attended church regularly. In 1873 nearly everyone in Oregon identified with a Christian denomination. Today community members have many different spiritual beliefs, and the nonsectarian culture of the Grange brings them together rather than divides them.

The National Grange Digest 1.12.1 states "Denominational religious or partisan political matters shall not be the subject of discussions in the work of the Order, and no religious or political tests for membership shall be applied."

The duties of the Chaplain are to deliver prayers, say grace, drape the charter when a member passes, and send cards to those who are sick or in distress. Prayers in the Grange manual are to a higher being and do not name a deity.

#7 GRANGE HALLS

State Master George Palmiter advocated that each Grange build its own hall because it gave that Grange stability and permanency in the community. Likely the oldest Grange hall in Oregon still in use is that of Columbia #267 in Corbett. It was built in 1898. The building is two stories with more than 3,000 square feet. The upstairs has a beautiful wood floor made from old-growth fir from nearby Bridal Veil Falls. For most Granges having a dance floor was nearly as essential as having an appropriate meeting space, a kitchen designed for multiple cooks, and a dining room large enough for a crowd.

Columbia #267 in Corbett built their hall in 1898.

Columbia's hall still serves their community.

In 1925 State Master Palmiter estimated that 136 Granges had their own halls valued, including contents, at $286,355. At that time there were 218 Granges. In 1939, State Master Ray Gill reported that 236 of 377 Granges had halls valued at $400,000.

Most halls were built by members who volunteered their time, tools, and skills. They loaned money or held dinners, card parties, dances, and bake sales to raise funds. A penny or silver drill at the end of each meeting may have raised only a couple dollars but over time every cent helped.

Halls were even built for Juvenile Granges. Ada #570 in western Lane County built one in 1936 and McKinley #582 in Coos County built theirs in 1942.

In 1932 the National Grange's slogan was "Name on Every Grange Hall." Grange halls are one of the best forms of advertising for the organization assuming the hall looks well maintained. In honor of Oregon's 100th anniversary in 1959, the State Grange sponsored a "Paint Up" program. Paint was provided at a low cost so that Granges could improve the exterior appearance of their halls. After COVID, "We Welcome Back the Community, Our Grange Missed You!" banners were distributed at State Session for delegates to take home and display on halls.

In some states, many Granges no longer have halls. If a Grange meets in members' homes, a church basement, or restaurant, it would be easy to decide that it is too hard to keep it going. Having a building that serves as a community center gives members an additional reason to carry on.

#8 CONNECTION

Rural families were isolated. The next farm was miles down the road. Farmers made a trip to town for necessities. They saw neighbors when they attended church services, but there the purpose was for them to hear the pastor's sermon. There was no opportunity to share the thoughts and ideas they had while milking the cows, plowing the field, weeding the garden, or canning fruits and vegetables for the winter.

The Grange offered an opportunity for rural families to socialize with others who shared the same lifestyle. During a potluck or coffee and cookies after a meeting, they could compare experiences dealing with pests, predators, and noxious weeds as well as share recipes, sewing patterns, and child rearing methods.

During the meeting, members could present their ideas for solving community, state, or national problems. They would bond further while working together to prepare and serve a dinner, make a quilt, or help a family in need.

During the pandemic, everyone experienced the effects of isolation on mental health. Coming together at the Grange, whether in person or by video conferencing, helped members overcome the loneliness they experienced. Likely this was the same effect early Grange members felt.

#9 FRATERNAL ORGANIZATION

Most Grange meetings across the country begin with the words, "The hour of labor has arrived. The work of another day demands our attention."

After the Bible is opened, the Chaplain recites a prayer. Members salute the U. S. flag. An order of business is followed. A brief closing ceremony concludes the meeting. In his 2012 Master's Address State Master Mark Noah stated, "These basic practices define and differentiate a Grange meeting from any other and are some of the common threads that bind us together in fraternity."

In 1979 State Master W. C. Harris reported that 500 organizations had died since the Grange was organized. He attributed the Grange's ritual and fraternal tie to be a reason for its survival. In 1982 Oregon delegates appealed to the National Grange that "to proceed with plans to forsake or radically change our ritualism would be an act of the greatest imprudence and that we firmly believe that to do so would be to seriously jeopardize the existence of the Order of Patrons of Husbandry."

In the First Degree the Overseer says, "The Grange is a great fraternity, and the lessons of its ritual are expressed by the use of symbols drawn from the field, the farm and the farm home." Grange rituals deliver moral lessons based on activities during each season on the farm. Some members complain that the language is antiquated and that the degrees are time consuming. A Welcoming Ceremony or Obligation Ceremony can be used to initiate new members. Modernized, streamlined versions of some ceremonies are available in the Alternative Manual.

In his 2012 address, State Master Mark Noah pointed out why the State Grange continues to set an example. "The words of the traditional Grange Manual have a unique rhythm and beauty and are preferred by many. The crisp floorwork of a correctly performed presentation of guests or the flag is impressive."

#10 MEMBERS' DEDICATION AND SACRIFICE

Throughout the Oregon State Grange's 150 history, many members have donated their time and talents for the benefit of the organization. In 1875 State Master Daniel Clark and his wife traveled from Oregon to

Charleston, South Carolina to attend the National Session. Their trip to Charleston took nearly a month. After a week of meetings, the Clarks sat on trains another 20+ days on their return trip home.

State Deputies left their farms and traveled over mountains and through forests to organize or reorganize Granges. They went by rail, horse and buggy, boat, car, and several even walked. Members often invited them to share a meal and spend the night on a spare bed or sofa.

Before good roads, getting to a Pomona meeting held at another Grange hall in the county was a challenge. State Secretary Mary Howard of Molalla #310 shared that in the early 1900s the trip to a Clackamas County Pomona meeting took three days: One day to get there, a second for the meeting, and a third to return home.

After World War II, the State Master, Lecturer, Secretary, and the Legislative, Agriculture, and Home Economics chairmen, Juvenile and Youth Superintendents conducted a conference in each of Oregon's 36 counties. Their road trip took three weeks before Thanksgiving and two after. Being able to present their programs in person and answer members' questions was worth the trip. But some missed a child's birthday or made other personal sacrifices.

Even after roads were improved, attending State Session on the other side of the Cascades was a difficult journey. A trip over the McKenzie Pass usually involved a flat tire, often on a hairpin turn.

Many members did whatever was necessary to get the job done. A lobbyist parked his motorhome in the closest RV park and walked two to three miles to the Capitol and back each day. Members spent their spare time building a Grange hall, preparing a meal, typing letters, writing newspaper articles, getting signatures on ballot measures, collecting recyclables, and volunteering as needed. Their efforts built the foundation and the organization's reputation that members enjoy today.

ESTO PERPETUA

Esto perpetua is a Latin phrase that means "let it be perpetual." Grange founders adopted it as a motto on December 4, 1867. The goal of this book is not to predict the accuracy of this motto but rather to recap the Oregon State Grange's first 150 years.

WHY DID THE GRANGE CATCH ON SO QUICKLY?

After the Civil War, Oliver Hudson Kelley, a Minnesota farmer who sometimes worked as a clerk in government departments to supplement his income, was sent to the south to assess the condition of agriculture. As expected, he found that fields and buildings were destroyed, and machinery was not up-to-date or in good repair. He also learned that farmers did not know the latest techniques or current varieties.

Kelley was not welcomed in the south until he revealed that he was a member of the Freemason fraternal order. He began to visualize a fraternal association of farmers. Their meetings would be a place to share what they learned from reading or their own experiments.

He sold the idea to six of his friends in Washington, D. C. On December 4, 1967, the seven men met in the office of William Saunders, the Superintendent of the Propagating Gardens of the Department of Agriculture. They organized the National Grange of the Order of Patrons of Husbandry. Saunders became its first Master and Kelley its first Secretary. In January the group organized Potomac Grange #1 to test their ideas, especially for ritual.

Kelley quit his job to become the organization's chief promoter. He set off with a train ticket to Harrisburg, PA with "good health, unlimited courage, and $2.50 in real cash!" He was a better writer than salesman.

His early efforts were mixed. But he succeeded in organizing Fredonia Grange #1 in New York state.

When he returned to his farm in Minnesota that May, Kelley was discouraged. He did not know that his wife Temperance had an inheritance of approximately $500 stowed away. That amount of cash gave Kelley the boost he needed to work the Midwest. Meanwhile Kelley's niece, Caroline Hall, agreed to manage his office and correspondence. She convinced him that the organization would not succeed unless an equal place was given to women.

The timing was right. The Homestead Act of 1862 brought easterners and immigrants west to claim 160 acres. While the extension of railroads provided farmers with a way to move their crops to market, they were run by monopolies who charged more for short hauls than for long hauls. Granges in Illinois pressured their legislature to set maximum rates for the storage of grain in elevators. This early success in 1871 was the best evidence of the power that organized farmers could have.

Five years later, the *Willamette Farmer* reported that Iowa had 1,622 Granges, Illinois 486, Missouri 376, Minnesota 252, and Nebraska 222. The total number of Granges in the U. S. and Canada was 4,034 with a membership of 175,000.

OREGONIANS READ ABOUT THIS NEW ORGANIZATION

Word of this new organization reached Oregon via newspapers. The first mention of the Patrons of Husbandry was in the February 18, 1870 issue of the *Oregon Weekly Statesman* (Salem). The article mentions that the Grange fostered agricultural pursuits, and protected agriculturists. But also, that it was a secret society that admitted women.

A more complete description of the organization appeared in January 21, 1871 issue of *The Oregon Republican* (Dallas).

PATRONS OF HUSBANDRY

"This is the name of an organization which is becoming quite numerous in our land; we hear of lodges being organized in all parts of the East.

"As it is comparatively unknown here, it would perhaps be interesting to our readers to know the object to be attained.

"This is a society designed to protect by mutuality of understanding, the business of agriculture, and to promote among them a greater and freer sociality of interests and acquaintance. The meeting of the lodges, or Granges as they are called, are made the occasion, not only for business consultation and conference, but also for social interchange, the wives and daughters being admitted to membership and elevated to office the same as the fathers and sons. An organization of this nature cannot but result in good to the farming community. The co-operative system is being engrafted into all branches of business. The capitalists form their boards of commerce, and other protective associations to protect their interests. The working men are uniting to secure ends which will ensure them success; and we think it right and proper that agriculturalists as well should benefit themselves by the co-operative systems.

"There is no place in the United States where it is needed more than in Oregon, and we hope soon to see lodges springing up in all parts of the state, and the farmers as well as all other classes, taking active steps to secure their best interests."

The April 29 issue of this newspaper published a letter to the Editor from Oliver Hudson Kelley. He lists the advantages of membership and adds:

> "We ignore all political and religious discussions in our Order, we do not solicit the patronage of any sect, association or individual, upon any grounds whatever, except upon the intrinsic merits of the Order.

A front-page article in the February 8, 1873 issue of the *Willamette Farmer* detailed requirements for organizing a Subordinate and State Grange and their relationship to the National Grange. The *Willamette Farmer*, *Oregon City Enterprise*, and *States Rights Democrat* (Albany) all published the Constitution of the National Grange in 1873.

THE FIRST GRANGES IN OREGON

The first Grange in Oregon was Marshfield in Clackamas County organized in December 1872 by W. J. Campbell. (In 1938 when Marshfield was reorganized, it was renamed Oregon Pioneer #1.) W. J. corresponded with O. H. Kelley for at least six months prior to the organization. Kelley wrote "As it is new in your state some latitude must of course be allowed to get it introduced when it will soon become popular." Campbell's latitude caused problems. All 30 charter members were male when Article 9, Section 4 of the National Grange Constitution specifically said, "Charter members shall be not less than nine men and four women, nor more than twenty men and ten women." Also, two of the charter members were "not engage in agricultural pursuits."

However, W. J. pressed on and reported to the *Willamette Farmer* in May 1873 that he organized six Granges in as many days in Polk and Linn Counties. Then in July he organized another nine Granges in Linn, Lane, Benton, and Yamhill Counties.

Meanwhile the July 18 issue of the *States Right Democrat* (Albany) reported that Elias Fanning also organized four Granges in a week in Linn County.

By August Oregon had 25 Granges, most of them in Linn County. The September 13 issue of the *Albany Register* announced that National Grange Deputy N. W. Garretson had called a meeting of the Masters of Subordinate Granges in Oregon and the Washington Territory, with their wives who are members, at Salem at 10 o'clock on Wednesday, September 24 for the purpose of organizing a State Grange of Patrons of Husbandry.

ORGANIZING SESSION OF THE OREGON STATE GRANGE

In 1873 the National Grange sent Deputy N. W. Garretson from Iowa to organize Granges on the Pacific coast. In September Oregon had 40 Granges in ten counties, enough to organize a State Grange. Five Granges in the Walla Walla area of the Washington Territory were also included.

The organizing Session was held at the Masonic Hall in Salem. Forty-two Masters and their wives represented 33 Granges in Oregon and seven delegates represented four Granges in the Washington Territory. They met from Wednesday September 24 through Saturday the 27th from 8 a.m. until their business was done in the evening with breaks for lunch and dinner. They took their business seriously. There were no banquets, receptions, programs of entertainment, or tours.

Garretson served as Master until Daniel Clark of Salem Grange #17 was elected and installed State Master. Garretson appointed members to fill the offices of Overseer, Chaplain, Steward, and Assistant Stewards so that they could practice the ritual of the opening and closing ceremonies. National Grange Deputy John H. Smith from California served as Secretary.

The second morning was devoted to adopting thirteen Rules of Order. Why didn't they use Robert's Rules? They were not published until 1876. Also, some of the rules adopted were Grange specific. For example, Rule

8 was "Members wishing to speak on a question shall rise in their places and respectfully address their remarks to the Worthy Master, confining themselves to the question and avoiding personalities."

A committee of delegates wrote the first By-Laws which the delegates adopted. Delegates elected twelve other officers, four of whom were from the Washington Territory, and six Executive Committee members. All were to serve a one-year term.

Instruction in Grange ritual was another objective of the organizing Session. N. W. Garretson instructed the delegates in the unwritten work and "informally conferred" the Fifth Degree, which was the state level degree at that time.

The first resolutions adopted were to build locks at Celilo Falls on the Columbia River and at Oregon City on the Willamette River so that produce could be transported to market more easily and cheaply. The Secretary was directed to send these resolutions to their Senators and Representatives.

Delegates also adopted a resolution that children over the age of three years (but under 16) not be allowed to remain in any Grange meeting after the gates were ordered closed by the Master. What prompted this resolution is not known.

The Committee on State of the Order proposed establishing a cooperative system of trade, purchasing farm implements, machinery, and sacks at the lowest prices, and selling grain and other products at the highest market rates. They proposed gradually substituting cash for the credit system, establishing Grange stores, and eventually shipping grain in bulk.

The latitude taken with the National Grange Constitution by W. J. Campbell, who organized Marshfield #1, was discussed. "It was moved and seconded that the Master of Marshfield Grange be instructed to withhold the unwritten work from two members of that Grange, who were taken into that Grange as charter members, although not engaged in agricultural pursuits." After considerable debate, the motion lost.

However, W. J. Campbell was reportedly so embarrassed that he never attended another Session.

Members were urged to subscribe to the *Willamette Farmer.*

A Resolution of Thanks declared Deputy Garretson an honorary member of the State Grange of Oregon and the Washington Territory. They presented him with a gold-headed cane and a set of gold sleeve buttons.

DANIEL CLARK

1st State Master, 1873-1876

When Grange Masters in Oregon and the Washington Territory met in Salem September 24-27, 1873 to organize a State Grange, they elected Daniel Clark (1824-1885) its first Master.

Daniel was born in Ireland. His family immigrated to Missouri when he was four. At age 19 he came to Oregon and settled in Marion County. He raised chickens and wheat as well as other livestock and crops on Pleasant Point Farm five miles south of Salem on Turner Road. He claimed to have supplied Joe Meek with flour for his long journey.

Daniel and his wife Harriet (1846-1932) were charter members Salem #17. In 1873 he was Salem's Master. During the State Grange organizing Session, Daniel was appointed Steward and served on the Credentials and By-Laws Committees. He was likely elected first State Master because of his prior experiences as President of the Farmers' State Convention, Oregon Agricultural Society, Oregon State Union, and Vice President of the Cheap Transportation Convention.

Shortly after being elected Master, Daniel headed to San Jose to attend the California State Grange Session. During his first year as Master, Clark spent 12 weeks traveling 2,500 miles in the work of the organization. His travel paid off because the number of Granges grew from 37 to 175 and membership totaled around 10,000.

Daniel's first National Grange Session was in St. Louis, Missouri in 1874. The following year his wife Harriet accompanied him to the 8th Annual Session in Charleston, South Carolina. After traveling from Salem to Portland by train, they boarded the steamship Oriflamme for San Francisco. Daniel reported experiencing seasickness from the time the ship crossed the Columbia River bar until it docked in San Francisco three days later. Meanwhile this may have been Harriet's first ever vacation given her work on the farm and raising their eight children.

The Clarks took the train from San Francisco to Des Moines where they stayed for three days with N. W. Garretson, the deputy who organized the Oregon State Grange. According to a letter written by Garretson and published on the front page of the *Willamette Farmer*, he was not expecting the Clarks. From Iowa the couple continued to Washington City and finally to Charleston. They left Portland on January 9 and arrived in time for the opening of the Session on February 4.

After serving as State Master for three years, Daniel was appointed Gatekeeper to fill a vacancy caused by death. The following year he was the delegate for Marion Pomona Grange.

In 1880 Daniel welcomed the delegates to Salem Grange on the first evening of the Session. Salem Grange provided "entertaining exercises interspersed with excellent music." Later that Session, he was elected to a two-year term on the State Grange Executive Committee. He chaired the committee on Cooperation at the 1884 and 1885 Sessions.

After serving as Master, Daniel tried his hand at politics. He supported Peter Cooper, the Greenback candidate running against Democrat Samuel Tilden. Clark proved his inexperience at politics; the topic of finance "proved to be a deeper subject than he could successfully handle." Clark was appointed by the State Legislature to a Tax Commission but died before the work was completed.

Daniel Clark passed on December 31, 1885, at the age of 61. He was survived by his wife Harriet and eight children. His coffin was followed by a large group of friends to the Salem Pioneer Cemetery where his I.O.O.F. brothers conducted the burial service.

At the 1886 Session, a condolence resolution was adopted: "That in the death of our Brother this Grange has lost one of its most earnest and trusted workers, the Order one of its truest friends, and the cause of agriculture one of its bravest defenders."

Harriet had to sell the 800-acre Pleasant Point Farm for $8,000, "a most splendid bargain." However, she and her school age children were allowed to continue living in the house. While she was helping a neighbor prepare dinner for their threshing crew, the house caught fire and burned to the ground.

In 1891 Harriet married N. W. Garretson, the National Grange Deputy that organized the Oregon State Grange. He was an insurance salesman. The Garretsons bought a corner lot in Salem and built a house. However, N. W. spent more time traveling than sitting by the fireplace with Harriet. In 1900 Harriet filed for divorce on grounds of desertion.

Daniel Clark Grange #162 was organized in Prairie City, Grant County, in 1874. It became dormant in 1890.

ONE STEP FORWARD, TWO BACK

1873-79

During 1873 and 1874, Granges spread rapidly throughout Oregon. By 1875 the 187 Granges in Oregon had a total membership of 10,885. But this early success did not last. The third State Master A. R. Shipley admitted in his 1879 Master's Address, "We organized in too great haste; there was too much enthusiasm and too little knowledge..."

The number of delegates to the 1874 Session jumped to 115. But in 1875 there were only 75. This was because the By-Laws had been changed and each Grange no longer had representation. Granges in each county sent representatives to their county courthouse to select one Master (and his wife) for every four Granges. For example, Linn County had 25 Granges, so they picked seven of their 25 Masters (25/4=6 + 1 for the remainder). Later the ratio was changed to one delegate for every six Granges.

Soon this scheme for controlling the number of delegates was not necessary because by 1879 there were only 65 Granges and a membership of 2,477. The number of delegates was 30, including wives, plus seven from County Councils or Pomonas.

The 1875 Session was held in Portland and 1876 in Albany. All others were held in Salem. From 1873 to 1877 Sessions were held in September. Beginning in 1877, they were held in May.

In 1875 the Executive Committee hired A. J. Dufur as a business agent. He purchased $60,000 worth of wagons and farm machinery directly from the factory. Had the 500 Moline wagons sold, this investment would have been wise. But apparently most farmers decided their current wagon was good enough. Their first effort at cooperative buying failed.

At the 1878 Session, delegates personally pledged $1,415 to debt relief. A special committee recommended that members' dues be increased 10¢ per quarter, and that each Grange pay $1.25 per member to settle the debt left by the agency. Delegates agreed to hire an agent in Portland and pay him commission, but not give him authority to incur any debt.

This buying disaster was compounded by a cooperative selling disaster. E. E. Morgan's Sons was the largest shipper of wheat on the west coast. Northwest Storage Commission and Shipping Company secured a ship owned by E. E. Morgan's Sons to transport a load of Oregon Granger's wheat to Liverpool. The ship sank. The State Grange agreed to pay those who lost wheat 47¢ per bushel, far less than the value of the wheat (60¢ per bushel). But the State Grange's loss could have been much worse. When E. E. Morgan's Sons filed for bankruptcy later that year, the California State Grange lost nearly $500,000.

By the 1876 Session, 78 Granges had closed, and membership dipped below 10,000. However, on the evening of the first day of the Session, representatives from each county reported on the condition of the Order. That day's journal says, "From the reports made, the Order was found to be in a better and more encouraging condition than was anticipated."

Of course, this loss of membership had a further impact on finances. The following year, State Master William Cyrus revealed in his Master's Address that Oregon had not paid dues to the National Grange in the past year. In 1878 the State Secretary delivered the bad news that 125 Granges were dormant, and some had not paid dues in two years. Membership had dropped to 4,195. The Treasurer was absent and refused to attend but gave the books to a Brother who reported that the balance on hand was $725.25. The Oregon State Grange asked the National Grange to allow biennial representation at the National Sessions until the State Grange's indebtedness was liquidated, which did not occur until 1884.

At the 1874 Session 23 resolutions were numbered, but others were introduced by committees and delegates. The following year, a motion passed that all resolutions "be reduced to writing and handed to the Secretary to be read."

Policy resolutions adopted during the 1870s were that a Granger's bank be established in Portland, the Oregon Legislature appropriate $100,000 for improvements to the upper Willamette River, that a canal or locks be built at Cascade Falls, a lighthouse built at Tillamook head, and that the State Fair be more of an agricultural exhibit.

Delegates adopted a resolution that "no Grange shall be organized within five miles of any existing Grange unless the consent of such Grange has been first obtained and natural obstacles render such new organization desirable."

In his 1875 Master's Address, Daniel Clark proposed the formation of Pomona or district Granges. The following year, he proposed the publication of a Grange newspaper and having the State Lecturer be in the field to encourage Granges.

WILLIAM CYRUS

2nd State Master, 1876-1878

William Cyrus (1820-1890) was Master of Santiam #37, served on the By-Laws Committee at the organizing Session, and elected the first Overseer of the Oregon State Grange. That October, State Master Daniel Clark appointed William Linn County Deputy. William's wife Jane (1828-1879) was the first Ceres of the State Grange.

William was born in 1820 in Grainger County, Tennessee. He and his family moved to Linn County via the Oregon trail in 1847 and settled in Scio. In 1866 he was elected State Senator from Linn County. In 1872 he was elected a County Commissioner.

In addition to being a farmer, William was a Director of the Home Manufacturing Company, which sold shares to build a factory to make agricultural wagons and equipment. The company closed before it made anything due to disputes over whether to locate it in Albany or Salem and the failure of some investors to buy the number of shares they pledged.

After three years as State Overseer, William was elected Master. He faced serious challenges. Early attempts at cooperative buying and selling had nearly bankrupted the organization. Only one new Grange in Idaho and one Pomona in Oregon had been organized. Membership was 4,195. In his 1878 Master's Address, William "cautioned Granges to emphasize the Social, Fraternal, and Educational benefits for members before Co-operation."

Four matrons attended the 1877 Session unaccompanied by their husbands who were Masters. William ruled that the matrons could not be seated. A. R. Shipley of Oswego Grange in Clackamas County hastily wrote a resolution to seat them, which was adopted.

Despite the state of the order and his controversial decision, William was re-elected. However, the following afternoon, "The Worthy Master thanked the brethren for their confidence and good will in electing him a second time to the office of Master, and very feelingly declined to accept the position." The *Salem Statesman* noted, "It is to be regretted that Mr. Cyrus was compelled to resign, as the affairs of that Order have prospered greatly under his administration."

William and Jane were named delegates again in 1879. However, on the first day of the Session, Jane was reported sick. Later "A gloom was cast over the assembly by the announcement that Sister Jane Cyrus was dead and buried." A resolution on her death was adopted by a rising vote.

William was elected to the State Grange Executive Committee in 1881 and served until 1885.

William died on the evening of June 6, 1890. He had been hoeing in his garden in the morning when he was struck with paralysis and became unconscious. He was survived by his third wife Martha (1837-1923) and seven of his eleven children. He is buried in Providence Cemetery in Scio.

At the 1891 Session, the committee on Condolence wrote, "He was a devoted Patron, and loved, practiced, and promulgated the principles of our Order. He was one who can truly say, if asked as to his stewardship at the gate of the Grange above, I have not defrauded; I have not been idle; I have not betrayed friends or trusts; I have helped the widows and the fatherless; I have kept the faith. He was a man of noble instincts and a high order of intelligence. His kind and generous face is missed from our assembly, and we mourn his loss, but his life and example remain a precious inheritance to the Grange of Oregon, and the record of his faithful and useful stewardship is a monument to his memory more enduring than marble, and will serve as a light and a guide to prevent from stumbling the feet of many in our Order as they travel along the path of duty."

A. R. SHIPLEY

3rd State Master, 1878-1880

Adam Randolph Shipley (1826-1893) was born in Uniontown, PA. At age 9 his family moved to Mount Vernon, Ohio. He studied law under Attorney General Taft and was admitted to the bar, but never practiced.

A. R., his first wife, and their child traveled the Oregon trail in 1852. Shortly after they arrived his wife and child died. Having only $5 in his pocket, he took the only job he could find, which was chopping wood. His next job was Postmaster of Portland, which he held for eight years.

In the mid-1850s A. R. advertised a catalog of books and stationery in the *Salem Statesman* and other newspapers. That business subsequently became J. K. Gill.

In 1862 A. R. bought a farm in the Oswego area, where he experimented with many different crops. He won a premium at the State Fair for six varieties of grapes. At an Oswego Grange Fair, he entered 12 varieties of apples, eight of pears, as well as multiple varieties of beets, turnips, onions, squash, beans, peas, strawberries, and raspberries. He tried growing sorghum, cornstalk sugar, and sugar beets. Over the years he added acreage and owned 1,000 acres at the time of his death.

A. R. was Secretary of the Fruit Growers and the State Horticulture Society. He was appointed to the grasses and seeds department of the State Board of Centennial Commissioners. In 1890 he was superintendent of garden products at the State Fair. He was often a presenter at Farmers' Institutes.

A. R. was a charter member and first Master of Oswego #175. He was a delegate to the 1874 Session at which he was appointed to the By-Laws Committee. For the 1876 Session, he served as Chaplain pro tem. He was named an incorporator of the Grange Cooperative Association and elected Overseer at that Session.

The following year A. R. was Master and delegate of Multnomah District Pomona, which included Granges from Clackamas and Washington Counties. When Master William Cyrus ruled that four sisters who were not accompanied by their husbands could not be seated, A. R. wrote a resolution to reinstate them.

When William Cyrus declined re-election as Master on the last day of the 1878 Session, A. R. was elected the third Master of the Oregon State Grange. A. R. took over an organization that was overwhelmed with debt and declining membership. In his first Master's Address, A. R. admitted, "Without necessary qualifications or experience, we rushed into business enterprises and then let them fall for want of united support, and that careful supervision necessary to success."

At the end of his term as Master, a resolution was adopted expressing thanks "for the very efficient and gentlemanly manner in which he has presided over the Grange and conducted the business."

A. R.'s wife C. E. (Celinda Elvira, 1826-1905) took the Fifth Degree in 1876. She served as Pomona pro tem in 1877 and then was elected Pomona. She was elected Master of Oswego Grange in 1881. At the 1886 Session, she delivered an essay on the history of the cooperative movement, which is printed in that Session's Proceedings.

A. R. was elected State Lecturer in 1880 and to the Executive Committee in 1885.

In 1891 A. R. was appointed by the Governor to the Board of Regents of Oregon Agricultural College. He was later elected its Treasurer. In 1983 $20,000 of college funds were invested in a Corvallis bank that failed. A. R. and two other bondsmen were held responsible. A. R. died of a heart attack a week later.

A. R.'s funeral was held in the Shipley home in Corvallis. After the service, Clackamas County Grangers formed a procession of 100 carriages to the Oswego Pioneer Cemetery where the Master of Oswego "conducted the service in accordance with the impressive ritual of the Patrons of Husbandry." A. R. was survived by his wife and six children.

The resolution written by the Condolence Committee noted that "we have lost one of our most ardent and honest workers in the Grange, one of the best, progressive citizens, an obliging neighbor, a kind friend, a thorough Christian, a loving husband and father, and withal a man of the people, whose wise counsel and upright example we can ill afford to lose..." It went on to say, "This State Grange has lost one of its ablest workers, the Subordinate Grange its staunchest friend and the whole State one of its foremost citizens, and his family a kind, true husband and father."

When C. E. died in 1905, she was survived by three of their six children.

1880-89

Membership hit its lowest point of 1,241 in 1880 but bounced back to 3,000 by the end of the decade. The number of Granges increased from 53 to 86, thanks to the work of State Lecturer H. E. Hayes who was then elected the fifth State Master.

All State Grange Sessions were held in Salem. In 1882 a past Master could be a voting delegate if the current Master was unable to attend. From 1888 on, any Fourth Degree member and their spouse could be delegates. The number of delegates ranged from 23 to 41 plus 5 to 16 Pomona delegates.

Delegates approved the State Master appointing deputies in each county to visit Granges and instruct members on the aim and purposes of the Grange, to resuscitate dormant Granges, and organize new Granges. But they cut the annual salary of the State Secretary from $300 to $100.

The most important accomplishment was the formation of the Lower Columbia Fire Relief Association. The company insured members' property valued at $155,000, reported no losses, and received new applications every week. The Association became a "valuable auxiliary of the Grange." This company subsequently became Grange Mutual Insurance Company (GMIC), which operated until it closed in 2002.

A resolution advocating direct election of U.S. Senators got favorable press. In 1906 Oregon voters were able to elect their U. S. Senators rather than have the legislature pick them. Delegates also favored the Australian ballot, which insured that each voter could cast his ballot in secret without intimidation.

The report of Session Education Committee recommended hiring competent teachers, requiring attendance of all children of school age, and not replacing textbooks so frequently. Delegates agreed that the General School Fund should be distributed so that each school district had sufficient funds to run at least six months of school. They also wanted the effects of alcohol on the human system to be taught, and tobacco to be prohibited on school grounds.

A committee was appointed each year to visit Oregon College of Agriculture and report their findings. Some years their report was favorable, but in 1888 it was, "At the present time there is less agriculture taught than ever."

Delegates favored labeling weights and measures of food products and identifying any alterations to them. They felt that an alien should be prohibited from owning land in the U. S. and especially opposed the immigration of Chinese. They also voted that citizens should not be allowed to own more than 640 acres, although some members did.

Transportation remained a concern. Delegates favored construction of two free roads from Salem through the Cascades. They requested that fares on railroads be 3¢ per mile and charges on the Willamette River be reduced by at least one-third.

Electing Judge R. P. Boise their fourth State Master brought prestige to the organization. The Judge was likely responsible for encouraging this period of legislative activity.

R. P. BOISE

4th State Master, 1880-1888 & 1892-1894

Reuben Patrick Boise (1818-1907) was born and raised on his father's farm near Blandford, Massachusetts. He graduated with honors from Williams College in 1843 and moved to Missouri to teach. Two years later he returned to Massachusetts to study law in the office of an uncle who was a city attorney. He passed the bar and practiced locally for two years.

R. P. came to Oregon in 1851 and established a practice in Portland. The Territorial Legislature elected him Prosecuting Attorney for counties west of the Willamette River. He assisted in compiling and updating Oregon's legal code.

R. P. acquired 640 acres in a donation-land claim near Dallas and moved his family there. He was elected by Polk County to the Territorial Legislature and to the Constitutional Convention, where he was chairman of the Legislative Department. President Buchanan appointed R. P. a Supreme Judge of the Territory. After Oregon became a state, he was elected to the Supreme Court and served on it for 16 years, three times as Chief Justice. He was well known for his dissenting opinions.

R. P. joined Salem #17 in 1879 and was elected Master. He was a delegate for Marion County to the 1879 and 1880 State Sessions and was appointed chair of the Good of the Order Committee both years.

In 1880 Salem Grange held a reception for delegates. "Brother R. P. Boise entertained with some very wholesome remarks." Later that Session, R. P. was elected Master of the State Grange. From 1880 to 1883 R. P. and his wife Emily (1828-1919) entertained delegates in their home one evening during Session.

R P.'s Master's Addresses were considerably longer than those of his predecessors or successors. His sentences were long and complex. In his 1884 Master's Address, R. P. said, "While we firmly adhere to the cardinal principles enumerated in our declaration of purposes that in the Grange there can be no partisan politics, yet as the church teaches pure morals and without partisan bias, seeks to advance Christianity for the good of all, so we too conserve those great interests of our class, which if properly guarded and fostered, will bless all mankind, must give heed to those public questions and laws which affect our calling; and we may without just cause or criticism from any other class or party, seek such political reforms as will promote our interests and relieve our industries from unjust burdens."

H. E. Hayes succeeded R. P. as State Master. However, in 1892 when H. E. felt forced to give up the office "owing to very severe illness in my family," delegates turned to R. P. to lead them for another two years.

R. P. took an interest in education. He was a member of Portland's first public school board. He served as a trustee of Pacific University, La Creole Academy in Dallas, and Willamette University. In 1886 as State Master, he became an ex-officio member of the Board of Regents of Oregon Agricultural College.

At the 1897 Session, Emily Boise served on the Women's Work Committee. The committee's report addressed the question, "What is Women's Mission?

Over the years, R. P. slowly acquired adjoining land until he owned 2,500 acres in Ellendale, west of Dallas. He retained his mental vigor, serving as an elected circuit judge until he was 86. He died in his home on April 10, 1907. He is buried in Salem Pioneer Cemetery.

During the memorial service at the next State Grange Session, R. P. was termed "The grand old man" of the Order; "Educated, a trained and tried jurist, he was ever a safe adviser and leader. A counselor the Grange could trust and rely upon. His word was his bond. Ripe in experience, wisdom, and observation he was worthy of our highest regard."

Boise Grange #256 was organized in Clackamas County in 1892 but surrendered its charter in 1896.

H. E. HAYES

5th State Master, 1888-1892

Henry Elizur Hayes (1831-1919) became the Oregon State Grange's salesman when he accepted the office of State Lecturer in 1882. At that point there were 50 Subordinate Granges in Oregon with a membership of 1,549. During the next six years, Hayes spent 753 days traveling for the Grange. He organized 28 Granges and re-organized 22. By then there were 69 active Granges in Oregon with a membership of 2,512.

In his 1888 Master's Address R. P. Boise said, "We have for the past four years put this work mostly on Brother H. E. Hayes, and in this work, he has been both diligent and efficient, and by his exertions this year in eastern Oregon, we have added to our number thirteen new Granges and revived two dormant ones."

H. E. was born in Hartford, Connecticut in 1831. He married Sarah Levina Woodruff (1835-1896), a Hartford teacher, on February 3, 1853. The following day, the newlyweds and her brother started their overland trip to Oregon, arriving in Oregon City that November. They bought horses and cattle along the way. They farmed a donation-land claim six miles west of Oregon City. H. E. was considered "a prominent fruit grower," but he also grew grains and vegetables and raised cows and pigs.

Hayes was a pioneer steamboat captain. However, little is written about that work except that he was known throughout Oregon "as one of the most efficient steamboat men."

In 1874 brother Hayes became a charter member and first Lecturer of Tualatin #111 (now Frogpond). He was a delegate for Clackamas Pomona in 1879. His wife S. L. was elected State Pomona at the 1880 Session.

In his Master's Address in 1889, Hayes stated that when the State Grange was organized the masses of farmers understood little about law making or the laws that govern them. "Today we formulate bills and force them to a final passage."

When Granges in the Washington Territory met to form the Washington State Grange, H. E. was its organizer. He appointed committees to draft by-laws and act on resolutions before they elected their first slate of officers.

In 1891 the Hayes moved from their farm near Stafford to Salem, probably because S. L. was reported have had "a nervous attack." In his Master's Address 1892, Hayes said, "Owing to very severe illness in my family during the greater portion of the Grange year, which is now closing, it has been impossible for me to reach in person very many of our Granges, or even to correspond by letter to so great an extent as in former years."

However, Hayes again accepted the office of Lecturer. Over the next two years he spent time in the Willamette Valley, Wasco, Gilliam, and Sherman counties, organizing fifteen new Granges and re-organizing three. Then in 1894 he was elected to the State Grange Legislative Committee for two terms.

Upon his election as State Master, H. E. became an ex-officio member of the Oregon Agricultural College Board of Regents. In 1891 he was appointed to the State Board of Equalization. The State Attorney General presented H. E. with a gold-headed cane of which he was immensely proud.

In 1994 H. E. ran for Congress on the Populist ticket while his son Gordon ran on the Republican ticket. Neither won. The son was a lawyer and judge, who often spoke to groups and reportedly enjoyed having an audience as much as his father did. The similarity ended there. There is no evidence that Gordon was ever a Grange member. He practiced family law, but also represented large companies including the Southern Pacific Railroad.

After H. E.'s wife Sarah passed in 1896, he moved in with his oldest daughter, who lived in the Mount Tabor area. His final years were challenging. When his youngest daughter died at the age of 32, he moved back to the farm with a nurse. He had smallpox and suffered a partial paralysis. He died October 21, 1919 at the age of 87. He was survived by a daughter and his son Gordon. He is buried in Robert Bird Cemetery in Wilsonville.

1890-99

Membership continued to be a problem. State Lecturer William Holder reported, "When I took the field one year ago, I must confess I was surprised at the condition of our Order in Eastern Oregon. Granges had been organized and left to die. No attention being paid to them. Not over one-fourth of the whole number had any life at all. The other three-fourths were in a comatose condition, and just merely existed, meeting, or rather three or four of their members managing to meet from three to six months apart."

State Masters Boise, Hayes, Voorhees, and Hilleary sent deputies to all parts of the state, but the number of Granges dropped from 93 to 59 and total membership declined from 3,000 to 2,340. The economy in this period was a factor. "Several more would have been organized but for the few dollars required, as the scarcity of money is keenly felt by farmers in rural districts."

Up to this point, all but two annual Sessions were held in Salem. In the 1890s Sessions were held in Hillsboro, Albany, The Dalles, Eugene, Oregon City, McMinnville, Corvallis, Forest Grove, and Portland. All delegates were from Oregon since the Washington State Grange had been organized in 1889 and all Granges in Idaho were dormant. However, regardless of the Session's location, the number of delegates ranged from 38 to 49. Pomonas did not have delegates during these years.

Although the National Grange gets credit for achieving Rural Free Delivery (RFD), members in Oregon did not have to fight for it. In his 1898 Master's Address William Hilleary reported that he now enjoyed free rural mail delivery, which was an experiment in Oregon. In fact, the first route in Oregon was from the Turner Post Office on October 16, 1897. That is where Brother Hilleary lived.

Freight rates were still an issue. Delegates pushed for a Railroad Commission with power to regulate both the rates of freight and fares. The commission they envisioned would consist of two farmers and one railroad man, which of course did not happen. But a commission was named. Its decisions were not always what members wanted.

Delegates were encouraged by the favorable responses they received from Oregon's Senators and Congressmen to a letter sent concerning permanent improvements needed to navigation on the Willamette River.

The Session Women's Work Committee wrote two resolutions that were adopted. One was that women should be able to serve on school boards. The other was to secure the right of suffrage for all women 21 years of age and older. In 1899 Sister Abigail Scott Duniway, considered to be Oregon's Mother of Equal Suffrage, wrote a resolution that was adopted, "That we fully endorse the action of the late legislative assembly in submitting to the voters at the next general election the pending constitutional amendment to extend the elective franchise to women." Oregon voters gave women the vote in 1912.

The 1890 Session sent greetings to the Oregon Woman's Christian Temperance Union, endorsing their work, "especially scientific temperance instruction in the schools." In addition, delegates took a firm stand in favor of prohibiting the manufacture and sale of intoxicating liquors.

Delegates passed a resolution that oleomargarine, butterine and other imitation butter compounds be colored pink so that consumers would not be deceived. They wanted fertilizer dealers to be required to have a state chemist analyze their products at their own expense and report the ingredients.

Brother William S. Uren, the father of the initiative and referendum, convinced the State Grange to champion both. The organization became recognized as one that gave the people a voice in government. No longer could the State Legislature shelve bills the people wanted or impose bills they did not want.

The State Grange's long-standing support for a graduated income tax began in this period as did their opposition to issuing bonds (deficit spending) to finance road construction.

JACOB VOORHEES

6th State Master, 1894-1896

Jacob Voorhees (1841-1928) was a charter member of Woodburn #79 in 1874. He served as Woodburn's Master and Secretary for many years. It is not known when his wife Anna (1846-1919) joined. However, in 1877 Anna was one of the four matrons who was not initially seated as a delegate by State Master William Cyrus because she was unaccompanied by her husband.

The Voorhees were selected to be delegates in 1883 but were unable to attend because Jacob had been shot three times by a discharged farm hand. At first it appeared as though his injuries might be fatal, but he recovered. Delegates to the 1883 Session sent Jacob a telegram expressing sympathy and good wishes from the State Grange. His assailant was captured working on a farm near Myrtle Creek and returned to Marion County. Whiskey was reported to be the cause of his action. In 1891 Jacob was a delegate to the State Temperance Alliance.

In 1886 Jacob was elected State Grange Assistant Steward. He was named chairman of the program committee for a Grange picnic held June 10-12 at Jefferson.

At the 1888 Session Jacob was appointed to the State Agricultural College Committee and elected State Overseer. He took the Sixth Degree in 1890, the second time that Degree was offered.

In 1894 the Voorhees were again delegates. He was chair of the Legislation and Transportation Committees, and she was on Cooperation. He was elected State Master. In his Master's Address the following year, Voorhees said, "It should be the business of every patron" to improve our rural highways, "by properly draining and grading our roads." He called for banishing narrow tires on freight wagons. "The most unnecessary and expensive tax we pay is using bad roads."

After his two-year term as Master, Jacob was elected to the State Grange Legislative Committee on which he served from 1896 to 1904. In this capacity, he got petitions signed for initiatives and referendums and worked with legislators and attorneys to get bills written for resolutions that were passed at State Session.

Jacob served as Secretary of the Lower Columbia Fire Relief Association and Grange Life Insurance Association and was a Director of the Grange Mutual Fire Insurance Company. He served on the Board of Regents for the Normal School at Monmouth as well as the Oregon Agricultural College.

Jacob was Marion County Deputy from 1896 to 1899 and State Deputy from 1901 to 1908. In 1906 State Lecturer Clara Waldo and Jacob tag teamed through Eastern Oregon. She went into a community and delivered an entertaining speech. He followed up enrolling members, handling organizational details, and instructing new officers on their duties.

Jacob was addressed as "Honorable" because he had been a State Senator from Marion County from 1882 to 1886. He was known for introducing a resolution to move the government school for Indians from Forest Grove to Chemawa.

Jacob was born and educated in Montgomery County, New York. He taught for several years before moving to Rochester, Minnesota, where he engaged in general merchandizing. He married Anna in 1868, and they came to Oregon in 1872. They settled on a farm on French Prairie in Marion County.

Jacob was the delegate for Woodburn Grange again in 1924 and 1926. He passed in 1928, leaving an estate valued at $2,000. He was survived by a daughter Mary, who was a Grange member, and three other children. Jacob and Anna are buried in Belle Passi Cemetery in Woodburn.

WILLIAM M. HILLEARY

7th State Master, 1896-1900

William Hilleary (1840-1917) was born in Burlington, Iowa. He crossed the plains with an ox team to California in 1861. Later that year he moved to Turner, Oregon.

In 1865 William enlisted in Company F, First Oregon Volunteer Infantry, and served in the Indian Wars. *A Webfoot Volunteer: The Diary of William M. Hilleary, 1864-1866* was published by Oregon State University Press in 1965. In it he described the battle of Burke's Creek and the raid at Harney Lake Valley.

William was Secretary of the First Oregon Cavalry and Infantry Veterans' Association, which meant he notified veterans of reunions and encampments. He was elected Adjunct of the Oregon Volunteer Veterans Association and then Commander the last time he attended.

After the war, William became a schoolteacher. He married Irene Cornelius (1847-1920) of Molalla in 1867. They would have celebrated their 50th wedding anniversary had he lived two weeks longer. They bought a farm south of Turner that they called "Red Oak." In addition to being a farmer, he was also a Justice of the Peace, Judge, and President of the Independent Telephone Company.

William gave the opening address at the Fruit Growers Congress. At Farmers' Institutes he spoke on "The Cow as a Mortgage Lifter." He won first prize at the State Fair on a bushel of oats and second prizes on popcorn and white beans.

William was a charter member of Turner #18 in 1874 and elected its Secretary. He was a Director of the Turner Storing and Trading Company, a Grange cooperative. He also served as President of the Patron's Life Insurance Association and a Director of the Lower Columbia Fire Relief Association.

In 1877 Irene was one of the four matrons who was not initially seated as a delegate by State Master William Cyrus because she was unaccompanied by her husband. Both attended the 1878 Session at which Irene served as Lady Assistant Steward pro tem and was then elected to the office. William was elected State Steward in 1880 and Assistant Steward in 1882. He served as Secretary from 1890 to 1896.

As Master, William was a strong advocate for rural free mail delivery, a postal savings bank, and a canal across Nicaragua. At several Sessions, William exemplified the unwritten work, "which he did very effectively." Irene sang a solo that was "well received."

In 1888 Irene read an essay she wrote entitled, "Tenacity of Purpose as Applied to the Grange." The following year she delivered the response to the Governor's Welcome. In 1897 she gave a long, detailed account of their trip to the National Grange Session in Washington City. She was well known for her literary ability.

William and Irene took the Sixth Degree in 1889, the first time it was offered. They attended the National Grange Session in Sacramento that year.

William and Irene became members of Surprise #233 in 1898.

After his term as Master, William was elected to the State Legislative Committee and served from 1900 to 1906. He was also appointed State Deputy in 1904.

William and Irene continued to own the farm after they moved to Brownsville, where their son Homer was Mayor and President of the Commercial Club.

William died at the age of 77. His funeral was held at the Brownville Presbyterian Church. A Grange graveside service was held at Twin Oaks Cemetery in Turner. He was survived by his wife, son Lloyd and two grandchildren. His son Homer and daughter Clara proceeded him in death.

TWO STEPS FORWARD, ONE BACK

1900-09

The first decade of the new century was a period of growth and increased activity. The number of Granges grew to 127 and membership increased by 6,000 to 8,085. The Executive Committee awarded cash prizes of $7.50 to the two Granges with the greatest gain in membership and the greatest percentage gain. They also gave $5 and $2.50 to the two members who secured the most "accepted" applications.

Another factor that may have spurred Grange growth was an inspection system. State Master Austin Buxton appointed inspectors to visit assigned Granges twice a year. The system was credited with saving four Granges from becoming dormant.

Improved communication also may have helped increase activity and membership. The State Lecturer edited an *Oregon State Grange Bulletin* which began as a quarterly and became a monthly with a circulation of 1,700. Later it was part of the *Pacific Grange Bulletin* that was published in conjunction with the Washington State Grange.

State Sessions were held in cities previously visited plus Independence and Hood River. The number of delegates ranged from 36 to 79. Pomonas did not have representation.

State Master B. G. Leedy got the National Grange to hold its Session in Portland in 1904. Delegates from 26 states arrived on special railroad cars, were greeted with typical Oregon hospitality, and shown that western Grange states were as good as those in other parts of the county. Local newspapers gave the Session front-page coverage.

The State Grange achieved its first real legislative success in June 1902 when voters approved the initiative and referendum by a wide margin. The initiative allows voters to introduce amendments to the state constitution or pass laws. The referendum gives voters the opportunity to overturn laws passed by the State Legislature. The initiative and referendum became known as the "Oregon System."

The State Grange first used the initiative in 1905. They secured enough signatures to place two initiatives on the June 1906 ballot: One was to levy a tax on the gross earnings of sleeping car, refrigerator, and oil car companies and the other to tax express, telephone, and telegraph companies. Both passed.

The following year the State Grange used the referendum on two bills passed by the legislature. They opposed building 15 armories for which only $100,000 had been appropriated and requiring railroads to give legislators and government officials free passes. Voters agreed and overturned both laws.

In 1906 the Good Roads Session Committee advocated a unified system of public roads: National roads to connect Oregon to neighboring states, state roads to link cities with national roads, and county roads to bring produce to market.

The Committee on the Agricultural College recommended that the number of farmers on the Board of Regents be equal to the proportion of citizens engaged in farming and to the amount of taxes paid by farmers. The Governor did not accept their request, but in 1906 he appointed State Lecturer Clara Waldo to the board.

The State Grange also backed the Recall amendment to the Oregon Constitution that passed in 1908. Oregon was one of the first states to allow voters to call an election to remove an official from office before the end of his term.

In 1909 the State Grange secured passage of the Water Code bill. This law regulates, controls, and distributes water, including requiring the issuance of water rights for surface water.

With these successes the Oregon State Grange became a force in the State Legislature.

1900-02 State officers taken in 1902: front from left to right Treasurer H. Hirschberg (who served 25 years); Flora Clara Swank; Master B. G. Leedy; Pomona Mrs. E. A. Niblin; Chaplain Oscar Eaton; seated in second row Secretary Mary Howard and Overseer Mary Jane Whitby; standing in the back center Ceres Mrs. N. E. Olin and Lecturer Austin Buxton; one of the two men on the far-right is Gatekeeper H. C. Wheeler, father of future State Master Allen Wheeler; others are Assistant Steward C. L. Shaw; Executive Committee members J. R. Booth and George Stephenson

B. G. LEEDY

8th State Master, 1900-1906

Byron Garber Leedy (1857-1923) attended 29 consecutive State Grange Sessions between 1894 and 1923. He performed the Master's part in the Sixth Degree during his terms and many after, conferring the degree on 2,576 members.

B. G. was the oldest of eight children born to Aaron and Elizabeth Ann (Garber) Leedy in Knox County, Ohio. His father was a charter member of Jefferson Grange, served as its Master, and was President of the Patrons Mutual Relief Association. B. G. joined the Grange in Ohio in 1877. He married Flora Young (1857-1944) the following year.

B. G. and Flora moved to Nebraska where they lived for four years before heading to Oregon. They bought a fruit farm at Taylor's Bridge over the Tualatin River in Tigardville (now Tigard). He grew strawberries, apples, peaches, and hay. The Gravenstein apples he sent to the Pan-American Exposition in Buffalo won a silver medal.

B.G. and Flora joined Butte #148 (now Tigard). They were delegates in 1896 and took the Fifth and Sixth Degrees. He was elected the first Master of Washington County Pomona in 1898. B. G. served as Washington County Deputy from 1896 to 1899.

B. G. was elected State Overseer in 1896 and served a single term before being elected Master. He proposed that each county have an agricultural exhibit at the 1905 Lewis and Clark Exposition. Expo leaders liked his idea, but they did not have space and the State Grange did not have money to erect a building.

His next project was to get the National Grange to hold its 1905 Session in Portland during the Lewis and Clark Exposition. The National Grange rejected his idea because they feared that hotel space would be limited and traffic a problem. Instead, the National Grange agreed to hold its 1904 Session in Portland. Meetings were held in the Armory. The Session did not start on time because workmen were still installing B. G.'s county agricultural exhibits. However, delegates were forgiving because Oregon Grangers met their special train at the station. They enjoyed a trip to Corvallis to tour of Oregon Agricultural College. Apparently, Oregon Grangers also were happy with B. G.'s performance because in 1921 when Oregon next hosted National Grange, they asked him to organize the delegates' banquet.

After serving as State Master for six years, B. G. declined re-election. But he was elected to the Executive Committee, on which he served ten years. In 1909 when his successor was unable to attend the Session, B. G. filled the chair. He regularly installed State Grange officers. He was a State Deputy from 1907 to 1912 and from 1915 to 1923. B. G. took charge of Grange Institutes that were held around the state to train Masters, Lecturers, and Secretaries.

B. G. and his family moved to Corvallis when some of his children were enrolled at Oregon Agricultural College. While there, he was elected to the Corvallis City Council and the Benton County Fair Board.

The Governor appointed B. G. to a committee to draft a workman's compensation law, and to the Lime Board to determine if there was a need for a state-run plant.

In addition to the Grange, B. G. was a member of the State Horticultural Society, American Threshermen, and Farm Bureau. He was President of the Farmers' League, a federation of the State Grange and the Farmers' Union. He was an incorporator of the State Grange Cooperative

Association and on its board of directors. He served as Secretary of the Tigard Farmers' Telephone Company. He was a Tigard School Board member in 1922 when they built a new building. He was President of the Tigard Community Fair.

B. G. died on November 18, 1923 at the age of 66. He is buried in Crescent Grove Cemetery in Tigard. Leedy Grange #339 organized in Cedar Mill in 1903 is named after him.

Flora attended State Sessions nearly every year between 1925 and 1939. In 1942 she became a Gold Sheaf (50-year) member. When she died in 1944, she was survived by their six children.

Son J. C. (Jay Clark) Leedy (1887-1971) and his wife Mildred (1893-1950) were members of Kinton #562 when Mildred was elected State Flora in 1918 and J. C. was elected State Assistant Steward in 1920. In 1930 they were members of Melrose #434 while he was Douglas County Agent. He was a delegate for Douglas County Pomona that year. Later when he was Secretary and Manager of the Oregon Turkey Cooperative, he spoke to the State Grange Farm-Labor Relations Committee. In 1960 J. C. and his second wife Enid were delegates from Fernwood #770 in Yamhill County. From 1961 to 1967 he was Yamhill County Deputy. He became a 50-year member in 1966.

AUSTIN T. BUXTON

9th State Master 1906-1910

Austin Todd Buxton (1872 -1918) was born on his father's farm in the unincorporated community of Buxton. In time Austin inherited the farm. It was described as the largest and best equipped in Washington County. The editor of the *Forest Grove Times* reported that the new barn had a concrete floor for the cow stable. Austin also had a silo and used all the latest methods. Austin's wife Orla grew beautiful roses and poppies that were such new varieties they had not yet been named.

Austin graduated from Tualatin Academy in Forest Grove and was valedictorian of the Oregon Agricultural College class of 1895. Austin was active in the literary society. He wrote and delivered orations, including one entitled "Hasten Slowly," which became the motto of his class. He won the honor of representing the college at an intercollegiate oratorial contest at Pacific University. Unfortunately, he became ill and was unable to deliver his speech. However, it was published in the newspaper and lauded for being the best written speech in the competition. Austin also participated in debates on the death penalty and other topics.

Austin's father Henry Buxton was elected the first Master of Forest Grove #67 in 1873. Austin was a charter member and first Master of Gale #282 (now Forest Grove) in 1896. He was a delegate for Washington County to the State Grange Session in 1897 where he took Fifth and Sixth Degrees. Austin spoke on "What Has the Grange to Offer to the College Graduate?" He was appointed Washington County Deputy from 1897 to 1899 and from 1901 to 1905.

Austin married Orla Robbins (1872-1956) of Molalla in 1895. She took the Sixth Degree at the 1895 Session, two years before he did. When he was Master of Washington County Pomona, she was Lecturer.

In 1897 Orla was on the Women's Work Committee whose report was entitled "What is Women's Mission?" Orla gave a series of lectures on domestic science and art for Oregon Agricultural College's six-week winter course. She was the first State Grange Home Economics Chair serving from 1910 to 1915.

Austin was elected State Grange Assistant Steward in 1898 and State Lecturer in 1900. From 1904 to 1906 he was a member of the Executive Committee. At age 34, he is the youngest member to be elected State Master.

While Master, Austin held six Grange Institutes around the state to train Deputies, Masters, Lecturers, and Secretaries. He initiated an inspection system. Austin called for legislation on water rights and encourage members to learn about denatured alcohol and to use it to light their halls.

Austin was unable to attend the 1909 Session due to illness. His absence may have predicted his future. He became seriously ill in 1917. The Buxtons moved to Molalla to be closer to a specialist who could treat his symptoms. The following April, doctors in Portland diagnosed cancer of the lower bowel. He was said to have looked upon his condition "with a philosophic light." He died September 17, 1918 on his father-in-law's farm after suffering from cancer for two years. Austin's funeral was held in the home of his brother Jacob Buxton in Forest Grove. He is buried in the Buxton family plot in Mountain View Memorial Gardens in Forest Grove.

Orla Buxton was a delegate for Molalla #310 in 1924 and while she served as Molalla's Master in 1931 and 1932. The State Home Economics Handbook published in 1954 was dedicated to her. She was remembered during the Memorial Service at the 1957 Session. Their son Oliver (1898-1974) was the delegate for O. A. C. Students #611 in 1923. In 2000 son Maurice (1902-2001) received a letter from the National Master for being an 80-year member.

1910-19

State Master Spence expressed concern that automobiles would "provide easy transport to the city for picture shows," and seriously affect meeting attendance. However, the number of Granges grew in the 1910s to 200 and membership exceeded 10,000 in six of the ten years.

Annual Sessions were held around the state, including in southern Oregon in Roseburg and Grants Pass, on the northern coast in Tillamook and Astoria, and in Monmouth and Hillsboro. There were 66 to 115 delegates from as many as 60 Granges in 29 counties. Beginning in 1918, there were 26 to 28 delegates from 15 Pomonas.

Delegates took their first stand in favor of public power in 1912. The Conservation Committee recommended legislation to make electrical power available to farmers, manufacturers, irrigators, and cities at the lowest possible cost. Their report was adopted.

Delegates voted to abolish the State Senate because it was not a representative body. They thought the Senate was redundant and an unnecessary expense. This position did not win them friends in the legislature or catch on with voters.

In 1913 the Agricultural College Committee gave an extensive report on its progress. There were 2,314 students from every county in Oregon. County field agents had been added. "The extension work carried on by the College is to be especially commended." However, delegates opposed the extravagance of a proposed forestry building.

Grangers were very patriotic during World War I. Six hundred young Grangers served in the Army or Navy and another 600 worked in shipyards, mills, or factories. Thirty percent of Granges purchased Liberty Bonds, 50% organized a Red Cross auxiliary, 50% had service flags in their halls, and all observed food conservation rules.

In his 1917 Master's Address Charles Spence laid out a case for financing the war by taxation rather than with bonds. Delegates agreed. They voted to forbid the use of grain in the manufacturing of alcoholic beverages and favored using war prisoners for farm labor. Delegates voted not to collect dues from members serving their country.

State Master Spence's focus was on marketing farm products for the best price. In 1918 he and a representative of the Federal Grain Corporation met with President Wilson and negotiated a 15 cent higher price per bushel of number one wheat shipped from the West Coast. In 1923 Governor Pierce appointed Charles to the new position of State Market Agent.

In his 1919 Master's Address, Spence noted that Grange work had suffered from the stress of the war and the influenza epidemic. "The sickness of many members and the death of a number, together with the ban on all meetings had the effect of suspending Grange work." However, he was optimistic that there was "an awakening" in the previous two months.

Delegates in 1919 voted against the production and use of tobacco. They favored U. S. involvement in the League of Nations. They also favored making the U. S. Employment Service permanent and voted to repeal the "so called daylight savings law."

In 1912 the State Grange got an initiative on the ballot to create a State Highway Department. The initiative was voted down, but the State Legislature later approved the department. Delegates favored hiring a State Highway Engineer, until they realized that he was primarily interested in building scenic highways for pleasure seekers.

The State Grange took a strong stand in favor of a "Pay as you go" policy for road construction. Members felt that issuing bonds would be a burden to future generations. In 1919 the Legislative Committee urged "every farmer who hates mud" to vote for the one mill tax bill on the June 3 ballot. The Market Road Law was termed "the best good roads bill ever (up to that point) passed by the Oregon legislature." Voters approved it 53,199 to 28,039.

CHARLES E. SPENCE

10th State Master, 1910-1923

Charles E. Spence (1865-1927) was born in Toronto, Canada. When he was six, his parents moved to Kansas where they homesteaded. Charles graduated from normal school, taught for six years, and worked on the railroad before moving to Oregon to teach at Beavercreek, outside Oregon City. There he married Anna Spangler (1862-1925), who had two children. They moved back to Kansas, where their daughter Echo was born. But then they returned to Oregon and bought a 70-acre farm at Carus in Clackamas County where he raised oats, red clover, corn, Jersey cows, Berkshire hogs, and draft horses.

The Spences joined Central #276 (now Beavercreek) in 1896. Charles and Anna were delegates to the 1902 State Session. He was appointed to the Legislation and Agricultural College Committees and Anna served on the Education and Resolutions Committees. They took the Fifth and Sixth Degrees. Daughter Echo took the Sixth Degree at the 1910 Session.

In 1904, Charles was appointed to a State Grange committee to update the organization's By-Laws and elected to the Board of Directors of Patrons' Insurance Association. The following year he was elected to the State Grange Executive Committee. Charles took charge of circulating petitions for initiatives the State Grange wanted to get on the ballot.

Charles was appointed to the Board of Regents of the Normal School at Monmouth. He served as Secretary of the Clackamas County Fair Association, the Beaver Creek Mutual Telephone Association, and a joint committee of the Oregon State Grange and the Oregon Federation of Labor to defend the initiative and referendum. He served as chairman of the legislative committee of the Oregon Taxpayer's League.

In 1910 Charles was elected State Master by two votes. He became known as one of the best lobbyists and debaters on topics ranging from good roads and how to finance them to abolishing the State Senate. Future State Master Ray Gill gave Charles credit for starting the movement for public ownership and development of power.

In 1918 Charles faced serious opposition for his position on the non-partisan league and for making a living off the job of State Master. His salary was $300 per year, but he traveled extensively so his expenses totaled $3,000. The challenge was not as serious as reported because he was re-elected by 70 to 39 votes. Charles' opponent was a lawyer. Many delegates wondered aloud why a farmers' organization should be headed by an attorney.

In the thirteen years that Charles was Master, he never performed the Master's part in the Sixth Degree. His wife Anna substituted for him in 1915, National Master Lowell in 1920, and B. G. Leedy all other years. One might conclude that Charles was not into Grange ritual. However, in 1921 he was elected Priest Annalist of the National Grange and Anna served as National Flora.

In his 1919 Master's Address, Charles said "The State of Oregon should have a market master whose duty it will be to organize producers of like products together, to standardizing the products, and to find a market as near the ultimate consumer as possible for those products." In 1923 Governor Pierce appointed Charles to the new position as State Market Agent. The position was not then fully defined but was intended to determine how to best market Oregon products.

Charles resigned as State Master at the 1923 State Session. "As indicated in my annual report yesterday, I believe it to be to the best interest of the Grange and myself and the office of State Market Agent that I resign as Master of the Oregon State Grange at this time. I will continue my interest in Grange work and will cooperate with the Grange in every way possible." A motion was made and seconded not to accept his resignation. After discussion, the motion lost. Nine brothers were nominated. On the first ballot, Charles received a majority of votes cast. Finally, his successor was elected. The State Grange gave Charles a gold watch, which he valued highly.

The Spences were delegates in 1924 and 1925. When Anna died in 1925, Charles moved to Gladstone to be near his daughter Echo Spence McMahon (1894-1994) and her family. He became ill in December 1926, was operated on in January, resigned from the Market Agent position in February, and died March 31, 1927. He is buried in Beavercreek Memorial Cemetery.

1920-29

The number of Granges in the 1920s reached 256. Membership steadily increased from 9,233 to 16,761.

Sessions were held for the first time in Bend, Newport, Dallas, Baker, Rainier, and Myrtle Point. Since every Grange could send two delegates, the number jumped from 190 to 330. Another 16 to 27 delegates represented Pomona Granges.

In his 1922 Master's Address Charles Spence reported on hosting the National Grange Session the previous November. He specifically mentioned the boat trip to municipal docks and Vancouver, flowers sent to delegates' rooms, the visit to a "modern monster sawmill in full operation," and the use of the Public Auditorium for the Seventh Degree. The Secretary's report noted that 577 Oregon members took the Sixth Degree at the Session.

The average number of resolutions submitted per year in the 1920s was 45, 73% of which set State Grange policy.

The State Grange took a firm stand against a sales tax, the first of nine times it was voted down by Oregonians. Members opposed the tax because they thought it was regressive. Instead, they favored a graduated income tax. In 1928 the State Grange struggled but succeeded to get enough signatures to place an income tax initiative on the ballot. However, it was voted down 53% to 47%. None of the eight measures on the ballot that election passed.

Delegates favored compulsory education for children between the ages of 7 and 16. They called for Congress to begin work on the first Monday in January and the inauguration be moved from March to January, making the President less of a "lame duck."

Delegates took a strong stand against driving under the influence of alcohol and felt that those convicted should be sentenced to not less than five years in jail. Punishment for the manufacture or sale of liquor should be one year in jail for the first offense and five years for each succeeding offence. They also opposed billboard advertising for cigarettes.

Before 1921, the State Grange favored consolidation of rural schools. At that time there were over 1,500 one-room schools in the state. But by 1923, delegates reversed their position because they wanted local school boards to have more control.

In 1923 delegates adopted a resolution calling for U. S. Supreme Court judges to be elected. They also felt that seven of nine votes should be required to declare a law unconstitutional. Their action was probably motivated by Muller v. Oregon and Bunting v. Oregon.

Delegates voted in favor of state ownership and development of hydroelectric projects. Opponents argued that the cost would drive up taxes. The *Oregon Statesman* (Salem) reported that the Session was evenly divided, but when the vote was taken there were few negative votes.

The State Grange began a campaign in 1929 to elect a Lieutenant Governor. Two Governors had resigned to take Senate seats, one resigned due to ill health, and James Withycombe died in office. Even though

Governor Patterson died on December 21, 1929, the measure on ballot the following November lost by 2,570 votes. Oregon still does not have a Lieutenant Governor.

In 1929 the Legislative Committee's report stated, "We believe the Grange's influence was greater at the Session than any other Session ever attended by us." The Grange created lobbying groups with the Brotherhood of Railroad Trainmen, Locomotive Firemen and Engineers, the Union Fisherman, and formed a Farm Bloc with other farm organizations.

In 1928 Oregon's Session was in Rainier while the Washington State Grange met in Longview. The Longview Chamber of Commerce served "a splendid banquet." Washington Master A. S. Goss spoke on the problems of agriculture and conditions of the order. Master Palmiter was too horse to speak so asked Executive Committee member and future State Master Ray Gill to speak for him. "Everyone who attended voted the joint meeting a great success."

GEORGE A. PALMITER

11th State Master, 1923-1930

George Abner Palmiter (1879-1938) was born in Manitowoc County, Wisconsin. He married Emma Groom (1873-1971) in 1901. They moved to California in 1910 where George was in the furniture business. In 1916 they moved to Hood River, bought an orchard, and joined Park #501 (now Rockford).

The Palmiters were delegates to the 1920 Session, but neither was assigned to a committee. In 1921, George was chairman of the Transportation Committee, and his wife Emma was on the Assessment and Taxation Committee.

George was elected State Assistant Steward at the 1922 Session. In his report the following year, he asked the Worthy Master to instruct members on the proper way to give the salutation. Today delegates are not required to give the salutation when entering or leaving State Session.

When State Master Charles Spence resigned because the Governor had appointed him State Market Agent, nine brothers were nominated, three of which withdrew. The Election Committee reported that Spence received a majority of the votes cast, but he asked to be relieved. George was declared elected.

George's first action was to announce a membership campaign. However, he was immediately sidelined with appendicitis. Nonetheless his campaign was successful. Membership was 9,701 when he became State Master; eight years later, it was 19,287.

George gave his all to his position. He concluded his 1927 Master's Address with an accounting of his time. He had spent 49 days at the Oregon Legislature, 25 days going to, attending, and returning from the National Grange Session in Portland, ME, 23 days circulating Income Tax petitions, 16 days visiting Granges in Idaho with their State Master, 6 days attending the California State Grange Session, three days each attending the Oregon Federation of Labor convention, Lecturers' School, and Masters' and Deputies' School, two days each at Grange Fire Relief board meetings, hearings on lime rates, and the Washington State Grange Session. He attended 77 Grange meetings, ten picnics, four Executive Committee meetings, and five Board of Regents meetings. He visited three Experiment Stations. The rest of his time was spent writing letters or sleeping.

In 1930 George received a majority of votes cast by members. He thanked them but resigned "owing to other business." He had accepted a managerial position with Farmers Automobile Inter-Insurance Company in Portland. His resignation was accepted. The State Grange presented him with a gold watch.

It does not appear that George stayed with the insurance company long. He was a State Deputy from 1931 to 1934 and was asked to be a field representative for Grange Supply Cooperative. In that capacity he set up Grange Co-op stores in Klamath Falls, Central Point, Coos Bay, Redmond, Hood River, Roseburg, Clackamas, and Enterprise. These eight stores purchased 150,000 gallons of gas, and $5,000 worth of tires, batteries, and auto accessories. The stores had a total membership of 870 and a $12,500 investment in storage facilities and equipment.

George was elected to the State Executive Committee in 1932 and re-elected twice. But he resigned in the fall of 1937, reportedly because he objected to the debt acquired from the new headquarters building. He noted that when he left office in 1930, the treasury balance was $25,000 and there was no debt. In 1937 the organization owed $6,000 and had no plan to pay it off.

When George filed as a candidate for Oregon Secretary of State in 1932, a supporter commented. "No man better qualified to fill the position." His talent "for detail" was evident during his terms as State Grange Master. He was not elected Secretary of State, but Governor Pierce appointed him to the State Industrial Accident Commission and later Governor Patterson named him to the State Board of Forestry.

George's wife Emma was also an active member. When Oregon hosted the National Grange Session in 1921, she distributed 30 boxes of Hood River's finest apples along with 2,500 information cards on cherries, peaches, and other Oregon agricultural products. Fittingly, in 1928 she was elected Pomona of the National Grange. She also served as Chair of the National Grange Home Economics Committee in 1934 and 1935.

George's career came full circle. He returned to the furniture business in St. Johns. The Palmiters joined Milwaukie #268. George was stricken with a cerebral hemorrhage while attending a meeting. He died later that night at his home. His ashes are at the Riverview Abbey Mausoleum and Crematory in Portland. He was survived by his wife Emma and six children. In 1942 Emma received her 25-year pin. She attended the 1949 and 1951 State Sessions.

A STUMBLE BEFORE MARCHING FORWARD

1930-39

In 1939 the number of Granges reached 377, the largest number in the Oregon State Grange's history. That year Oregon had 22,583 members and led the nation in Grange growth. State Master Ray Gill reported that 236 Granges had their own halls, valued at $400,000.

The number of delegates ranged between 342 and 455 representing 75% of Granges from all 36 counties. In addition, 38 to 55 delegates represented 30 Pomonas. The number of resolutions Granges submitted ranged from 51 to 99 with an average of 69, 73% of which set State Grange policy.

Redmond, Medford, Silverton, Pendleton, Lebanon, and Klamath Falls hosted a Session for the first time. The *Evening Herald* (Klamath Falls) noted in 1938 that the Grange Session was different from others. Grangers really work at their Session. Grangers were up and at it at 8 a.m. each morning. Midnight was the usual quitting time, but on the last night they stayed until 3 a.m.

The State Grange felt the effects of the great depression that lasted nearly ten years. Dues were reduced, the *Grange Bulletin* had fewer advertisers, and the State Grange got a short-term loan of $4,000 to cover milage and per diem for delegates. The number of deputies was reduced, and their travel limited. Instead, eight state officers travelled in two cars to conduct a conference in all 36 counties. Average conference attendance was 100 with 80% of Granges attending.

The *Grange Bulletin* printed 307,868 copies which required 17 tons of paper. The advertising manager obtained 12 national advisers. More importantly he began the Sales Slip Program that financed the publication when advertisers were scarce. A member in each Grange got local businesses to buy a two- or three-line ad. Then members saved sales slips for their purchases from those advertisers. Granges were paid $1 for every $2,000 in sales slips. By 1957 the Sales Slip Program turned a profit of over $111,000.

In 1937 the State Grange conducted a vote by mail on four questions: Should the length of the State Session be increased? Should the salary of the State Secretary be increased? Should mileage for delegates who travel to Session by "stage" or train be increased? Should the number of members on the State Agriculture Committee be increased? A majority of the 221 responses agreed with all four questions. Clearly, at this point members did not see the economy as a serious problem.

In 1936 State Master Ray Gill often quoted National Master Taber, "Oregon has the best-balanced Grange work of any state in the Nation." Gill advocated that Granges increase their summer activities with picnics, bonfires, and special programs to maintain the habit of getting together. He challenged Granges to give scholarships to 4-H Summer School at Oregon State College. The State Lecturer reported that 32 Granges had orchestras, 35 choruses, 36 quartets, and 31 dramatic clubs.

4-H Summer School attendees that were sponsored by their local Grange.

Oregon ranked fifth in the nation in the number of Juvenile Granges and in 1931 held a State Juvenile Grange Session for children between the ages of five and fourteen. Ninety children participated. In 1938 YGAs (Young Granger Auxiliaries later changed to Young Grangers of America) were formed in Granges that had at least ten members who were teens or in their early 20s.

Oregon was the first state to organize Home Economics Clubs. Many clubs donated $1 to the Charles E. Spence Educational Memorial Fund that loaned money to members who were pursuing a post-high school education.

The State Agriculture Committee reported that every Grange had an Agriculture Committee. Granges in Wallowa, Douglas, and Baker counties marketed livestock. Deschutes, Grant, Josephine, and Lane Granges pooled orders for lime, seed, sacks, twine, and other commodities to reduce shipping costs. The State Agriculture Committee sponsored a prune marketing meeting that led to the formation of the North Pacific Prune Exchange.

In 1938 Oregon hosted the National Grange at the Multnomah Hotel with two conferrals of the Seventh Degree at the Portland Auditorium. Prior to this Session, 28 meetings were held around the state so that 1,843 members could receive the Fifth and Sixth Degrees before the Session. Oregon had 3,777 candidates for the Seventh Degree, again exceeding previous records.

In 1938 the State Grange purchased three buildings at 12th and Salmon in East Portland for $5,000 to house the offices of the State Secretary and Oregon Grange Wholesale. The Wholesale began selling gasoline and oil to members in 1934. It secured a contract with the Massey-Harris Farm Machinery and Tractor Company and sold nearly $10,000 worth of machinery and parts in three months. The following year, the Grange Wholesale Manager reported that total sales volume was $250,000, with huge increases in sales of tires, fertilizer, and machinery. $10,000 worth of capital stock certificates had been sold at $10 each.

Legislatively, the Grange continued to work for public power. Bonneville Dam was being constructed. In 1930, voters approved the Oregon Water and Power Utility Districts (P.U.D.s) Amendment. Two years later they approved the Oregon Hydroelectric Power measure, often called "The Grange Power Bill," by 38,000 votes.

The State Grange also successfully fought the sales tax three times in the 1930s (1933, 1934, and 1936). They supported an initiative that only taxpayers be allowed to vote on bond and tax measures.

At the 1932 State Session, delegates heard a guest speaker who convinced them to oppose any monopoly, but especially chain stores. They also voted that the *Grange Bulletin* discontinue advertising contracts with chain stores when they expired.

Delegates supported the League of Nations, World Court, and the World Disarmament Conference and opposed compulsory military training in tax-supported schools. They favored laws that prevented the sale, exportation, or manufacture of firearms, munitions, explosives, gas, powder, and airplanes except for national defense. They thought preference should be given to American manufactured goods over foreign-made goods. Delegates supported Old Age, Survivors, and Disability Insurance (Social Security). They also favored abolishing the Electoral College.

When the State Grange re-affirmed its strong opposition to alcoholic beverages and resubmission of the 18th Amendment, voters did not agree. As early as 1938 delegates favored heavy fines and long prison sentences for the use, sale, or possession of marijuana.

Since the State Grange failed to abolish the State Senate, in 1934 State Master Ray Gill called for abolishing the State House of Representatives. He claimed, "We would not think of having two boards of directors to conduct a private business." That position also did not catch on.

C. C. HULET

12th State Master, 1930-1932

Charles Clair Hulet (1882-1956) burst upon the Oregon State Grange scene, left just as quickly, and then reappeared 20 years later.

C. C. was born in Russell, Kansas. He graduated from a Methodist seminary but became an ordained Presbyterian minister. He joined the Grange while serving as a pastor in the Seattle area. When he came to Oregon, he was first a Sabbath School Missionary. He called on six hundred families and started ten Sunday Schools.

In 1925 while C. C. was the pastor of churches in Merrill and Malin, he was involved with the Klamath Irrigation District. He and the Mayor of Malin attempted to conduct a district meeting to recommend to the Interstate Commerce Commission which railroad should build a trunk line to that area. The newspaper headline was "Meeting Gets Out of Control." The next week C. C. resigned as pastor of the Merrill church.

C. C.'s next church was in Myrtle Point. He was elected Master of Myrtle #289. He attended the 1928 Oregon State Grange Session, took the Sixth Degree, and invited delegates to hold the 1929 Session in Marshfield (now Coos Bay).

On May 27, 1929, State Deputy Hulet wrote to the Marshfield Chamber of Commerce, "The State Grange cannot and will not come to any city where they are not welcome or where there is a feeling that they are being 'dumped'; therefore, the State Grange convention will not be held in Marshfield this year." Apparently, the Chamber and the Grange did not agree on which would handle housing for Session goers. The Session began in Myrtle Point sixteen days later. C. C. was Myrtle Grange's delegate.

The following year, George Palmiter was elected State Master but resigned because he had accepted a managerial position with Farmers' Automobile Inter-Insurance Exchange in Portland. C.C. was the delegates' second choice.

In 1930 the Hulets lived in Albany. C. C. set up an office for the State Grange at 705 W. 6th Avenue SW.

C. C. performed the duties expected of a State Master. He visited Granges, organized new Granges, and spoke at labor and FFA conventions, the State Fair, and picnics. Newspapers often included a small article on another page that while visiting a town, Reverend Hulet delivered the sermon at the local Presbyterian Church and stayed night at the parsonage.

C. C. represented Oregon at the National Grange Session in Rochester, N. Y. He convinced the National Grange to add an Agriculture Committee and was named its first Chairman. Oregon was recognized that year for leading the nation in membership growth.

In July 1931 Governor Meier called a "tax reduction conference" that gave a platform to C. C. and others with political ambitions. C. C. was known to be interested in running for Congress in 1932. The *Oregon Statesman* described C. C. as "an ardent organizer in Grange work, knows how to talk the language of farmers, fights utilities, banks, and high taxes–all the bogies of the Grange crowd–and is rising rapidly in public attention."

C. C. announced in the February 20, 1932 issue of the *Grange Bulletin* that he planned to resign April 1 to run for Congress. Earlier he had claimed that running for office would not interfere with his work as State Master, but the State Executive Committee apparently thought otherwise. They did not mind him preaching a sermon while traveling for the Grange, especially when his night's lodging was provided. But they were concerned that his political positions might differ from Grange policy. In fact, he supported a 2% sales tax and declared that prohibition was a failure and should be resubmitted to the voters. As newspapers predicted, C. C. came in third in a four-man race.

Overseer M. C. Glover became Master on April 1. C. C. attended the 1932 Session. His name does not appear in Grange Proceedings again until 1951.

Minnie Patterson Hulet (1882-1950) was more active in the Women's Christian Temperance Union than the Grange. C. C. and Minnie had a son and two daughters. William and Evelyn took the Sixth Degree at the 1931 Session. In November 1932 C. C. filed for divorce from Minnie in Reno on grounds of cruelty.

The 1940 census shows C. C. living in Plympton, Multnomah County with wife Ruth and adopted son Donald. In 1951 C. C. and Ruth A. Hulet were delegates from Lents #351 to the State Session in Portland. He was presented to the Master's station along with other past state officers.

C. C. was remembered during the Memorial Service at the 1957 Session. He is buried in Lincoln Memorial Park in Portland.

M. C. GLOVER

Matthew Clyde Glover (1883-1959) has been omitted from lists of past Masters of the Oregon State Grange, likely because he served only 77 days, from April 1 to June 17, 1932.

M. C. was a charter member of Eagle Creek #287 and served as its first Secretary in 1901. He took the Sixth Degree at the 1903 Session in Oregon City. He served as Eagle Creek's Master from 1913 to 1915. He and his wife Eva (1881-1953) were delegates to the State Session in 1914. He served on the Finance Committee and she on the Pure Foods Committee.

In 1918 M. C. was elected Clackamas County Pomona Master. At the Session that year, M. C. was elected State Steward. He was re-elected in 1920 and in 1922 he was elected Overseer.

M. C. served as Clackamas County Deputy from 1919 to 1923. During the 1924 Session, he was sent to Vancouver to meet National Grange Master Taber at the Washington State Grange Session and drive him to the Oregon Session in The Dalles. He must have made a good impression because he was subsequently named a National Grange Deputy. During that time, he organized eight Subordinate Granges. From 1923 to 1928 he was a special Juvenile Deputy and organized 17 Juvenile Granges. In 1929 and 1930 he was again a County Deputy.

When C. C. Hulet resigned on April 1, 1932, M. C. assumed the responsibilities of State Master. In his first column as State Master published in the *Grange Bulletin*, M. C. asked for help identifying weaker Granges. At his first Executive Committee meeting as Master, he claimed that only first-time delegates should be appointed to Session committees. His opinion was overruled.

In his Master's Address, M.C. noted that KOAC cost taxpayers $100 per day and questioned whether enough listeners were being reached to warrant such an expenditure. Delegates took issue with his opinion and adopted a resolution in favor of retaining the station as part of the Oregon Agricultural College.

After performing all the duties of State Master for 77 days, M. C. happily resumed the office of Overseer. When he retired in 1934, he was presented an Indian blanket.

M. C. continued to attend Sessions in the late 1930s. He was presented to the Master's station along with other past state officers and introduced as past Steward and Overseer. Only one year was he identified as a past Master. His obituary page in the 1960 *Proceedings* says he was a past State Overseer.

In addition to his Grange involvement, M. C. was President of the Eagle Creek Council of Defense and Secretary-Treasurer of the Ag Council, which later became the Farm Bureau. He served on the Clackamas County Tax Board. He chaired the County Budget Committee and the Farm Crops Committee for an Agricultural Economic Conference. In 1932 Governor Meier appointed M. C. to a nine-member state advisory board for the Highway Commission. Their mission was to lower vehicle registration fees.

M. C. died September 9, 1959 and is buried next to his wife Eva in the Beavercreek Memorial Cemetery. They were survived by two children.

M. C. should be included with other State Masters because he performed the duties of the office and his accomplishments were similar to others who have held the office.

RAY W. GILL

14th State Master, 1932-1942

Raymond Walter Gill (1882-1963) was born on a farm in the Montavilla District of Portland and lived there his entire life. He and his brother Edward farmed 74 acres and grew 15 varieties of grains, 36 of vegetables, 12 of cantaloupes, and 15 of squash and pumpkins. Ray was considered a champion cabbage grower; he dry-farmed 24 acres of cabbage in 1909. He also developed many varieties and colors of dahlias and was President of the Oregon Dahlia Society.

In 1910, Ray and Edward co-founded Gill Bros. Seed Company. They had their own breeding program, trial grounds, and production fields. Ray gave talks on the relation of seed strains to yield and quality of vegetables.

Ray was a charter member of Russellville #353 in 1905. Only four of Russellville's charter members were over the age of 30. He was 20 when he was elected Master. Ray and his wife Nina (1891-1984), called Nan, attended their first State Grange Session in 1905. They took the Sixth Degree in 1906.

Ray was elected Multnomah Pomona Master in 1910. While he was Master, the Pomona established a public market on the east side of

Portland. Ray and Nan were Multnomah Pomona delegates between 1918 and 1924. At the latter Session, she was elected Lady Assistant Steward.

In 1918 Ray was elected to the State Grange Legislative Committee. This position was a natural fit because he had written many resolutions; in 1931 he served one term in Oregon's House of Representatives. After that term, *The Capitol Journal* called Ray the most frequent speaker at public hearings on proposed legislation.

Many State Masters have served as State Overseer before being elected Master. Instead, Ray served three terms on the State Executive Committee and was a State Deputy for nine years.

During his five terms as State Master, Ray traveled throughout the state speaking at Grange meetings, picnics, and to other groups. He was an outspoken advocate for public power, electing a Lieutenant Governor, abolishing the state house of representatives, and against the sales tax.

Ray proudly quoted National Master Taber's claim that, "Oregon has the best-balanced Grange work of any state in the Nation." Ray began the tradition of the State Master giving a Good of the Order Address that focused on internal Grange issues. He urged Granges to build their own halls and provide scholarships to 4-H Summer School.

In 1938 Ray's re-election appeared to be in jeopardy. Opposition began with apple growers in Hood River County who feared a shippers' strike. Ray maintained close ties with leaders of organized labor. However, despite newspaper reports of his opponent's claim that he was winning, Ray received 5,740 votes to 3,010 in the preferential vote of members and 444 to 22 votes of delegates. Ray considered it a "vote of confidence."

After being State Master, Ray was again elected to the State Grange Executive Committee from 1942 to 1963. When the State Grange purchased a new headquarters building, Ray and Nan loaned the organization $5,000 without interest or a repayment date requirement.

Ray was often mentioned as a candidate for Governor, U. S. Senator, and National Master. A June 6, 1934 *Capital Press* headline was "Gill Aspires to be National Master of Grange in America." The article detailed, "This explains why the Republican candidate for Senate from

Multnomah and Clackamas counties is not running for Governor as an Independent. Session goers reasoned that Ray's recent trips to New England and east coast Grange states were indication that he hoped to replace National Master Tabor, who has served for a dozen years." The article went on to claim that being National Master would pay better and his term would last longer.

In fact, Ray Gill was elected to the National Grange Executive Committee from 1937 to 1945, one term of which he served as Chairman. Being elected to a fourth three-year term was unprecedented. Nan was elected Pomona of the National Grange and appointed Home Economics Chairman.

In addition to his Grange involvement, Ray served as President of the Gresham Fair Association and on the boards of Multnomah County Fair and Russellville School. He was a Director of the Oregon Grange Fire Relief Association and a member of the Executive Board of Farmers Automobile Inter-Insurance Exchange. Other organizations to which Ray belonged included the Portland Rotary, Masons, Order of Eastern Star, Al Kadar Shrine, Eastside Commercial Club, and Portland Chamber of Commerce.

Ray Gill could not attend the 1963 State Session because he was hospitalized. He died on August 8, 1963 and is buried in Lincoln Memorial Cemetery on Mt. Scott in Portland. He was survived by his wife, daughter Helen Miller, and granddaughters Cheryl and Patty. Nina was a 75-year member in 1980 and Helen a 75-year member in 2009. Both granddaughters participated in Junior and youth activities. Cheryl's name was drawn for a $200 Home Economics college scholarship in 1967 and Patty's in 1973.

1940-49

Although there were 23 fewer Granges (371 to 354) by the end of the 1940s, Grange #900 was organized. Membership reached its peak of 32,069 in 1948.

Sessions were held for the first time in Milwaukie and Coos Bay. There were 266 to 401 delegates plus 39 to 58 delegates from 26 to 34 Pomonas. The low numbers were likely due to gas rationing.

The 1940 Session was interrupted to listen to the President's radio broadcast on the war, "which made us realize what a grave situation the war has now reached." Two years later in his last Master's Address, Ray Gill stated, "When war was declared the National Grange immediately took up Red Cross and first aid programs. In Oregon these activities were along with many others such as the promotion of increased agricultural production as requested by the Secretary of Agriculture, also Victory Gardens, nutrition studies, salvage collections, promotion of war bond sales and organization to meet rural transportation problems."

Ray Gill advised farmers to look for new crops and new uses for the crops they were growing. His successor Morton Tompkins used the term "chemurgy," the science of turning crops into marketable synthetics like Russian dandelions into rubber or milkweed into life preservers. While this sounded a good idea, chemurgy did not always work. In 1947 delegates asked manufacturers to recall canning jar lids made during the war with synthetic rubber or rubber substitutes because 85% of them did not seal.

The Oregon Grange Wholesale Manager reported that although dollar volume was up 47%, tire business was down 50% due to rationing, and steel products were impossible to find. After the war, sales exceeded $1,000,000, more retail stores were opened, and a frozen locker plant was built in Umatilla County.

In the 1940s the number of resolutions averaged 91 per year, which was considerably higher than in the previous decade (69). Eighty-one percent of the resolutions were written to set policy.

Delegates voted to establish a Columbia Valley Authority modeled after the TVA, build Hells Canyon Dam on the Snake River, and protest Pacific Power and Light's charging "loss leader" rates in The Dalles attempting to destroy the Northern Wasco P.U.D.

Building dams for flood control was on everyone's mind. Delegates approved the Willamette Valley Flood Control Program that included 16 reservoirs. They supported a Flood Relief Program to be administered by the Oregon Department of Agriculture, with grants and loans from the federal government and tax relief for those affected.

Delegates supported a resolution that bridges and ferries across the Columbia River be toll free and favored the federal government purchasing the Hood River Bridge and Bridge of the Gods to make them toll free. Delegates favored making gross weight and length limits for trucks uniform with adjoining states and standardizing highway signs and route numbers throughout the country. Delegates favored requiring all traffic coming to a complete stop when a school bus was loading or unloading children. Surprisingly many state legislators thought this action would increase danger to children.

Delegates reaffirmed the State Grange stand against a sales tax. However, since Rogue River Valley #469 in Josephine County voted to support the sales tax initiative, newspapers expected "a substantial group of Grangers" to favor it. After a morning of debate only 20 delegates voted against the Grange State position.

In 1943 a Post War Session Committee was added to consider resolutions on how to achieve peace, employ servicemen, provide veterans' services, and deal with the "Japanese problem." Specifically, delegates supported the United Nations. They favored employing servicemen to construct irrigation, drainage, and flood control projects. They recommended re-opening Camp White as a veterans' mental hospital. Delegates approved the immigration of 200,000 displaced European agricultural workers but opposed the return of any Japanese from relocation centers. After three hours of debate, they voted to appoint an interim committee to recommend what to do about those of Japanese ancestry.

In his 1943 Good of the Order Address, Morton Tompkins stated "The time has come when the Grange must adopt modern methods of putting its message before the public." In response, the State Grange produced programs on KEX in Portland that were carried by every radio station outside Portland. Seven were 15-minute dramatized plays. Nine were five-minute programs built around Grange accomplishments. Later a series of eight public-relations advertisements were placed in 68 newspapers. The Executive Committee budgeted $1,336 for radio advertising to defeat a senate bill that was termed "the hydro power grab." Their budget paid for a five-minute talk on 20 stations and three 100-word announcements on 60 stations.

In April 1945 a resolution was sent to Granges on holding the Session later in the year due to war travel restrictions. An overwhelming majority voted to delay. In September the Office of Defense Transportation turned down the State Grange's application to hold a meeting. That ban was later lifted but by then it was too late to reschedule. The State Grange did not hold a Session in 1945.

In 1944 the State Juvenile Grange was unofficially organized. Delegates elected officers who conducted meetings, learned Grange rituals, and presented guests. They had craft and nature study classes. Scrapbook, poster, and essay contests around a theme, like Birds of Oregon, were judged and prizes awarded. By 1948, Oregon had 75 Juvenile Granges with a membership of 1,550. In addition to supporting the war effort, many sent packages of food and clothing to families in need in European countries.

YGAs had over 600 members in 54 Granges and 18 Pomona. When Oregon hosted the National Grange Session in Portland in 1938, Oregon youth were well represented.

The Home Economics Committee compiled a cookbook and sold 3,000 copies. Members from 33 counties entered the canning contest sponsored by White Satin Sugar, which awarded major appliances to the winners. Many of the 255 Home Economics Clubs purchased war bonds, gave parties or monthly dinners for servicemen, or helped with school lunch programs by volunteering in the kitchen, donating food or home canned goods.

The 1948 Session was held in Astoria despite the devastating Columbia River flood that wiped out the city of Vanport just west of Portland on Memorial Day. State Master Morton Tompkins announced that the

Session would observe "regular" time. Each city in Oregon could determine whether to use standard or daylight time. Portland, Salem, Bend, and Klamath Falls went to daylight time. A judge ruled that the city of Dallas would use "God's time." Railroads and Oregon State Grange did also.

In his 1948 Master's Address, Morton Tompkins stated, "Of all the problems which face the world today, conservation of our natural resources is of top-ranking importance, but in comparison to the magnitude of the problem, we are doing very little about it." In response, delegates proposed what became known as the Grange Timber Severance Tax bill. It would have levied 25 cents per thousand board feet to reforest devasted areas, finance wood utilization research at Oregon State College, and establish an extension forester in each county. The initiative on that year's ballot, which passed narrowly, was far more modest.

MORTON TOMPKINS

15th State Master,1942-1950

Morton Tompkins (1885-1956) was born in Oregon City to Josephus and Sarah Tompkins, well-known Oregon pioneers. Morton began his working life in sawmills and logging camps in Columbia County. He met and married Maud Wilson (1888-1974) in St. Helens in 1903.

After the Tompkins lost their eldest son Lester to appendicitis, they moved to Grand Island in the Willamette River near Dayton where his parents and brother Jake lived. Morton grew peaches, filberts, tomatoes, onions, musk melons, and cantaloups. He advertised his "ripened on the vine melons" in the *Salem Statesman*. Morton managed the Grand Island Co-op Cannery that employed 60 and in 1931 packed 15,000 cases of tomatoes.

When they moved to Grand Island, access was by ferry. In 1915 Morton got the Oregon Legislature to approve construction of a bridge. Morton was active in the Grand Island Improvement Club and Maud was usually an officer in the Mothers' Circle.

The Tompkins joined McMinnville #31 in 1922. He was elected Master in 1925 and Lecturer in 1928. He and Maud were delegates to the 1925

State Session at which they took the Sixth Degree. Morton served as Agriculture Chairman of Yamhill Pomona from 1933 until 1936.

Morton served two terms (1929 and 1931) in the State House of Representatives. He was credited with Oregon's School Bus law. Governor Meier appointed him to the first advisory committee for the new Oregon Department of Agriculture.

In 1931 State Master C. C. Hulet appointed Morton to a State Bank Committee and to a committee on Columbia River and Willamette River navigation. Morton was elected to the State Grange's Legislative Committee from 1932 to 1942. He was a very active lobbyist, especially for public power and against a sales tax.

Morton served as chairman of the State Agricultural Committee from 1936 to 1942. He chaired weed and flood control committees, served on a farm-labor relations committee, substituted for State Master Ray Gill on a Surplus Agricultural Products Marketing Commission, and attended over 100 meetings at which growers reported their interest in improved product marketing.

In 1934 Morton was elected State Overseer, an office he held until he was elected Master in 1942. In his first Master's address, Morton proposed extending Oregon's successful absentee balloting system to allow every voter in the state to receive and cast their ballot by mail. His vote by mail proposal was adopted by the delegates and reported on the front page of *The Salem Statesman*, but neither the State Grange nor the state of Oregon acted on his idea until 1998.

In 1943 Morton was one of six American farmers selected to tour England as a guest of the British government. Morton spoke on his experience at numerous meetings throughout Oregon.

Morton's wholehearted support for the Columbia Valley Authority came under attack when it was revealed that he had received compensation from the Bonneville Power Administration seemingly in exchange for the Grange's support. The *Bend Bulletin* and *News-Review* (Roseburg) ran editorials against Morton. The final straw was when Morton named 22 members of the Oregon House of Representatives who voted to change petition requirements for Oregon's initiative. Many members felt that he was becoming too political.

In the 1950 preferential primary Overseer Elmer McClure led by 400 votes even though he and Morton agreed on most policy questions. But another factor may have been that Elmer was 12 years younger than Morton. The *Oregon Journal* reported that Elmer McClure was expected to provide "less belligerent and arbitrary leadership." The State Grange had become "more interested in legislation and ideology than agricultural technology, the economy, and the social status of its members."

Morton concluded his 1950 Master's Address with, "During my term of office the Grange has served through a major part of a world war, has gained 55% in membership and comes to this convention in good financial condition."

Morton was elected to the board of Grange Mutual Fire Insurance. But when a member of the Executive Committee passed, he was not elected to fill that position.

Over the years Maud provided Grangers with ideas for table decorations, party favors, and bazaars. In 1951 she opened a commercial hobby store in Salem. She was a popular craft instructor at Juvenile Grange Camp. She played the piano for group singing and a march when campers carried their trays down the front steps of the log lodge and around the building to the dish washing porch.

Morton died on February 14, 1956 in Salem at the age of 70, and was buried in Hopewell Cemetery in Dayton. He was survived by his wife, sons Russell and Joe, and daughter Lorene Reierson. In lieu of flowers, the family requested donations to the State Grange Juvenile Camp.

During the Memorial Service at the 1956 Session, long-time State Secretary Bertha J. Beck delivered this eulogy:

"Yes, we have lost Brother Tompkins in person, but we know that his kindness, his good deeds, his influence, will live on, not only in the lives of members of the Grange, but in the lives of all others associated and working with him.

"Yes, we owe much to the memory of Morton Tompkins – our friend and our brother."

MARCHING TO SUCCESS

1950-59

Through the 1950s the number of Granges declined slowly from 354 to 331. The number of members also dropped steadily from 31,406 to 26,042. In 1954 a membership contest offered the grand prize of one-week's stay for two at Harrison Hot Springs in British Columbia. The winner undoubtedly enjoyed the vacation, but that incentive program did not solve the membership decline problem. Since the Home Economics Committee had a reputation for getting things done, the State Executive Committee turned over the membership gain contest to them. But State Master Elmer McClure also recommended that each Grange adopt a goal of having a net gain of one new member each year.

Six of the ten Sessions were held east of the Cascades. Ontario and LaGrande hosted for the first time. The number of delegates ranged from 280 to 363 plus another 51 to 60 Pomona delegates.

In the 1950s the number of resolutions averaged 74 per year, 80% of which set State Grange policy.

The health of Granges during this period was good. The State Lecturer reported that a third Lecturer's school was added with a total attendance of 244. Booster Night programs were held by 142 Granges, although only 72 entered the Booster Night contest. There were entries from 161 Granges in the community service contest, 177 had a youth chair,

100 a Health & Safety chair, 57 a drill team, 99 a degree team, 21 a drama group and 25 a music group. The average meeting attendance was 28.

In 1950 the State Grange held meetings in cities prior to the November election to explain farmers' opposition to daylight savings. Apparently, these meetings were effective because standard time was upheld by 59% of the voters in that election and the next two.

The Executive Committee approved funding a page in the Voters' Pamphlet against a measure that would have allowed the legislature to use the emergency clause to immediately enact tax laws. Voters agreed 73% to 27%. However, voters did not agree with the Grange on other measures. In 1959, Elmer McClure expressed fear that there was a new apathy among members: "Oh, what's the use: You can't win, anyway!"

Bonneville Dam had proven its worth in producing hydroelectric power at low cost. Members expected similar results from McNary and The Dalles Dams that were completed in the 1950s. But they were disappointed when Secretary of Interior, former Governor Douglas McKay, authorized the Idaho Power Company to build three dams in Hells Canyon. In his 1959 Master's Address, Elmer McClure claimed that "the people of Oregon have been subjected to the most intense campaign of brainwashing" by private power companies.

Legislatively, the State Grange continued to be effective in Salem. The Grange's Financial Responsibility bill became law. State Master McClure reported, "The Grange was widely complimented by Legislators and state officials for sponsoring this constructive and important legislation."

Master McClure called the small, family-sized farmer the forgotten man in American agriculture. He claimed that "the greatest source of help for agriculture lies in the field of science."

The State Agriculture Committee held district meetings to explain several federal price support programs. These meetings were attended by 450 members and non-members. The committee worked closely with the State Extension Service on a "show window" of water conservation devices including dams, farm ponds, grassed waterways, and drainage projects.

Master McClure expressed concern that the new State Forestry Board was composed primarily of loggers and lumbermen who were interested in cutting and marketing rather than growth and preservation.

The *Grange Bulletin* sponsored a Public Relations contest that was entered by more than 80 Granges. Each Grange kept a scrapbook of local newspaper coverage of their activities. The *Grange Bulletin* made a profit by advertising Grange tours to Hawaii, Canada, New England, and the National Grange Session.

The Home Economics Committee conducted canning schools to increase the number and quality of entries in the White Satin Sugar Canning Contest. In 1956 there were 2,500 entries from all counties. The HEC also sponsored cotton apron, crochet, baking, and craft contests.

In 1957 the Home Economics Committee made the Spence Memorial Scholarship their project. They received 53 applications and drew the name of the winner. This led to the HEC raising money to award a $200 scholarship in each of six districts and one at large. The names of the seven winners were drawn during the HEC breakfast in the school cafeteria at 7 a.m. Four hundred members had their fingers crossed that a name from their Grange would be called. They also hoped to win a door prize of a bag of sugar.

By-Laws for the State Juvenile Grange were written and adopted. For many years children read these By-Laws aloud before they elected their officers. As many as 132 children attended the State Session. Over 100 entries in various contests were judged. However, in 1959 the Session was the first week of June. Most schools were still in session. Leaders had trouble getting a full set of officers.

A Juvenile Camp Committee recommended Skyline Camp, 12 miles west of Bend, as a permanent camp site. July 4th weekend work parties were devoted to getting the facility ready for campers and making needed improvements. Volunteers built four cabins with eight bunks each in the girls' and boys' areas. More than 64 children registered so first one week was added and then two. Members volunteered to be cooks, counselors, and craft instructors.

Skyline Camp was the site of week-long Juvenile/Junior Camps from 1952 to 1974. The Grange had to give up the lease when the U. S. Forest Service required $10,000 worth of improvements to the lodge.

Six youth degree teams competed. An all-star team comprised of the best performer for each office was named. The all-star Chaplain was an exchange student from Germany.

In 1959 the first Education Committee was appointed. The committee recommended that the State Board of Education be elected, and the Board appoint the Superintendent. They favored the school year being 180 days of classroom instruction, but the local school board be allowed to set their start and end dates.

For Oregon's Centennial in 1959, the State Grange was invited to set up a farmstead at the State Fair. Members moved an abandoned log cabin to the fairgrounds and furnished it with historic implements and household items. The log cabin became the most popular exhibit at the fair.

At the beginning of the decade, Oregon Grange Wholesale Cooperative had 4,500 individual farmer members and 12 retail stores. Gross sales were $1.8 million. However, when Grange Wholesale no longer carried farm machinery, there was a serious financial loss. The new manger proposed that each Grange name an agent who would order a carload of fertilizer, feed, fence posts, or freezers (30 per car) shipped by rail directly to the Grange, saving handling and other costs. That manager and new idea did not last long.

Grange Wholesale was reorganized as Oregon Grange Supply in 1955. The Supply bought for 35 locally owned and operated retail stores, and member-buying pools. The State Grange purchased the former Wholesale building and rented it to Grange Supply. Business quickly bounced back. The big money makers were Shell petroleum products and the Unico line of farm supplies.

Although Grange Mutual Insurance suffered $124,000 in losses in 1958, the company was able to help three fire districts purchase new equipment and presented the State Grange with a check for half of 1% of earned premium income. Grange Insurance Association wrote policies for 13,000 Oregon members. Grange Mutual Life added polio and dread disease coverage, which helped their bottom line.

ELMER MCCLURE

16th State Master, 1950-1962

John Elmer McClure (1897-1976) was born on a wheat ranch near Pendleton. Whether this is the same ranch he owned in the 1940s and 1950s is not known. The McClure family moved frequently before settling in the Portland area around 1908. The children graduated from Portland public schools, and Elmer attended the University of Washington. Like their father, the four McClure sons worked as steamboat engineers.

Elmer and his wife Icelia (1904-2004) joined Harding #122 in 1930. At that time McClures lived on a farm nearby. When Elmer was elected Master, they were delegates to the 1933 State Session where they took the Sixth Degree.

In 1935 Elmer was appointed a State Deputy, a position he held for nine years (1936-39 and 1943-47). During that time, he traveled throughout the state, speaking on legislative issues, installing officers, organizing Granges, and dedicating halls.

In 1941 Elmer served on the State Grange Legislative Committee. In addition to tracking bills, speaking at hearings, and following amendments, the committee produced a mimeographed circular with the Grange position on major bills for both legislators and Grange Legislative

Committees. He served on the Legislative Committee again in 1973 and 1974.

Elmer became Executive Secretary and Manager of Grange Mutual Insurance Company in 1946. He served as State Grange Overseer from 1942 to 1950, and then he was elected Master over incumbent Morton Tompkins.

Delegates at the 1950 Session voted to invite the Grange Insurance Association (GIA), the Washington State Grange's insurance company, to write auto policies for Grange members in Oregon. Elmer spoke against this proposal. In his first *Grange Bulletin* article after becoming Master, he made clear that he would follow the vote of the delegates. "The basic policies of the State Grange are established by the delegate body at the annual convention of the organization. A State Master is charged with carrying out those policies. That I intend to do to the very best of my ability."

In his first Master's Address, Elmer called enforcement of state and local liquor and gambling laws "lax." The *Roseburg News-Review* termed his Address "a fiery speech." The following year he criticized former Governor McKay, then Secretary of Interior, for giving away the Hells Canyon Dam site to the Idaho Power Company. The next year he condemned Senator McCarthy as "a power-drunk man making a deliberate attack on democracy."

Elmer's dream was to have a headquarters building large enough to house the State Grange offices and affiliate businesses with space to generate rental income. His dream became reality when the Dairy Cooperative building became available. It was located between S. E. Main and Madison between 11th and 12th. Elmer convinced Evening Star Grange, Grange Mutual Insurance, Grange Insurance Association, and others to loan the money needed for a down payment and to remodel the interior. The new headquarters was dedicated by National Master Herschel Newsom and Senator Mark Hatfield on October 1, 1961.

Elmer concluded his final Good of the Address with, "It is most gratifying to me to know that I am turning over the organization in much stronger condition than when I took office twelve years ago. At that time, the State Grange had a net worth of around $15,000. Today, the State Grange has a net worth of well over $100,000."

After serving as Master, Elmer was elected State Representative from Clackamas County in 1963 but served only one term. He was elected to the State Grange Executive Committee from 1962 to 1966. In 1967 he was elected President of the Oregon Roadside Council.

In addition to his Grange offices, Elmer served as Secretary of the Oregon Anti-Tax Committee, Secretary-Treasurer of the Hells Canyon Association, Director of the Farm Co-operative Council, and Secretary of the Council of Electric Consumers. He was co-chair of VOCAL, a 50-member board of directors that oversaw collective bargaining and picketing by farm laborers. Governors appointed Elmer to the Industrial Safety Advisory Commission and Reapportionment Advisory Board. He headed an Oregon State College task force on forest taxation.

Elmer died December 30, 1976 following complications from surgery. He is buried in Redland Pioneer Cemetery.

Elmer's wife Icelia lived another 28 years, making her a 74-year Grange member. She was raised on a farm in Redland. As a young girl, she cooked for her family and farm hands. She always had home canned fruits and vegetables in her pantry and later a freezer filled with produce from her garden. She was known for having a green thumb that earned her many blue ribbons at garden shows and fairs.

Icelia served on the State Grange Home Economics Committee and on the National Grange Juvenile Committee. She and son Bobby took the Juvenile Degree at the 1949 Session. In 1957 Bob was elected State Juvenile Overseer. When Icelia passed away in 2004, she was survived by sons Delmar and Robert.

1960-69

During the 1960s the number of Granges declined from 328 to 298 and membership slipped from 26,451 to 25,439. In 1961 State Master McClure reported that 2,351 new members were initiated but the net gain was only 41. Clearly retaining members was an issue.

Sessions were held for the first time in Beaverton, North Bend, Gresham, and Ashland. The number of delegates ranged from 184 to 311 plus 44 to 56 Pomona delegates.

Finances were also a concern. In his 1964 Good of the Order Address, Master Allen Wheeler discussed the cash flow issues created by the purchase of the new headquarters building and hosting the National Grange Session. Two years later he noted that the State Grange had created a budget for the first time and stuck to it.

In 1963, State Master Wheeler cautioned delegates not to report the small number of farmers in attendance or focus on the declining farm population but rather tell the story of agriculture's importance.

The State Agriculture Committee was comprised of representatives of different types of agriculture: Field crops, horticulture, livestock, dairy, and poultry. Its members attended different commodity group meetings. Speakers at Session Agriculture Conferences were from other farm organizations and agricultural experimentation stations. In 1969 the committee recommended that every Grange initiate or promote a rural-urban activity to improve communication between farmers and consumers. The committee worked to increase Land Products exhibits at the State Fair and supported an agricultural wing at OMSI.

The State Grange's stand on public power focused on two issues. In 1963 Oregon had only four operating Public Utility Districts while Washington had 22. This was because Oregon required two votes to establish as P.U.D.: One to approve it and a second to raise revenue for it. In 1973 the Legislature finally passed a P.U.D. law like Washington's.

The second issue was building an intertie between the Bonneville Power Administration and California. The State Grange supported a federally funded intertie but wanted it to give preference to the Northwest. In 1964 the Pacific Northwest–Pacific Southwest Intertie was funded by Congress. It became operational in the 1970s. However, it is not exactly what the Grange had in mind. It serves states other than California as well as both private and public companies and is not based on the differing seasonal needs of the Northwest vs. the Southwest.

In 1961 the State Grange took a position on ten of fifteen initiatives and referendums on the ballot, including a measure to prohibit commercial fishing for salmon and steelhead in inland waters. The sales tax was on the ballot again. Opponents claimed that since the Grange backed taxes on gasoline and cigarettes, the organization supported a sales tax. Voters once again rejected a sales tax 89% to 11%.

In 1960 Master McClure reported that the Legislative Committee's job had become more difficult. Legislators were not as available because they were commuting to Salem from their homes. Only one farmer (Don Willner, who later became the State Grange's attorney) was on the House Agriculture Committee although a majority on the Senate Agriculture Committee were farmers.

Legislative successes were passing the fraternal property tax exemption and killing a bill that would have allowed legislators to use the emergency clause on all tax measures. Its defeat gave the people a vote before a tax went into effect.

The average number of resolutions 90, but 81% aimed to set State Grange policy. Over 700 resolutions were adopted.

In 1963 Grange Mutual Insurance had 1,100 Columbus Day Storm claims and paid out $58,587. Unlike other companies, their policies did not have a $50 deductible. Their total loss that year was nearly $500,000. Grange Insurance Association came to Grange Mutual's rescue, but in 1968 GIA's losses were 64%. Meanwhile, Grange Mutual Life continued to increase the number and value of its policies in force.

A front-page article in the *News-Review* (Roseburg) in 1960 announced that the State Grange Home Economics Committee was holding a Cookie Fair during the Session being held at the Douglas County Fairgrounds. Entries were for sale to the public with proceeds going to a scholarship for each district. By 1967 the HEC had 437 dozen entries in the Cookie Fair. The committee published a 70-page Cookie Book.

The State HEC chair calculated that Home Economics Clubs contributed $63,204 to their Granges' treasuries in the previous three quarters. To celebrate the National Grange's centennial in 1967, the committee dressed in period attire and made aprons for the State Officers like those worn by officers 100 years earlier. In 1968 the committee's name was changed from "Home Economics" to "Committee on Women's Activities." Clubs donated to Care, March of Dimes, and Muscular Dystrophy as well as to newly organized Junior Granges and Grange camp.

In 1965 the name "Juvenile Grange" was officially changed to "Junior Grange." The National Grange Master reported that Oregon was fourth in the nation in number of Junior members. The children were excited to be on TV when Governor Mark Hatfield visited their Session in 1963.

Youth state officers were elected in 1963. One afternoon during Session these officers performed a seating drill, opened the Grange in the Fourth Degree, presented guests, and then closed the Grange. Later officers were selected rather than elected, and they opened the Session one morning. Oregon's Outstanding Young Couple was named National Grange Outstanding Young Couple.

State Master McClure urged Pomonas to find a purpose. Multnomah County Pomona was the first to establish a credit union. County Conferences organized by Pomona Masters and County Deputies were well attended.

The original log cabin at the State Fairgrounds was too small to accommodate crowds of visitors. Wallowa County members dismantled the log hall that had been the meeting place of Pine Grove #644, carefully marked each piece, and loaded them onto a truck donated by Grange Wholesale. In Salem, another team assembled the pieces to create a "permanent feature" at the fair.

In his 1969 Good of the Order address, Allen Wheeler announced that although the National Grange had approved exemplifying the first four degrees in one 24-hour period, he would not grant permission for Oregon Granges to do so. The founders' plan was for Granges to confer the First and Second Degrees at one meeting and the Third and Fourth at a subsequent meeting.

ALLEN P. WHEELER

17th State Master, 1962-1970

Allen Prentice Wheeler (1901-1993) was born in Pleasant Hill, Oregon. In his youth he raised White Leghorn and Buff Orpington chickens. He entered them at the Lane County Fair, Oregon State Fair, and the Oregon Poultry Show in Portland and they won prizes. While State Master, Allen was referred to as a sheep rancher.

In 1900 Allen's father H. C. Wheeler was a delegate for Lane County and was elected State Gatekeeper. He served one term. In 1920 H. C. was elected to the State Legislative Committee, which gave him a good idea of how the State Legislature worked. He was elected to two terms in the House of Representatives. After his service in the House, H. C. again served on the State Legislative Committee for another two years.

H. C. arranged for his son to be a Messenger in the Oregon House of Representatives in 1931 and Sargent of Arms in the Oregon Senate from 1933 to 1939.

Allen married Effie Gibson (1894-1991) on June 12, 1925; they often celebrated their wedding anniversary during State Grange Sessions. They joined Goshen #561 in 1927 and were delegates to the 1929 Session, where they took the Sixth Degree. In the early 1930s, Allen was chairman of the Division of Labor Committee whose duty was to assign resolutions to committees.

Allen was elected Lane County Pomona Master in 1939. He and Effie were Pomona delegates for many years. He presented Lane County's invitation to hold the 1943 Session in Eugene.

In 1940, Allen was elected State Assistant Steward. After serving two terms he was elected to the State Executive Committee for two terms.

During his time as State Master, Allen dealt with a declining number of family farmers, challenges to field burning, and two ballot measures that the Grange defeated: A proposed new State Constitution and a sales tax. His successes were establishing county conferences, solving the financial crisis caused by the new headquarters in Portland, and having a net gain in membership. His legacy included an officers' seating drill, the Sunday evening church service, and beginning each Executive Committee meeting with a prayer.

Before announcing that he would not seek re-election, Allen concluded his 1969 Good of the Order address with, "This experience has been the most challenging, the most demanding, and the most rewarding of any work which I have ever entered into."

In 1966 Allen was elected Chaplain of the National Grange. This was an appropriate office since he had attended Eugene Bible University, served as President of Lane County Christian Endeavor, and was a lifelong member of the Disciples of Christ Church in Pleasant Hill.

After serving as State Master, Allen was again elected to the State Executive Committee in 1974 and served until 1978. Then he was State Chaplain for two terms. The Wheelers were delegates until 1988.

In addition to his Grange work, Allen was instrumental in re-establishing the Lane County Fair. He served as the Fair's manager in 1938 and 1939. In 1986 the agricultural building at the fairgrounds was named the Wheeler Pavilion in his honor.

Allen served as one of two Lane County Commissioners from 1941 to 1948. He was known for the efficient way he distributed road equipment.

Allen was elected Lieutenant Governor of the Kiwanis in 1948. He was a long-time member of Masonic Lodge No. 112 in Creswell.

Allen was appointed to the Lane County Tenant Farmer Advisory Board, State Bureau of Land Management Advisory Board, and a Legislative Interim Commission on Technological Employment.

Allen's obituary notes that he was a farmer who enjoyed politics and liked to sing. He led group singing at several State Sessions and sang solos and duets for Memorial Services, CWA Breakfasts, and Session breaks.

Allen is buried next to his wife in Pleasant Hill Cemetery. Allen was survived by daughters Catherine and Alene.

1970-79

At the end of the 1970s there were 20 fewer Granges (294 to 274) but 5,000 more members (25,876 to 31,052). The State Grange had a net gain in six of ten years. What accounted for the increase is not clear. The Membership Committee presented plaques to Granges that had a 10% or greater gain and to members who brought in ten or more members. They had slogans like "Keep the members we have and get one to five new members in '75." Did that make the difference?

In his 1970 Good of the Order Address, Master Allen Wheeler talked about making "insurance members" into active members. While all three insurance companies increased their customer base, all suffered losses, which led to higher premiums. In 1974 Grange Mutual reported that many of their insured "cashed out their policies."

Sessions in the 1970s were held in southern Oregon and the Willamette Valley in cities that had hosted previously. The number of delegates ranged from 231 to 277 plus 48 to 54 Pomona delegates. If a Master was unmarried, the Grange could elect a second delegate.

The average number of resolutions per year was 84, 77% of which aimed to set Grange policy.

Legislative efforts were disappointing. Master W. C. Harris focused on restricting corporate farming. He formed a coalition with other organizations, but they did not get enough signatures to get a measure on the ballot. They did succeed in getting a bill introduced in the legislature, but it did not pass.

The legislature passed a field burning bill Grange members said they could live with, but Governor Straub vetoed it, and there was not enough support to override his veto.

The Agriculture Committee recommended that the State Grange take the lead among farm organizations in developing and carrying out an educational program to inform the public on why farmers got only $300 of every $750 spent on food. In 1977 the committee reported a year of change not only due to the draught, but because a resolution passed the previous Session required one committee member be from each district. As a result, three of their active members had to be replaced.

In 1975 Oregon's CWA director was named National Grange Director of the Year. Club members not only raised money for their own Grange but also for Parkinson's disease, CARE in South America, and State Grange debt relief. Members made carpet slippers and therapy balls for the V. A. Hospital and some clubs sent cookies, washcloths, or ketchup packet to service men in Vietnam. They collected 15,000 eyeglasses and cases for VOSH (Volunteer Optometric Services to Humanity), and they recycled 4,000 used hearing aid batteries.

Deaf awareness became a major focus of the CWA. Speakers at their annual breakfast inspired attendees to donate to the National Grange Deaf Fund, a southern Oregon school for the deaf, and scholarships for hearing impaired students.

Oregon's CWA finally exceeded its National Grange sewing contest quota with 1,965 entries. The State CWA co-sponsored bread baking contests with the Oregon Wheat League. They sponsored more contests: Beach and tote bags, dressed dolls, patchwork pillows and quilts, macrame, and tea towels.

The Youth department's focus was on raising money for the Youth Travel Fund to send Oregon's Outstanding Female, Male, and Couple to that year's National Grange Session. Youth sold chair cushions, cards, candles, and jewelry.

Fall, spring, and couples' youth conferences were well attended and memorable, especially one at Drewsey #738 in Harney County. Apparently, youth did not expect an outhouse and a hot and cold running creek. Some learned sign language so that they could enter the Sign-A-Song contest. The Youth Committee sponsored a bowling tournament, which became the first scheduled event at each Session.

Junior Grange leaders (the new name for Matrons and Patrons) had their hands full with 150 contest entries including 30 competing in talent. New contests were woodcarving and decorative mobiles. National Grange introduced a merit badge program for which Oregon Juniors earned 80 badges in one year. Tours were popular, especially those to The Dalles Dam (a busload plus seven cars), Oregon Zoo, Grandma's Cookies, and Woodland Deer Park. Juniors appreciated being invited to watch the Rosebud Drill during the Sixth Degree if they promised to be really quiet.

The U. S. Forest Service demanded that the State Grange make an estimated $10,000 worth of repairs to Skyline Camp. The organization could not afford that so gave up the lease and sold the contents of the lodge. The Executive Committee struggled to find another facility, director, and counselors.

The Lecturer's Program at the 1974 Session had a centennial theme in honor of the State Grange's 100th anniversary. The State Secretary gave a history and Clackamas County youth modeled fashions through the years. Lecturer's schools had to be canceled due to the gasoline shortage, but were well attended when resumed. The Lecturer reported nearly 200 entries in art and photography in 1978.

The *Grange Bulletin* found it harder to get advertising from farm equipment companies, who were putting their money into TV advertising. The paper also lost $1,000 worth of drug store advertising when the National Grange promoted a prescription service. In 1974 the *Grange Bulletin* faced a paper shortage, so each issue was limited to 12 pages. The exception was the June 4, 1974 Centennial issue. The *Bulletin* advertised a 16-day tour to cattle ranches in Argentina with stops in Peru and Brazil.

A tour to Japan sold 179 seats on a Pan Am 707 so another tour was scheduled for the following spring.

In 1971 Grange Supply was sold to Farmers Union Central Exchange. Sixty local Grange stores remained independent. Grange members continue to serve on their boards. Central Exchange (CENEX) had a 28,000 barrel per day refinery and several producing wells. The Wholesale's six fertilizer plants and feed mill became part of Farmers Union Central Exchange's operation. CENEX presented a check to the State Grange for 5% of the profits in Oregon, which ranged from $5,400 to $20,461.

TED SIMS

18th State Master, 1970-1974

Theodore O. Sims (1904-1992) belonged to seven Granges over his seventy years as a member.

Ted was born and raised in Scio. He was the youngest of eight children, an honor roll student, and a basketball and track star at Scio High School. After graduation, Ted took a job in nearby Mill City and then in Cushman near Florence. His return home for Christmas in 1925 was a big surprise to his family. He brought along his bride Mable Hartley Sims (1900-1994). Not only had none of them met her, they did not know that he had married.

Mable, a teacher in Reedsport, was originally from Medford. At the end of the school year, the Sims moved to Jackson County where he farmed. They became active members of Jacksonville #700 in 1928. Ted was elected Master in 1929. They were delegates to the 1930 Session where they took the Sixth Degree. At the 1933 Session, Ted spoke against raising dues.

Mable was Lecturer. She played the piano and sang at Grange and their church. Their daughter Joyce was also musically talented. Mable enjoyed putting on programs and leading group singing. Ted was the insurance agent. Both were on committees, a degree team, and organizers of events.

In 1937 Ted was elected Master of Roxy Ann #792. Why they switched Granges is not clear. Then in 1943 Ted was elected Gatekeeper of Central Point #698. There he was appointed to the Dramatics Committee and was on a drill team. Mable and Joyce were not mentioned as Central Point members. Both continued to provide music for their church. Ted's obituary makes no mention of this Mable or marriage so apparently it did not end well.

In 1947 Ted moved to Corvallis to work at the Children's Farm Home. Later he bought a farm on Peoria Road. The following year he married Mable Johnson (1903-1978). They were delegates from Mountain View #429 in 1949.

In 1954 Ted was elected Master of Western Star #305. The Sims were delegates for the next five years. When he became Linn Pomona Master in 1960, they were Pomona delegates for four years.

Ted served as State Overseer and State Deputy from 1963 to 1970. He traveled extensively, installing officers, delivering speeches for Booster Night programs, and awarding 25- and 50-year certificates and pins. At that time Ted and Mable were members of Lake Creek #818.

While State Master, Ted set a goal of 30,000 members by the State Grange's 100th anniversary. His goal was not quite reached. Ted reported that the State Grange was in the best financial position it had ever been. A dues raise was not needed. The organization just needed more members. During his time as Master, Mable served as his Secretary, which helped the organization's budget. She was given a rising vote of thanks for her work during their final Session.

After his terms as Master, Ted served on the Executive Committee from 1974 to 1980.

When Mable passed in 1978, Ted moved to Albany where he met and married Virginia Bohles (1908-1978). She was active in the Eastern Star and he in the Masons. Ted and Virginia became members of Fairmount #252 and Benton Pomona. In the 1980s they were delegates from both.

The 1984 Session was Ted's last. He was escorted to the Master's station with other past state officers. Ten years later he died at the Albany Care Center and his ashes are interred in the mausoleum in Crystal Lake Cemetery in Corvallis.

W. C. HARRIS

19th State Master, 1974-1984

W. C. Harris (1914-1990) was the middle child of seven born to Walter and Cora Harris in Boone County Arkansas. He married Lida Ann Ware (1915-2001) in 1937. They moved to Springfield in the 1940s.

During World War II, W. C. served in the U. S. Army Air Corps based in Italy. He flew 51 combat missions and received the Air Medal and Purple Heart. While W. C. was in Europe, Lida worked as a welder's assistant in the Long Beach shipyards.

When W. C. was discharged, he and Lida returned to Oregon and lived at Star Camp while he worked in a sawmill. He was Deputy Coroner when they bought a home in Springfield. Finally, they settled in Noti, an unincorporated community in the foothills of the Coast Range between Eugene and Florence. They won prizes for rye, other grasses, and eggs at the Lane County Fair. She won many awards for baking and canning.

W. C. was shot in the stomach in a hunting accident near their home. He was transported in critical condition to Sacred Heart Hospital in Eugene. Fortunately, he recovered. The shooter pled guilty and had his hunting license suspended for ten years.

In the fall of 1956 W. C. and Lida joined Elmira #523. Although Elmira had more than 200 members, W. C. was soon elected Master. Their first State Session was in 1964 in Eugene. In addition to being delegates, Lida was on the Memorial team and W. C. was on the Installation team.

When W. C. was Lane Pomona Master in the late 1960s, he and Lida were Pomona delegates. W. C. was appointed to the State Agriculture Committee and read the committee's report because the Director was absent.

In 1970, W. C. was elected State Overseer. The following year his officer's report was the shortest of any officer; just four sentences. He also served on the Legislative Committee and was a State Deputy.

Lida was Marshal when W. C. was installed State Master. After installation, a large group of Lane County members marched to the Master's station and presented W. C. with a brief case and gave Lida a corsage. In 1976 Master Harris was presented with a plaque that read "Head Fella."

W. C. built a coalition of organizations to fight two issues. With the AFL-CIO, Farmers' Union, and the National Farmers Organization, he spearheaded a petition drive for an initiative to restrict corporate farming. The group became known as Save Oregon's Family Farms. He was elected its President. They came up short of the required 62,646 signatures. However, the group got a bill introduced in the next legislature. Their major opponent was J. B. Wyckoff, an agricultural economist at the Malheur Experiment Station, who published a 31-page booklet on the topic. Wyckoff established that only 3.5% of farms met the corporate definition in the legislation. A Freedom to Farm group claimed that the Grange was a suburban social club, who did not speak for farmers.

When the sales tax again threatened, W. C. formed a coalition with the American Federation of State, City, and Municipal Workers, Oregon Fair Share, Gray Panthers, and Farmers' Union. The likelihood of the tax passing in the 1980s was greater due to the number of voters who had moved into the state from states that had a sales tax. W. C. declared war on the sales tax at a rally attended by 150 citizens in Portland. Once again, the Grange position prevailed.

The 1978 State Power Committee lauded the State Master as "Another great leader in this fight; one who is perhaps more responsible than any other person for the present petition drive, is our own Worthy Master, Brother W. C. Harris." This praise was due to W. C.'s work to pass the P. U. D. law, which made it easier to form public utility districts.

The following year, W. C. concluded his Good of the Order Address with, "I believe the time has come for you to elect someone else to serve as Master." Members did not agree. He was re-elected for two more terms.

In 1976 the National Grange elected W. C. Chaplain and in 1978 and 1980 he was elected Steward. Lida served on the National Grange Women's Activities Committee.

After his ten years as Master, W. C., and Lida were delegates from Elmira, and he again served on the Legislative Committee.

Funeral services for both W. C. and Lida were held at Elmira Grange, and both are buried in the Sailor Cemetery in Noti.

STAYING IN STEP

1980-89

During the 1980s the number of Granges dipped from 272 to 262 and the number of members from 30,675 to 25,842. Although the National Grange Secretary reported that Oregon was the fifth largest Grange state, Oregonians were worried. In his 1984 Good of the Order address, W. C. Harris reported that he had interviewed those who dropped and found some who joined for insurance found cheaper coverage elsewhere. The Membership Committee sold "I'm proud to be a Granger" license plate holders. Delegates set a goal of organizing one new Grange each year. In 1988 delegates approved Life Memberships based on age: Those 61 and older paid $150 while those 14-35 paid $325. The following year 36 Life Memberships were purchased.

Due to inflation and the cost of hosting the National Grange Session, the Executive Committee had to decide whether to raise dues, cut programs, or reduce the size or frequency of the *Grange Bulletin*. They chose the latter. Beginning August 1, 1982, the Bulletin was published monthly, the sales slip program was eliminated, and the Editor's and Advertising Manager's jobs were combined.

Delegates reacted to what was happening in the country. They approved President Carter's stoppage of wheat sales to Russia, boycott of the Summer Olympics, and handling of the Iran hostages. They opposed the Oregon Senate opening with a prayer by a member of the cult of Rajneesh, who worshiped a human guru.

State Sessions were held for the first time in Woodburn, Canby, Hermiston, and Enterprise. The number of delegates ranged from 223 to 285 and 42 to 50 Pomona delegates. The number of resolutions ranged from 81 to 122 with an average of 100, 69% of which were to set policy.

The Governor signed a Grange backed bill that required one vote, rather than two, to form and fund a Public Utilities District. Thirteen counties were trying to organize P.U.D.s. The State Energy Committee urged Pomonas to teach non-Grangers in these counties how to succeed. Meanwhile, attempts were being made to overturn the Preference Clause, which would give private power companies equal access to electricity generated by the Bonneville Power Administration. The committee urged an "avalanche of letters to Congressmen voicing our opinion against this move."

Governor Attyeh's "Oregon Plan" included a 5% sales tax, which members termed "a tax shift," since it was based on ability to buy rather than ability to pay. Again, it was defeated by voters 78% to 22%.

The Youth Committee reported increased participation at events held throughout the year. They hosted Western Regionals attended by youth from nearby states. Multiple softball and volleyball teams competed, and they began sponsoring a golf tournament the day before the State Session began. The winning Youth Installation team had the honor of installing the State Officers. To raise money for the Youth Travel Fund, youth hosted a banquet and sold tickets on a treasure chest. The Outstanding Young Couple was crowned during a coronation ceremony. G.R.O.W. Club (Go Right On Working) held its first meeting.

In 1984 Oregon had the largest Junior membership in the nation. Every year they added new contests: Decorated cookie containers, dried arrangements, quilling, decoupage, string art, patchwork pillows, Junior yell, tree cone creations, seed pictures, hand puppets, Halloween masks, Christmas stockings, and bird feeders to name a few.

CWA was changed to GWA (Grange Women's Activities) to avoid confusion with Christian Women Clubs. They also added new contests. Members made 1,778 stuffed toys and after judging donated them to the Ronald McDonald House.

Community Service became a standing committee. In 1989 the committee reported that members from 57 Granges in 21 counties drove 6,260 miles, worked 13,393 hours, and donated $10,776. The committee began presenting a Volunteer of the Year award.

In 1983 Federal ID numbers were assigned to Granges, which created confusion. Three Granges indicated that they made more than $10,000 per year, which raised concern that the Oregon State Grange might lose its nonprofit status.

More than 400 attended Grange Day at the Capitol. Governor Atiyeh and several legislators spoke. Over 6,000 signed the register in the new Log Cabin at the State Fair but not all visitors signed. Since two historic cabins had not lasted, members constructed this cabin from a kit.

Volunteers welcome visitors to the Log Cabin during the State Fair. Photos of Grange halls and event flyers illustrate active Granges throughout the state.

MORTON V. WOLVERTON

20th State Master, 1984-1988

Morton Verrel Wolverton (1916-1993) was born in Lostine in Wallowa County. He married Freda Ilene Norman (1919-2011) in 1938 in Walla Walla. They were residents of Hermiston for 30 years. When Mort retired from Boise Cascade in Wallulla, Washington, the Wolvertons raised goats. They expected to raise a few for their own personal use. To their surprise, they discovered that immigrants from Mexico wanted both goat meat and milk. Their goat farm exceeded their expectations.

Mort and Freda joined Columbia #867 in 1966. They attended their first State Session and took the Sixth Degree in 1968 at Gresham. Mort was appointed to the State Youth Committee that year. He helped lead the floorwork portion of the fall youth conference.

Mort was Umatilla County Deputy from 1969 to 1982. He served as Installing Officer and Freda as Chaplain of a team that installed officers throughout Northeastern Oregon. At the 1978 Session in Eugene, his team installed the State Officers.

Degree teams were another of Mort's passions. He generally served as Master but would take any office that needed to be filled. When necessary, he got the job done even if he had to recruit officers on the spot and improvise degree paraphernalia.

Mort could also be counted on to perform for Lecturer's programs, including the State Lecturer's program. He was known for several readings such as Rindecella, the Stuttering Auctioneer, and Midnight Gallop. He once gave a demonstration of how to put on a ladies' girdle. He loved to tell stories and get a laugh.

Mort was elected State Steward in 1974. He served as State Deputy for Eastern Oregon from 1982 to 1984.

While State Master, Mort spoke clearly and directly. He called the decrease in membership a "backdoor loss." Granges were failing to collect dues from their current members. He warned that active members, who used to be middle aged, were becoming senior citizens.

In 1985 Mort successfully led the campaign against a 5% sales tax. He urged Granges to hold candidate forums. He challenged Pomonas to develop goals and not just get together for potluck dinners.

Maybe one of his most important appointments was naming Freda the first State Community Service Director. Under her leadership, the committee developed a handbook, report forms, and named a Volunteer of the Year.

After being State Master, Mort was elected to the State Executive Committee and served on it until his death. He headed the host committee for the 1993 Session held in Pilot Rock. During that Session, he collapsed and was taken by ambulance to St. Anthony's Hospital where he died of a heart attack. The Resolution of Thanks included, "Twenty-five years of devotion to the Oregon State Grange culminated here in his beloved Umatilla County doing what he loved best in life. His dedication to the Grange way of life and storytelling will be missed by every Granger in Oregon."

Mort's funeral was held in the Columbia Grange hall the day after the Session so that Grange members from across the state could attend. He is buried in Echo Memorial Cemetery in Umatilla County with their three infant children. Freda, son John, and several grandchildren survived him.

The following year Freda presented the State Grange with a framed photo of Mort surrounded by Grange pins and a gavel. She said that it captured who he was because "Morton was the Grange." Freda remained an active member of Columbia Grange for another 18 years. Her memorial service was also held in Columbia's hall where she was remembered as a "wonderful, humorous, and much-loved lady with an artistic flair and a true love for life." Freda is buried next to Mort in Echo Memorial Cemetery.

WAYNE JOHNSON

21st State Master, 1988-1992

Wayne Johnson (1924- 2006) was born in Moab, Utah, the eighth of twelve children. His parents must have run out of middle names because he never used one.

Wayne enlisted in the U. S. Navy in 1941 and was released September 1945. He moved to Oregon in 1955, where he married Della Trowbridge (1926-2000).

Wayne and Della joined Rogue River Valley #469 near Grants Pass in 1955. He served as Master for three years.

The Johnsons attended their first State Session in 1960 at Roseburg. They were Josephine County Pomona delegates since Wayne had been elected Master. The whole family took the Juvenile Degree. Two years later the Session was in Grants Pass. Wayne was Overseer for the Fifth Degree while Della was Ceres and on the Rosebud Drill team. Wayne and Della were elected State Assistant Steward and Lady Assistant Steward that year. They were the first couple elected to those offices and served three terms.

Wayne was appointed Josephine County Deputy in 1966 and served until 1974. He organized Illinois Valley and Deer Creek Juvenile Granges.

Their son Karl was State Juvenile Steward and Assistant Steward. Then he was State Youth Steward and Master, while his younger brother Ron was State Youth Assistant Steward. All three of their children were Sixth Degree members.

Wayne was elected State Steward in 1976-78. He issued an invitation for State Grange to meet in Josephine County again in 1977. At that Session he was Master of the Fifth Degree team. For the Lecturer's Program, he and Della performed an old-fashioned minuet with seven other couples, and he played his guitar. Wayne was elected State Overseer in 1978 and served one term.

Following Wayne's retirement, the Johnsons moved to Chiloquin and became active members of Winema #948 in Klamath County.

Wayne was elected Master of the Oregon State Grange in 1988. In that role he led the fight for repeal of the LCDC (Land Conservation and Development Commission). In a Letter to the Editor in the *Albany Democrat Herald*, he laid out the reasons. He claimed that Board members appointed by the Governor were making administrative rules that had the effect of law and that based on LCDC decisions only the rich could become farmers.

In his final Good of the Order Address, Wayne admitted that when he took office, he had no idea how widespread and serious some problems of the organization were. One of his goals was to promote ritualistic work, encourage full exemplification of degrees, and eliminate blatant disregard for the Constitution and By-Laws he claimed had been prevalent over the previous 20 years.

Wayne opposed selling the Portland headquarters building and moving State Grange offices to Salem. The mortgage on the headquarters building had been paid. The assessed value was $791,000, and he predicted it would increase due to the new convention center, OMSI, and remodeled Lloyd Center. He thought that rental income was necessary because the State Grange could not live on dues alone.

In 1991 Wayne was elected Chaplain of the National Grange. Regarding ritual, Wayne said he had heard complaints that it was antiquated and time consuming. He rejected them as excuses for failure to memorize or perform the ritual properly. "I will oppose the adoption of a concept of fully open meetings."

In 1993 the Johnsons were delegates from Sandlake #546 in Tillamook County. In 1997 when the Session was in Sutherlin, Wayne performed in an instrumental trio for the Lecturer's program, was on the Memorial team, and Spector for the Fifth Degree. He is listed as being from Evergreen #460 and Kellogg #811. He was Douglas County Deputy.

When Della passed in 2000, donations were collected for a Memorial Life Membership. At the time of Wayne's passing, he was a member of Pleasant Valley #348 in Multnomah County. He died on March 10, 2006, in Roseburg at the age of 81. A cenotaph in Roseburg National Cemetery commemorates their 54-year partnership.

Wayne was survived by daughter Virginia Facer, sons Ronald and Karl, six grandchildren, and six great-grandchildren.

1990-1999

The number of Granges declined in the 1990s from 261 to 246 and the number of members from 26,017 to 22,887. Still the Grange claimed to be the largest fraternal organization in Oregon, and Oregon was the second largest Grange state in the nation.

Sessions were held for the first time in Pilot Rock, Clatskanie, Sutherlin, and West Linn. The number of delegates ranged from 133 to 262 plus 25 to 30 Pomona delegates. In 1987 delegates voted to stop paying delegates mileage and $30 per Session.

Beginning in 1991 delegate packets were handed out during registration. Up to that point, resolutions were distributed after the Session officially opened.

The number of resolutions in the 1990s ranged from 66 to 119, with 52% setting Grange policy. In 1994 the State Overseer challenged members to submit resolutions that dealt with the real work of the Grange:

Farm, family, and community. His challenge was not heard. Only in 1998 were there significantly more resolutions that advocated policies.

Yet local and national issues affected members. The Northern Spotted Owl was declared a threatened species, which immediately affected 9,700 jobs in the Pacific Northwest. Measure 5 aimed to equalize funding for school districts, but since it cut taxes, some rural schools had to cut programs. The flood of 1996 focused attention on the need for dams. In his 1998 Master's Address, Ed Luttrell declared that the Grange must make protection of Oregon's best farmland a priority. Delegates opposed a national war tax to finance Desert Storm.

Delegates opposed deregulation of electric energy to provide large industries with an immense amount of cheap power. They voted to rescind support for NAFTA. They opposed breaching dams on the Columbia and Snake Rivers. They opposed converting existing freeways to toll roads.

The Legislative Committee threw their support behind the proposed Coos Bay to Ontario Expressway. Some legislators supported it as an alternative to I-84 which could be closed due to snow, ice, and wildfires. Although they formed a ROADPAC and produced a video, not enough members backed the expressway.

On the other hand, members quickly got behind a resolution to require newborn hearing screenings. Although the first bill that passed the state legislature was vetoed by the Governor, the second went into effect in 2000. In 1998 the National Grange recognized Oregon as one of the five top states for deaf activities.

In 1995, the State Grange headquarters building in Portland was sold for $625,000. The organization purchased a 5,660 square foot building at 643 Union St NE in Salem for $350,000. Bekins Van Lines moved the furniture and volunteers handled the rest.

The Agriculture Committee established a coalition of farm organizations to provide a solid voice for agriculture in opposition to Coho and Chinook salmon being declared endangered, closing the OSU School of Veterinary Medicine, and defunding FFA programs. The committee manned an information booth at the State Fair on Measure 38 "Don't Fence Oregon," which would have prohibited livestock along waterways. Voters rejected the measure. The committee had two booths at Ag Fest and served an Ag Awareness lunch at the Capitol for legislators and their staff members.

GWA added lots of contests: Baby quilts, embroidery, crochet, counted cross stitch, tole painting, candy, jam, jelly, Christmas tree ornaments, aprons, beads, teddy bears, and one called "potluck" for entries that did not fit any other contest. Clubs donated 186 baby blankets to a Teen Parent Program and supported abused children and cancer patients. The By-Laws were changed to make clear that all money earned by a GWA club was to be reported to the Grange and turned over to the Secretary, except the club could "retain a sum not to exceed seventy-five dollars ($75.00) for incidental expenses."

Oregon's Youth Directors were named State Directors of the Year in 1994, 1997, and 1998 by the National Grange. Fall, spring, and couples' conferences were well attended. Golf and horseshoes competitions were added. Goodie Baskets became the primary fundraiser. Each district filled a basket. Tickets were $1 each. The drawing was held during State Session. In 1993, $1,800 was raised and in 1999 the return jumped to $4,300. However, an attempt to add a "Senior Youth" category had limited success.

In 1990 there were only two active Junior Granges. Two years later there were 12 with 500 members. The new Junior Director explained, "Young people bring to Grange a vitality for life, an eagerness to learn, the willingness to do whatever is asked. Grange training teaches them to relate to people of all ages, to become involved in community service, and to promote Grange."

CENEX financed Junior Camp. The Director created Camp Co-op with a store and bank to teach campers cooperative buying and selling. Over 100 attended in 1993. After the Grange lost its lease on Skyline Lodge, delegates were in favor of moving the camp around the state, just like State Session. But by the end of the 1990s delegates changed their minds. It was hard to get enough campers when the dates and location changed each year.

The Lecturer's Committee eliminated judging. Contest winners were determined by People's Choice votes. Skit writing and poster contests were added.

The Education Committee increased the level of their support for Ag in the Classroom from bronze to gold.

Life memberships were set at $200 regardless of the purchaser's age. Memorial Life Memberships were $100, Junior Life Memberships $10, and Honorary Junior Life Memberships $50.

In 1994, the *Grange Bulletin* eliminated advertising by insurance and travel companies to retain its 3rd class postal rate. It was not enough. In 1997 the *Bulletin* began publishing every other month.

The Community Service Chairman reported huge numbers: 600,064 miles driven, 113,819 hours worked, and $91,000 donated and $31,000 for the value of donating the use of their hall to other groups. In 1999, the Community Service Chair urged those attending the Session to bring non-perishable items to donate to a foodbank in the host area. That year she presented 10,446 pounds of canned goods to the Central Oregon Community Action Network.

The Energy Committee recommended installing natural gas in newly built homes and converting electricity to gas wherever possible. They studied electric cars and gasohol. They supported the Trojan Nuclear Power Plant, wind farms, and Emerald PUD's Short Mountain Methane Power Plant. In 1996 the committee sponsored a tour to the methane gas plant at the Coffin Butte Landfill.

The Executive Committee minutes listed Granges that had closed, and disbursement plans for the property. A Y2K Committee was appointed; they did not expect problems, and none occurred.

The State Master held Visioning Conferences; at State Session Pomona Masters shared their vision statements.

Hands Across the Border was held with Granges in Western Idaho in 1995.

The Oregon State Grange Foundation was incorporated on August 1, 1993. By 1997, it had $4,243 in assets.

In 1998, four teams exemplified the first four degrees as they were done in 1873.

DALE W. MORRIS

22nd State Master, 1992-1996

Dale Wesley Morris (1917- 2016) was born in Derby, Iowa. He enlisted the in Army in 1942 and served in the Rolling W division. After completing his service, he moved to Eugene, where he met Mickey (Dorothy) Joll (?-2015). They were married in the First Christian Church of Eugene in 1948 and left immediately on a honeymoon trip through the Midwest, probably to Iowa to meet Dale's family.

Dale studied engineering while in the Army and later continued his studies in Iowa and Maryland. He worked in the equipment rental and leasing business, specializing in heavy equipment.

Dale and Mickey joined Irving #377 in 1975. He was a delegate to the State Session in Klamath Falls where he took the Sixth Degree. Dale and Mickey were Irving delegates and then in the mid-1980s they were Lane County Pomona delegates.

Dale was a Grange Insurance Association agent. In the early 1980s he was a member of GIA's Board of Directors.

In 1984 Dale was elected to Position 1 of the State Executive Committee. When Oregon hosted the National Grange Session in Eugene in 1985, Dale was chair of the host committee. At State Session the previous June, he reported on the status of the planning committees and the schedule of events. He took care of every detail and made sure that the Session ran smoothly.

Immediately after he was installed Master, Dale urged members to be willing to try new ideas and show pride in being Grangers. Although he had been a member for 17 years, Dale had not served as a committee director or held an office other than two terms on the Executive Committee. He did not always appreciate Grange traditions. For example, some were upset that he did not appoint all delegates to Session committees. Also, Multnomah Pomona expected to use the Portland headquarters auditorium for their degree day, but Dale wanted to rent it to an outside group to get more revenue and finance a youth trip to Western Regionals in California.

While Dale was State Master, the headquarters building in Portland was sold and the office in Salem was purchased. Dale managed all the details from environmental cleanup at the old site to finding a renter at the new facility.

In his final Good of the Order Address Dale said, "Those who are not impressed with ritualism are quick to point out that the young member does not like the procedure. Wrong! I find the Youth are very much into and like the ritualism and appreciate good form."

He concluded another Good of the Order Address with, "And to the nicest person in the world, my gratitude and love, who typed as many as 25 letters in one day. She set aside her plans on a minute's notice to go to a Grange meeting. I appreciate you, Mickey."

Dale was a member of the Scottish Rite Freemasonry for 72 years. His obituary notes that he was influential in many organizations that provided scholarships. His memorial service was held at Irving's hall. He was survived by two sons and a daughter. He is buried at Lane Memorial Gardens.

In 2017 the Oregon State Grange Foundation at the request of Lane Pomona Grange started a "Grangers Attending State Session" (GASS) fund. It was a memorial to Dale and others who passed the previous year. When interest reaches $25, that amount is given to a member whose name is drawn during the Annual Foundation Luncheon.

EDWARD L. LUTTRELL

23rd State Master, 1996-2000

Edward Lee Luttrell (1960-) was born in St. Helens and grew up on a small farm in Scholls in Washington County. He was an active 4-H and FFA member and joined Scholl #338 at age 14.

Ed became very active in State Grange youth programs. He served as Gatekeeper and Master on degree teams from Washington County and when he moved to Clackamas County, he was Assistant Steward, Overseer and Master of their teams. He was a member of drill teams in both counties. He participated in the public speaking contest, winning first place in 1977 and 1994. He served as State Youth Master in 1980.

Ed attended a meeting of Winona Grange #271 and complemented Winona member Celia Fox on her prepared speech. Celia's entire family were active members of Elmira #523 in Lane County. She and her sisters joined Winona when they moved to the Portland area to attend secretarial school and find good jobs. Soon Ed and Celia reported how interesting it was to visit other Granges. Celia was also on degree and drill teams and served as Youth Master in 1985. When Ed and Celia were named Oregon's Outstanding Young Couple in 1988, they represented Oregon at the National Grange Session.

Over the years Ed and his children were delegates from Eagle Creek #297, Boring-Damascus #260, and Clackamas Pomona #1. In 1988 Ed was elected State Gatekeeper. He served as State Youth Director from 1990 to 1992 and *Grange Bulletin* Editor from 1992 to 1996. The children were Junior officers and Charlotte held several youth offices, including Master.

In his final Master's Address, Ed stated that "The future of Oregon agriculture is dependent upon protecting our prime commercial farm and forestry lands and encouraging small scale agricultural operations on our secondary lands." He added that the Grange must demand a rewrite of the Endangered Species Act to require peer reviewed research.

In his 1998 Good of the Order Address, Ed reported that the Grange was the largest fraternal organization in Oregon. He set a goal of having no Granges with fewer than 40 members. He concluded his final Good of the Order Address stating, "I am proud to be a Granger. I am proud to have served you."

Ed spearheaded a campaign to replace the sashes worn by National Grange delegates which were in poor condition. Clackamas Pomona alone raised $16,000 and replaced nine sashes. Other Oregon Granges replaced an additional five. By the 2000 National Grange Session, all sashes had been replaced.

The National Grange hired Ed to be Leadership/Membership Development Director from 2001 to 2007. He presented workshops in Oregon and other states. At the 2007 National Session in Sparkes, NV, Ed was elected National Grange Master. He served eight years.

Ed then became Executive Director of the Pacific Northwest District of Kiwanis International. He has since moved to North Carolina and remarried. He is author of three books, including *Farm Grown Leadership* on traits a leader needs based on his farm and Grange experiences.

MEETING CHALLENGES OF A NEW CENTURY

2000-2009

The number of Granges began the 2000s at 246, dipped to 190 and then ended at 202 thanks to a Grange Renewal Committee reorganizing many. The number of members slid steadily from 20,431 to 6,500. The biggest dip was between 2002 and 2003, a drop from 16,099 to 9754. Grange Insurance Association no longer required policy holders to be Grange members. Grange Mutual Insurance Company closed in 2002. The company had taken a $1,500,000 bank loan earlier and if that loan were called, GMIC would have been forced to declare bankruptcy. Dues raises may also have accounted for membership losses.

Sessions were held for the first time in Phoenix, Joseph, Reedsport, Molalla, Jefferson, and Prineville. Since Pomonas were not issuing invitations, a Special Committee on Hosting Sessions was appointed. They recommended that districts host in a six-year rotation starting with District #5 in 2008.

The number of delegates ranged from 107 to 207 and Pomona delegates from 27 to 41. The By-Laws were changed so that the Master's spouse was no longer automatically the second delegate. If the Master was unable to attend, the Grange could elect any two Fourth Degree members to be voting delegates.

The number of resolutions ranged from 42 to 120, with 54% aimed at setting Grange policy. State Master John Fine expressed disappointment in the number of resolutions dealing with agriculture. In 2006, he concluded his Master's Address with the observation that previously resolutions proposed solutions to problems rather than opposing solutions proposed by others.

During this period drought was a concern. Delegates favored reversing the action of the Ninth Circuit Court and permanently restoring the flow of water from Klamath Lake to farmers served by the irrigation system. The State Grange created a GRANGEPAC for this purpose. The effort was too little too late.

In 2002 the State Grange joined a coalition to fight reintroduction of wolves into Oregon. They advocated the formation of P.U.D.s for PGE customers in Multnomah, Clackamas, and Yamhill Counties after the bankruptcy of Enron. This effort was not successful. Delegates also favored a P.U.D. to manage Bull Run's water supply.

The Legislative Committee continued to support the ROADPAC until it became clear that it lacked state-wide support. The State Grange became the chief petitioner for a measure on the November 2002 ballot that would have required the number of signatures for initiatives and referendums from each county to be proportional to those who voted in the last Governor's election. However, they failed to get enough signatures to get the measure on the ballot let alone enough to meet the standard they proposed.

National Grange made major changes in the early 2000s, including discontinuing contests, reducing the number of committees, and forming Action Granges. In Oregon 11 Granges became Action Granges.

In 2001 State Master Mike Stewart made ten recommendations, five of which were not adopted by delegates. However, several years later they discontinued paying per diem and requested a committee be appointed to shorten the State Session.

Hosting the National Grange Session in 2002 together with declining membership and an increase in National dues, put a squeeze on finances.

The Kickoff Banquet and dressing to fit the theme of the day with judging and prizes began during the 2000s. In 2005 the first Tribute to Veterans was held during State Session. Veterans marched to the anthem of their branch while Juniors gave each a small flag.

The Foundation provided Granges with $17,891 for hall repairs in 2005 and started the Fraternal Concerns Fund in 2007 to help members who experienced a property loss.

The Deaf Activities Committee was renamed Deaf Awareness and Family Health. The Governor finally signed the Newborn Hearing Screening law. The committee gave $200 each to three Granges to upgrade their sound systems. They donated $5,000 to Dogs for the Deaf for a dog that was named Granger. The committee together with the Foundation raised $10,000 for a cochlear implant for a member.

Although there were fewer than ten active Junior Granges and fewer than 100 members, 40 Juniors went to camp and 25 attended State Session. Camp was shorter because CENEX cut funding. The highlight of a State Session was riding the Crooked River Train, for which 28 Granges contributed $1,265 to buy the tickets.

In 2000 Clackamas County's All-Night Scavenger Hunt in the Portland metro area won first place at National Grange for the Most Creative Youth Night Program. The hunt was a city-wide tour using public transportation.

The Community Service Committee started the BOOK project, which provided agriculturally oriented books to first graders. In four years, the BOOK project purchased 7,000 books that were given to 110 schools. In 2004 the committee began supporting the dictionary project Words for Thirds. The committee collected $4,500 for Northwest Medical Team for the earthquake in the Indian Ocean, more than $2,000 for Katrina victims, and $600 for the Future Farmers of America Seeds of Hope program to rebuild FFAs in Mississippi and Louisiana.

The Grange Women's Activities Committee's name was changed to Grange Worker's Activities so as not to be sexist. Many members and

Granges sponsored contests by donating the prize money. GWA also donated to Katrina victims and to abused children.

The Membership Committee introduced a jigsaw puzzle theme with Fellowship, Community, Leadership, and Service pieces. Family Plan and Associate Business memberships were introduced. The Agriculture Committee had a booth at the FFA convention and mailed 3,000 letters to those who requested information.

MIKE STEWART

24th State Master, 2000-2002

Michael Bruce Stewart (1941-) and his wife Gaye were members of Rickreall #671 and Polk Pomona #3. State Master Dale Morris appointed them State Youth Directors in 1993. The Stewarts approached the task with creativity and flair. They gave new meaning to "We've never done it this way before."

To raise money for the Youth Travel Fund they introduced Goodie Baskets. Each district filled an actual basket with items that fit a theme. Tickets were sold and a drawing held. The first year the youth raised $1,800. In time "basket" was a misnomer because no basket was large enough to hold camping gear, a kayak, or playhouse furniture.

Mike and Gaye organized a caravan of 39 youth to the Western Regional Conference in Anaheim. They added the bunny hop and line dancing to the Youth Coronation Ball. The softball tournament had 65 players. Fifteen teams competed in the bowling tournament. "Find Clyde" was a challenge in each issue of the *Grange Bulletin*. The Stewarts led a "Building Your Team" workshop at a National Grange conference for youth directors in Kansas City. The National Grange named them Youth Directors of the Year in 1994, 1997, and 1998.

When Polk County hosted the State Session in Independence in 1996, Mike was Master of the Fifth Degree team and Gaye was Chaplain. Having anticipated every possible problem, they ran a smooth Session.

In 1999, Mike was elected State Secretary. His statement included that he was Polk Pomona Master and President of the State Grange Foundation. He also stated, "My professional work experience includes 30 years as a business manager in public higher education with responsibility for accounting, budget preparation, personnel, and department management. My work style includes the use of volunteers and I have the desire and ability to work with all people." He was elected, but since he was a full-time administrator at Western Oregon University, he was not able to work simultaneously at the State Grange office. The Executive Committee made the State Secretary's position honorary and named him interim office manager. He served one year before being elected State Master.

Mike broke with the long-standing tradition of delivering a Master's Address for an external audience and a separate Good of the Order Address for members. Instead, his "Master's Annual Report" was an internal document. Emboldened by the National Grange's renewal, Mike made ten recommendations. Delegates rejected six of the ten: Collect dues before December 31; raise Pomona dues to $1 per year per member; empower the Executive Committee to deal with affiliate companies; discontinue payments to delegates, officers, and directors; cease stipends to four directors; and shorten the State Session. Delegates may have agreed with one or two of these but the last was too much.

Mike appointed Gaye State Membership Director. At the 2001 National Grange Session, she was elected National Pomona.

National Grange accepted Oregon's invitation to meet in Portland in 2002. During the June 2002 State Session, host committee chairs met with the National Master to report progress and ask questions. It seemed curious that the only question either of the Stewarts had concerned flowers for the Seventh Degree.

At the beginning of the Executive Committee meeting on July 13, 2002, Mike read his resignation letter which cited "health and personal reasons." Then he passed the gavel to Overseer John Fine.

Mike has since retired from Western Oregon University. He serves as Parliamentarian of the Oregon State Federation of Garden Clubs.

JOHN FINE

25th State Master, 2002-2006

John Maurice Fine (1949-) began his Grange career as a Juvenile member. His parents' Grange did not have a Juvenile Grange, so they loaded the kids in the car and drove them to the nearest one.

John's first State Session was in 1967 at North Bend. There he took the Sixth Degree. He competed for Outstanding Young Man but did not have quite enough experience. However, two years later he was named Oregon's Outstanding Young Man and traveled to the National Grange Session in Daytona Beach, Florida. He was Overseer of the Youth officer team in 1969 and Master in 1970 and 1971.

In June 1971 John graduated "with high scholarship" (3.25 or higher GPA) in agriculture from Oregon State University. A loan from the Charles E. Spence Grange Memorial Educational Fund helped finance his education. That year John was a delegate for North Douglas #936 to the Session held in Roseburg. He was Steward of the Youth Degree team that won first place and performed at the Session. He was also on the Douglas County Pomona team that exemplified the Fifth Degree. John was on the host county's executive committee.

Upon graduation, John returned to Douglas County and started the ag program and FFA chapter at Glide High School. In 1975 he started a program and FFA chapter at Camas Valley High School. In 1992 John was named Ag Teacher of the Year by fellow ag teachers. At the time he retired from teaching, John was the only ag teacher to have started two new programs.

In 1973 John and his wife Kay were Junior Camp directors. The following year they were elected State Assistant Stewards. After three terms, John was elected Overseer for the first time. Then John was elected to Position 1 of the Executive Committee. In 1994 John was presented with a big bunch of balloons celebrating his 20 years as a state officer. He was only 45.

In the 1980s John was a delegate for Douglas County Pomona. His children Kris and Johnny were State Junior Grange officers. In 1991 Kris was a marching candidate for the Sixth Degree. When John installed the State officers in 1992, Kris was Marshal. John and Kris entered public speaking contests. In 1995 Kris was named Female Ambassador and was a legislative intern. John was appointed State Education Director.

John married Peggy (1950-2020) in 1994. He was elected Overseer again in 1998 and Kris was elected State Flora. She was a member of Mid Valley "O" #960 while a student at OSU majoring in agriculture. In 2001 she was a delegate for Vale #696 in Malheur County which was closer to Jordan Valley where she was teaching.

John was appointed to the National Grange Task Force on Renewal. They recommended Action Granges, fewer committees, no contests, and other changes to bring the Grange into the new century.

When Mike Stewart unexpectedly resigned during the July 2002 Executive Committee meeting, John and Peggy scrambled to make sure Oregon was ready to host the National Session in Portland just four months later. The session ran smoothly.

The following year Peggy was elected National Flora. She resigned a year later when John was elected to the Board of Directors because by tradition two officers from the same state cannot hold office at the same time.

In his first Master's Address, John reported that the State Grange had formed coalitions with other agricultural groups for the common good of all parties. He touted the Grange to School program which was designed to give teachers more time with their students.

John and Peggy introduced ideas they picked up from other State Granges they visited: The Kickoff Banquet, a theme of the day with prizes for those who dressed appropriately, and a Tribute to Veterans.

After John completed his terms as Master, he was again elected to the State Executive Committee serving from 2006 to 2008 and 2018 to 2022. He was State Agriculture Director from 2010 to 2014. Peggy was Co-Junior Director from 2010 to 2012 and State Chaplain from 2012 until her death.

John served as Chair of the Oregon Sheep Commission and on the State Advisory Committee to the Director of Extension. John was presented an Honorary American FFA degree at a National FFA Convention in 2000.

Currently, John is Secretary of Riversdale #731 and Master of Douglas County Pomona #13. His children and grandchildren have held offices in both.

PHYLLIS WILSON

26th State Master, 2006-2010

Phyllis Adele Booth Wilson (1942- 2020) was born in Nebraska. Phyllis and her husband Mark moved from Puyallup to Coos Bay in 1969. Mark was a Greyhound Bus driver for the Portland to Coos Bay route. They joined Sumner #865 shortly after they bought a 110-acre cattle ranch. When Phyllis called about the insurance, she learned they needed be Grange members or buy their insurance from another company.

Phyllis remembered her first Grange meeting which was a joint meeting with the 4-H. Soon her two children became 4-H members. Phyllis was elected Sumner's Lecturer in 1972 and Secretary in 1977.

In addition to her Grange work, Phyllis was President of the Sumner PTA, a volunteer firefighter for the Sumner Rural Fire Department, and Secretary of the Coos County Fair Board.

In December 1979 Phyllis's daughter Kelli, a Junior at Marshfield High School, was killed in a car accident. As often happens, the Wilson's marriage did not survive, and they lost the ranch.

After Sumner Grange closed in 1988, Phyllis joined Greenacres #834. She and another member agreed to visit other Granges. Since Phyllis was working, the friend made their potluck dish while Phyllis drove.

In addition to serving as Master and Secretary of Greenacres, Phyllis also held those offices in Coos Pomona. In 1992 she was appointed Coos County Deputy.

Phyllis' first State Session was in 1981 at North Bend. She was a member of the Rosebud Drill team and took the Fifth and Sixth Degrees. She was a delegate for either Greenacres or Coos Pomona throughout the 1990s.

In 1996 she was elected to a five-year term on the Oregon State Grange Foundation board and served as its Treasurer.

When Mike Stewart abruptly resigned and John Fine became Master, Phyllis was interviewed and selected to be State Overseer. She served as Overseer from 2002 until she was elected Master.

In 2006 Phyllis retired from the Coos-Curry Housing Authorities (HUD) where she served as Assistant to the Director. She moved to Salem to assume the duties of State Master. Her first challenge was to find a host for the 2007 State Session because no county had issued an invitation. She convinced Marion County Pomona that they were up to the task and that Jefferson High School would be a good venue.

Renting the back portion of the Salem office was another challenge. Doing so required electrical upgrades, new carpeting, a new door, security system enhancements, and new heating and air conditioning systems, all of which cost more than expected.

Another challenge was a front-page article in a local newspaper that was picked up by the Associated Press. The article quoted a member as saying, "I don't think we're too long for the world." Phyllis also expressed frustration that she could not find members for a Leadership Team she hoped to start.

In her final Good of the Order Address, Phyllis reported that four dormant Grange properties had been sold and three others had pending sales. But these sales were not easy due to zoning, asbestos, and DEQ regulations. Still, it was necessary to limit the State Grange's liability for these unoccupied properties.

Phyllis was elected National Chaplain in 2008 and served until 2011. After her term as Master, she was elected State Secretary. She resigned during her third term because her son David became seriously ill with Lewy body dementia. She could not leave him home alone when she went to Salem for Executive Committee meetings.

When she took David to the doctor, the appointment became more about her stress level and health than about him. She finally found a care facility for him, but he was not happy there. David passed in 2019 and she in 2020. Both are buried in Sumner Pioneer Cemetery along with her daughter Kelli.

2010-19

The number of Granges dropped in the 2010s from 185 to 165. The number of members declined from 6345 to 4587. In 2017 committee directors launched GrangeUp, a membership drive in which state officers, directors and their district chairs personally delivered boxes of materials and banners to every Grange in the state. They announced that monetary prizes would be awarded to the three Granges with the highest percentage gain. In addition, the State Grange would serve an ice cream social at the Grange in each district with the highest percentage gain. For the first time in 26 years Oregon ended the year with a net gain in membership.

Sessions were held for the first time in Seaside, Canby, Talent, and Florence. Banquets became luncheons because venues required their caterers to prepare meals and dinners were priced higher. The ceremonial parts of the Session were held on the weekend so more members could take the degrees. The first four degrees were conferred on Sunday afternoon although there were only a few candidates.

The number of delegates ranged from 74 to 140 with 13 to 29 representing Pomonas. The highest number of resolutions was 80 and lowest 16. Every year more resolutions aimed to set Grange policy than change By-Laws or internal procedures.

The Agricultural Committee had a booth at the OSU Small Farms Conference, which was attended by 900 with an average age in their 30s and 40% were women. They also attended the Women in Sustainable Agriculture Conference in Portland.

Agriculture conferences at State Session featured speakers on the Oregon Wolf Management Plan, Oregon's Friends of Family Farmers, and Healthy Forests, Healthy Communities. Their "Duck Pond" booth at the FFA convention was popular. Volunteers helped children transplant 5,000 tomato, green pepper, or marigold starts at Ag Fest.

Green Grange Summits were held in halls in Washington, Lane, and Jackson Counties. Green members were advocates for organic agriculture, sustainability, environmental justice, and local resilience. They were frustrated by their initial attempts to pass resolutions. But in time they succeeded in passing a resolution opposing the cultivation of genetically engineered seed in Oregon. They also got agreement that milk products from cows given Recombinant Bovine Growth Hormone (rBGH) should be labelled and neonicotinoids should be added to the restricted pesticides list.

The Legislative Committee handed out 40 dozen homemade cookies during the short legislative session while the Lobbyist, Ag Director, and committee members discussed Grange policies with legislators and their staff.

Session committees on Natural Resources and Agriculture reviewed their sections of the State Grange Legislative Handbook and recommended deleting policies statements that were no longer current. In 2016, delegates agreed to sunset policies in the Handbook that were ten years old unless they were reaffirmed by delegates.

In 2017 the Legislative Committee alerted delegates that Senate Bill 181 put the property tax exemption of non-profit organizations at risk. The committee distributed postcards to attendees to send to their state representatives. The lobbyist started a Capitol Granger email service to keep interested members up to date on the legislative session.

The National Grange introduced the Junior 1+ program for children aged 5 through 14 in 2014. White Eagle #683 was the first in Oregon to add Junior members to their quarterly report. By 2019 there were 94 Junior members of 37 Granges.

During the 2012 State Session, Juniors sold candy to raise money for Samaritan's Purse. The $500 they collected went to purchase goats and provide food for impoverished children and nursing mothers. Delegates who forgot to turn off their cell phones during Session contributed $60. In 2013 the Juniors' field trip was to the Oregon Zoo. They delivered a $1,350 donation from Session attendees for the family farm at the Zoo. Their visit was covered by a Portland news station.

Since most Juniors had never seen the Junior Degree, in 2019 their State Officers did not spend time learning it. They performed a seating drill and opened the Grange. Then the State Master Susan Noah and the State Assistant Stewards demonstrated the Junior 1+ Obligation Ceremony. The Junior session focused on conducting a meeting, making motions, giving reports, singing Grange songs, and understanding each officer's role. Attendees created Minecraft projects.

Some youth served as delegates while others performed community service projects like helping at the Humane Society or a soup kitchen, cleaning a beach, and making and delivering skid resistant socks for seniors at an assisted living center. One year they wrote and published a daily newsletter. Another some bonded by sharing a vacation rental.

Beginning in 2018 youth conducted a Keeping Oregon Warm campaign. The first year over 30 Granges donated 472 hats, 316 pairs of gloves, 176 scarves, and 85 pairs of socks which were given to the host district to distribute.

In 2013 two youths traveled to the Kelley Farm at Elk River, Minnesota to be officers of National Grange teams that exemplified the first four degrees as they were done in 1873.

GWA added contests for Juniors, paper craftsmanship, dried foods, sugar-free baked goods, and hand-dipped chocolates. Entries in Pillowcases for our Troops and Veterans were sent to active military personnel or a veterans' shelter in the host district. GWA conferences were hands-on workshops. Participants made jewelry and bookmarks using Grange symbols.

Grange Insurance Association had difficult years. GIA stopped insuring commercial property including Grange halls. When gas prices were low, people drove more and had more accidents. Technological advancements improved safety but also increased the cost of claims. Despite losses the company retained its A- rating. However, GIA cut the amount they distributed to State Granges in the West.

In 2011 the Community Service Committee held a Ducks versus Beavers competition for the State Session food drive. Beavers won with donations totaling 18,519 pounds. The committee collected 5,728 Campbell's Labels and Box Tops for Education. Schools could redeem them for supplies, books, or equipment. One year Community Service reports were received from 64 Granges showing that 909 of their 1852 members worked 109,909 hours on their service projects and 2,829 non-members spent 35,462 hours helping.

The Veterans Committee raised money for Joys of Living Assistance Dogs. A large group marched in the Veterans Day Parade in Albany. The committee set up a "Table of Remembrance." In 2018 the committee sponsored a tour of the U. S. Coast Guard Astoria Air Station.

Demonstrations were added to each day's program at the Log Cabin at the State Fair. Giving out backpacks with school supplies proved to be an incentive for fairgoers to visit the cabin.

In 2012 ballot Measures 82 and 83 would have authorized a privately-owned non-tribal casino called "The Grange" to be built in Wood Village. Grange halls that were visible from a highway displayed a "We are the real GRANGE" banner. The National Grange reached a settlement with the casino developers before the election. However, both measures were soundly defeated. Since then, the National Grange has made sure that entities using Grange trademarks are licensed and pay an annual fee.

A Communication Team was formed. They created a public Facebook page, conducted conferences during Sessions, and installed displays at 24 libraries around the state for the National Grange's 150th anniversary. The grand finale was a month-long exhibit at the Multnomah Central Library, which had 12 large display cases.

Since 2015 two issues of the Grange Bulletin each year have contained four-color pages (back, front, and middle section). One hundred Community Granges have submitted stories. Beginning in 2016 a special election issue was published. The *Awards, Contests, and Scholarships* booklet has been published annually.

The State Grange provided a matching grant program for a new or refurbished Grange hall sign. Then a matching Grant program was introduced to improve the exterior appearance or make major hall improvements. Granges could match up to $5,000 per project with cash, labor, donations, or another grant. In the first three years, grants were made to 36 Granges totaling $141,149.

In 2012 delegates voted to give Granges the option of allowing renters to serve alcohol, a proposal that had been voted down several times previously. The By-Laws were changed in 2019 to allow alcoholic beverages under certain conditions at Grange sponsored activities.

LARRY REA

27th State Master, 2010-2011

Larry Dean Rea (1939-2020) was born and raised in Rainier, where he broke javelin records while in high school. He went on to Oregon State University, where he set several meet records.

In October 1960, Larry married Margo Ann Hudkins (1939-2006) of Salem. They took a brief honeymoon trip to the Oregon coast while he was awaiting orders from the U. S. Air Force. He took pilot training at Webb Air Force Base in Texas, graduated with honors, and was awarded silver pilot wings.

After his Air Force service, Larry was a pilot for Northwest Airlines before joining the Oregon Air National Guard. He flew the F-101, F-102, and F-4, became a flight instructor, and Chief Safety Officer.

Meanwhile Larry finished his education at Portland State University, earning a master's degree in science education. He worked for the Fish and Wildlife Commission and as a realtor for his father-in-law's firm. In 1971 Larry and Margo adopted son Chris and later Tim.

Larry and Margo were members of Fern Hill #592 in Columbia County although they lived in Gresham. Larry's parents and extended family were Fern Hill members. Larry and Margo were delegates for

Fern Hill or Columbia Pomona from 2000 to 2004. Larry was named Assistant to the State Master in 2000 and Webmaster and State Deputy the following year. In November 2006 Margo died of breast cancer while Larry was traveling for the State Grange. He never recovered from losing her.

Larry was elected to Position 2 of the State Executive Committee in 2006 and served until he resigned prior to the 2007 Session.

A small group of family and supporters came to the 2010 Session to see Larry installed as State Master. His heart was not in the job. He spent most of his time researching butterflies and birds on the internet. He talked about Margo every day. He was slow to make decisions. He discussed what he planned to say in his Master's and Good of the Order addresses, but he did not put anything on paper. As he rambled, State Secretary Phyllis Wilson began recording what she could so that committees would have some text to review.

In his Master's Address, which usually deals with external issues, Larry complained that email addresses were not accurate and proposed having a media person. He reported that he got rid of the Master's cell phone because it was too costly. In his Good of the Order Address, he urged Granges to consult the By-Laws and "get some paint and paint your hall."

On the afternoon of December 29, 2011, Larry walked out the door brief case in hand. Office staff and volunteers sensed that he did not intend to return. His resignation was effective December 31, 2011.

In addition to his Grange work, Larry was Chairman of the Board of the Malheur Field Station and an Oregon Master Naturalist. He was an excellent photographer of nature. In 2017 he and his cousin had a photo exhibit at Urban Grange Coffee in Salem.

Larry died at his home in Gresham January 21, 2020. A memorial service was held a month later at the Methodist Church in Rainier.

MARK NOAH

28th State Master, 2012-2012

Mark William Noah (1953-) was installed State Master on January 1, 2012 at Sunnyside Grange #842 by National Master Ed Luttrell. Friends who were available on New Year's Day witnessed the event.

Mark met Susan Cramer on a University of Oregon biology field trip to the coast. He quickly learned that he would have to join the Grange if he hoped to see her because her calendar was filled with Grange meetings and activities. Mark joined the Cramer's Grange.

Mark's first State Session was in Oregon City in 1974. He was an Executive Committee member on the Lane County Youth Degree team, State Youth Gatekeeper, and took the Sixth Degree. Mark was on installation and drill teams and won talent and public speaking contests. He was often a delegate for Mohawk-McKenzie #747 or Lane Pomona. In 1978 Mark served as State Youth Master.

In 1987 Mark and Susan were named Oregon's Outstanding Young Couple and represented the state at the National Session in Redding, California. From then on, he has attended the National Session every year. He has often been Oregon's second delegate and served as secretary of his assigned committee.

In 1990 Mark was elected State Assistant Steward. In 1996 he was elected to Position 1 of the Executive Committee, and in 2006 he was elected State Overseer.

During the 166 days Mark served as State Master, he continued his full-time job in the Occupational Skills Training program at Chemeketa Community College. Since he could work for the State Grange only 20 hours a week, Mark proposed that he be paid 50% of the Master's salary plus expenses.

When Mark came in the front door of the State Grange office, he would announce, "I'm here for 15 minutes." Employees and volunteers had their questions ready, and Mark answered, which allowed them to proceed with the task at hand. Given his schedule, he asked Ed Luttrell to take the part of Master in the Sixth Degree. He performed all the other duties of the Master: Conducted Executive Committee and Session meetings, wrote and delivered Master's and Good of the Order Addresses, visited Granges, and presented awards. However, he seemed genuinely happy when his successor was installed.

SUSAN NOAH

29th State Master/President, 2012-2022

Susan Marie Cramer Noah (1954-) remembers sitting on the piano bench with the Musician and picking out the Opening and Closing songs for Mohawk-McKenzie #747 meetings that her parents attended.

Susan's first State Session was Ashland in 1969 where she was Pomona of the Lane County Degree team that put on the Fourth Degree. From then until the late 1980s she was on either a winning drill or degree team. She also entered the talent contest and won her division.

Susan was State Youth Lecturer in 1974 and 1975 and Lady Assistant Steward in 1976 and 1981. She was named Outstanding Female Granger in 1973 and represented Oregon at the National Session. In 1987 Susan and her husband Mark were named Oregon's Outstanding Young Couple and represented Oregon at the National Session in Redding, California. Since then, Susan has not missed a National Session.

In 1986 Susan was elected State Lady Assistant Steward. She served ten years. Then she was elected State Lecturer for the first time and served four terms. In 1998 Susan was chosen by the National Grange to serve on the Lecturer's Advisory Committee. From 2004 to 2010 Susan was State Secretary. Then she gave Lecturer another try.

After graduating from the University of Oregon with a degree in geography, Susan worked as a bookkeeper for Springfield Lumber Products. In the early 2000s, the Executive Committee hired Susan to set up the State Grange's chart of accounts and prepare for an audit. Her accounting experience was useful then and when she was State Master.

Susan had barely organized the State Master's office in 2012 when she was hit with the news that a Canadian developer had gotten ballot Measure 83 on the November ballot. It would have authorized the State Lottery to issue a renewable 15-year lease to turn the former Multnomah Kennel Club in Multnomah County into a casino. The name they selected was "The Grange." Susan, with help from the National Grange, fought the measure as a trademark violation. Voters rejected the measure 70% to 30%.

Susan instituted a matching grant program for Community Granges primarily to improve the external appearance of their halls. To date the program has given out $432,000 to 92 Granges.

In 2017 the committee directors devised GrangeUp. They and their district chairs delivered a box of materials and a banner to every Grange and announced that the three Granges with the highest net gains would receive cash prizes. In addition, the State Grange would serve an ice cream social to the top gaining Grange in each district. The highest percentages of gain were 105%, 90%, and 85%; 75 Granges had a net gain.

Then the COVID pandemic hit. Most Granges did not meet for months. Some met via video conferencing. Many Granges got out of the habit of meeting and performing community service. Since having to cancel events and rentals seriously affected Granges' finances, the State Grange offered two $500 Emergency COVID Grants. The State Session was postponed until September. It was a shortened Session with 54 delegates attending in person, wearing masks, and maintaining six-foot distances. Another 47 attended via video conferencing. The effects of COVID are still being felt.

During Black Lives Matters protests many members began questioning the use of the terms Master and Overseer. The alternative titles of

President and Vice President had been approved years earlier. Although the delegates indefinitely postponed a resolution to substitute the alternative titles, Susan began implementing them herself.

Susan's dog Bailey's column in the *Grange Bulletin* likely had more readers than her column did.

Susan was elected National Pomona before being elected a member of the National Executive Committee and serving as its Secretary.

After ten years as State President, Susan was elected to Position 1 of the State Executive Committee. When Oregon's GWA Director resigned unexpectedly, Susan volunteered to do the job although some would say she's probably the least domestic Sister in Oregon.

Susan made the office of State Master look easy. Although she has small feet and many pairs of footwear, she left her successor "big shoes" to fill.

2020-2023

Today the State Grange has 163 Granges with 4587 members. Oregon was the top state in the nation in membership growth between July 1 2019 and June 30, 2020. At the 2022 National Session, Oregon was recognized for having a net gain for four of the last six years.

The 150th Session will be held in Rickreall. The number of delegates in the 2020s has ranged from 76 (low due to COVID) to 102 with 12 to 20 Pomona delegates. The number of resolutions ranged from 22 to 49, 68% of which were aimed at setting Grange policy.

Everything changed in March 2020 when COVID-19 was declared a pandemic. Schools were canceled. Those who could, worked from home. Most ordered groceries and other necessities online. Stores ran out of toilet paper. Yeast was hard to find because many were making their own bread. Most Granges did not meet or met via video conferencing. The Executive Committee gave COVID grants totaling $56,040 to 78 Granges who could not hold their usual fundraiser or lost income from rentals.

At the May 2020 State Executive Committee meeting, the decision was made to postpone the State Session scheduled for June. It was held September 17-20 at the Klamath County Fairgrounds with chairs six feet apart, everyone wearing masks, and microphones sanitized between speakers. No meals were served onsite, no degrees were conferred, and only a few contests were judged. Friday there were 54 delegates onsite. The highest number of delegates attending by video conferencing was on Friday with 47. Fourteen members watched portions of the session via online video sharing.

Before the Session opened, attendees observed a moment of silence for those affected by the wildfires burning across the state. Attendees donated ten cases of water, individual packets of beef jerky, and approximately $200 cash to wildfire evacuees. Donations to the Oregon State Grange Foundation's Fraternal Concerns Fund for members who lost homes totaled $3,805 with another $1,500 pledged.

The investment earnings on the Life Memberships Fund paid more than the $45 dues each Grange paid per member per year to the Oregon State Grange. Granges with lots of Life Members paid no dues for one or more quarters.

The 2021 and 2022 Sessions almost returned to normal with good attendance, a Kickoff banquet and luncheons, degrees, and contests. Delegates voted to support adding apprenticeships and mentoring to the Farm Food Corps program sponsored by Senators Wyden and Merkley. They opposed The Abuse, Neglect, and Assault Exemption Modification and Improvement initiative, which has been postponed until 2024. At the 2022 Session delegates voted to change from six districts to five.

Since there were only 22 resolutions submitted, the 2021 session closed a day early. Many delegates used the time to shop in Joseph, enjoy Wallowa Lake, or ride the tram. Those from the Willamette Valley returned home to an unexpected heatwave with temperatures reaching 116 degrees F.

To raise money for 150th anniversary celebrations, the State Grange sold 150 candles on a cake, the first going for $1 and the 150th for $150.

Delegates look forward to celebrating the anniversary with a Celebration Dinner during the 150th State Session, a Celebration in Salem on September 24, and erecting a monument on the State Capitol grounds to recognize the service and sacrifice of all Oregon veterans.

JAY SEXTON

30th State President, 2022-2024

Jay Sexton (1958-) was born in Parkersburg, W.V. and raised in western New York state. After earning a BS degree at SUNY College of Environmental Science at Syracuse, he came to Oregon to study forest entomology at Oregon State University. Instead, he was hired by the University as a field research technician in forest ecology, mainly investigating decomposition and nutrient cycling. One week he gathered samples along the McKenzie River and the next in Mexico's Yucatan. He retired in 2012 after working outdoors for 30 years.

Jay and his wife Toni Hoyman joined Marys River #685 in Philomath in 2010. Neither had ever been in a Grange hall before joining. They quickly became active members. They were delegates to the State Session that year; Jay served on the Legislation committee and Toni on Agriculture. Both took the Sixth Degree.

The following year the State Session was held at the Benton County Fairgrounds. Jay volunteered to chair several host committees, including food services. The Resolution of Thanks says, "To Jay Sexton, ticket taker extraordinary, for his work with the caterers to provide our meals." He arranged for OSU catering to deliver meals. The consensus was that the food was excellent, although the portion size was what attendees should eat, not what they would have eaten had there been more. Jay made sure that food containers were recycled, and food waste was composted.

Marys River Grange was near closing when Jay and Toni joined. The Grange got a matching grant from the Oregon State Grange to make needed improvements to their hall. They sponsored community events, asked attendees to join, and got good local newspaper coverage. They challenged Rockford #501 in Hood River to a membership contest.

In 2014 Jay was appointed Director of the State Agriculture Committee. Since Jay was not a farmer, his appointment was controversial. However, he successfully organized the Grange's outreach at Ag Fest, the State FFA Convention, and OSU's annual Small Farms Conference. He and the committee participated in Ag Awareness Day at the State Capitol and hosted a day at the Log Cabin at the Oregon State Fair. He served as Ag Director until 2018.

Jay is currently President of Willamette #52. Its hall needed extensive repair and refurbishing. To replace the roof, a project that is expected to cost more than $110,000, Toni has applied for and gotten grants of $12,000 from Oregon Cultural Trust and $25,000 from the Ford Foundation. Donations have come from unexpected sources.

In May 2022, Benton County honored Jay and Toni for "reinvigorating Willamette Grange and their exhaustive efforts to raise funds for and organize the restoration of the Grange building." Not only have they improved the appearance and utility of the hall, but the surrounding community has joined. Membership has tripled.

Before being elected State President, Jay was elected Vice President in 2018 and served until 2022. He read the daily announcements with appropriate humor.

Jay probably found being State Master more challenging than he expected. His predecessor had been on the job for ten years and made it look easy. Meanwhile he had never worked in an office, let alone managed an organization as complex as the State Grange. His plans for the day were often interrupted by a phone call or email from a member who thought they needed his immediate attention to resolve a crisis. Meanwhile Jay has had great success revitalizing several Granges who were ready to give up. He helped them reidentify their purpose and plan an event to fulfill it. He traveled to visit them in an electric car.

In addition to his Grange work, Jay has served as Chair of the Philomath Planning Commission, and as a member of the Benton County Planning Commission. He ran for Mayor, twice, losing one close election. He served as a member of the Benton County Natural Areas and Parks Advisory Board and on the College of Philomath Community Corporation Board. Jay has been President of the Willamette Disc Golf Club.

Jay and Toni enjoy disc golf, gardening, and spending time with their four sons and three grandchildren. The sons and their wives are all Grange members.

STATE SESSIONS AND DELEGATES

State Grange Sessions have been held in 27 of Oregon's 36 counties. Marion county has hosted the most since 16 of the first 18 Sessions were held in Salem. Lane and Clackamas counties have each hosted ten or more Sessions.

In the early years Sessions were held in Grange halls or halls of other fraternal organizations. Government buildings were also used. From 1926 on, the most common venue has been schools. In recent years, Sessions have been held at fairgrounds and convention centers.

In many years, counties competed to host. The Pomona Master or County Deputy read letters or telegrams from county officials. Speakers sold the advantages including sightseeing opportunities. In 1891 delegates voted whether to meet next in Albany or The Dalles. Albany won 21 to 20.

In time invitations became bribery or performances. In 1928 delegates from Coos County handed out cheese and promised they would feed visitors cheese every day. A "noisy delegation from Lane County with balloons, horns, basketballs, a banner, and great deal of noise marched in and invited the delegates to Eugene" in 1977.

The Oregon Caves Cavemen, dressed as descendants of Neanderthals, initiated the State Master and others in 1972 when Grants Pass presented their invitation.

To give time to organize all the details of a Session, delegates voted in 1977 that invitations were to be for two years hence. As time went on, fewer Pomonas had the funds or leadership to host. When no invitation was received, the State Master or Executive Committee had to convince a Pomona to find a venue, appoint committees, staff a kitchen for onsite meals, exemplify the Fifth Degree, and perform other hosting duties.

When the Master in 2006 called for invitations, there was no response. A Special Committee on Hosting State Sessions was appointed and recommended that hosting be by district in a six-year rotation starting with District #5 in 2008. Since the number of districts was reduced to five in 2022, hosting will be every five years.

COMMUNITY GRANGE DELEGATES

In 1873 delegates were Masters and their wives. In 1875 the By-Laws were changed to a proportional system. Granges in each county sent representatives to their county courthouse to select one Master and his wife for every four Granges. That ratio was later changed to one for every six Granges. However, soon this scheme for controlling the number of delegates became unnecessary as the number of Granges grew smaller.

Beginning in 1878 past Masters and their wives were allowed to be delegates if the current Master was unable to attend. Since 2000 the second delegate has not automatically been the Master's spouse but any legally elected member.

Year	City	Place	Delegates	Granges	Counties
1873	Salem	Masonic Hall	42	33	10
1874	Salem	Reed's Opera House	115		
1875	Portland	Masonic Hall	75		20
1876	Albany	Odd Fellows Hall	54		16
1877	Salem	Salem Grange	48		18
1878	Salem	Salem Grange	37		12
1879	Salem	Old Legislative Hall	30		10
1880	Salem	Old Legislative Hall	23		8
1881	Salem	Old Legislative Hall	26		11
1882	Salem	Salem Grange	26		7
1883	Salem	Salem Grange	34		15
1884	Salem	Salem Grange	32		12
1885	Salem	Salem Grange	30		12
1886	Salem	Salem Grange	36		10
1887	Salem	Salem Grange	35		10
1888	Salem	Salem Grange	34		14
1889	Salem	Senate Chamber	41		11
1890	Salem	Salem Grange	45		14
1891	Hillsboro	Hillsboro Grange	49		15
1892	Albany	Knights of Pythias Hall	46		15
1893	The Dalles	Knights of Pythias Hall	48		14

1894	Eugene	Mount's Hall	39		13
1895	Oregon City	United Workmen Hall	38		12
1896	McMinnville	Wright's Hall	39		13
1897	Corvallis	Fireman's Hall	41		13
1898	Forest Grove	Masonic Hall	41		13
1899	Portland	Auditorium	40		12
1900	Independence	Opera House	38		12
1901	Albany	G. A. R Hall	36		13
1902	Salem	Senate Chambers	46		13
1903	Oregon City	Woodman Hall	55		13
1904	Corvallis	OAC Agriculture Hall	56		15
1905	Forest Grove	Masonic Hall	57		16
1906	Albany	United Workmen Hall	59		17
1907	Hood River	Odd Fellows Hall	64		18
1908	Eugene	Odd Fellows Hall	74		19
1909	McMinnville	Burns Hall	79		23
1910	Oregon City	County Court House	83		25
1911	Corvallis	Odd Fellows Hall	101		28
1912	Roseburg	Armory	115		29
1913	Albany	Moose Hall	106		27
1914	Monmouth	Normal School Gym	96	59	27
1915	Tillamook	Odd Fellows Hall	101	55	21
1916	Grants Pass	Waldorf Hall	112	60	24
1917	Astoria	Moose Hall	120	66	26
1918	Salem	Legislative Hall	107	61	26
1919	Hillsboro	Moose Hall	102	58	24
1920	Bend	YMCA Gymnasium	190	127	28
1921	Eugene	Elks Lodge	218	136	25
1922	McMinnville	Woodman Hall	192	118	26
1923	Newport	Armory	245	148	29

1924	The Dalles	Auditorium	224	150	31
1925	Dallas	Armory	275	174	30
1926	Baker	High School	275	169	31
1927	Corvallis	Agricultural Hall	282	169	33
1928	Rainier	High School	284	182	33
1929	Myrtle Point	High School	330	209	35
1930	Redmond	Gymnasium	342	219	35
1931	Medford	High School	408	242	36
1932	Silverton	Eugene Field School	398	246	36
1933	Pendleton	Happy Canyon	418	246	35
1934	Roseburg	High School	483	246	35
1935	McMinnville	High School	415	261	34
1936	Lebanon	High School	421	261	35
1937	The Dalles	East Port Dock Building	421	269	35
1938	Klamath Falls	High School	455	283	36
1939	Corvallis	Men's Gym	445	259	35
1940	Salem	Senior High School	401	247	36
1941	Newport	Natatorium	379	238	36
1942	Milwaukie	High School	291	211	35
1943	Eugene	Woodrow Wilson Jr Hi	345	183	34
1944	Grants Pass	Junior High School	266	192	34
1945	**No Session due to WWII**				
1946	Baker	Junior High School	369	228	35
1947	Bend	High School	378	234	35
1948	Astoria	U. S. O. Building	288	187	33
1949	Coos Bay	Marshfield HS	353	230	36
1950	Ontario	H. S. Auditorium	340	207	35
1951	Portland	Russellville School	360	228	36
1952	La Grande	Eastern Oregon College	327	307	35
1953	Medford	Medford High School	325	200	35

1954	Albany	Union High School	363	224	35
1955	Klamath Falls	High School	289	191	32
1956	Pendleton	High School	298	187	35
1957	Bend	Junior High School	282	179	34
1958	Eugene	Lane Cty Fairgrounds	283	182	34
1959	Baker	Junior High School	280	173	34
1960	Roseburg	Douglas Fairgrounds	258	167	33
1961	Beaverton	High School	281	181	35
1962	Grants Pass	High School	287	178	32
1963	Oregon City	High School	311	189	35
1964	Eugene	Willamette High School	278	173	34
1965	Pendleton	Armory	184	163	31
1966	Silverton	High School	284	166	32
1967	North Bend	Junior High School	287	177	32
1968	Gresham	High School	246	158	32
1969	Ashland	Junior High School	226	140	28
1970	Hood River	Wy-East High School	263	160	30
1971	Roseburg	Douglas Fairgrounds	249	153	30
1972	Beaverton	Highland Park School	231	143	30
1973	Grants Pass	High School	240	142	29
1974	Oregon City	Senior High School	259	156	28
1975	Klamath Falls	Mazama High School	241	147	30
1976	The Dalles	High School	261	165	32
1977	Grants Pass	High School	271	164	32
1978	Eugene	Willamette High School	276	166	32
1979	Gresham	High School	277	165	32
1980	Woodburn	High School	223	150	32
1981	North Bend	High School	261	157	29
1982	Rainier	High School	254	155	27
1983	Ashland	Junior High School	267	150	30

1984	Newport	High School	285	166	32
1985	Canby	High School	267	152	30
1986	Albany	Linn-Benton C. C.	250	139	27
1987	Hermiston	High School	246	141	32
1988	Roseburg	High School	271	153	28
1989	Enterprise	High School	252	145	28
1990	Ontario	High School	233	132	28
1991	Eugene	Willamette High School	245	139	27
1992	North Bend	Junior High School	253	138	30
1993	Pilot Rock	High School	232	125	30
1994	McMinnville	High School	262	146	30
1995	Clatskanie	High School	231	121	29
1996	Independence	Central High School	220	121	25
1997	Sutherlin	High School	195	111	27
1998	West Linn	Athey Creek School	133	121	28
1999	Redmond	Deschutes County Fair	194	112	27
2000	Grants Pass	High School	202	119	29
2001	Baker City	High School	207	121	27
2002	Eugene	Willamette High School	202	123	27
2003	Phoenix	High School	137	82	23
2004	Joseph	High School	107	*	*
2005	Reedsport	High School	139	82	20
2006	Molalla	High School	102	58	19
2007	Jefferson	High School	124	*	*
2008	Prineville	High School	118	*	*
2009	Pendleton	Convention Center	110	*	30
2010	Roseburg	Junior High School	131	83	23
2011	Corvallis	Benton Cty Fairgrounds	119	64	22
2012	Seaside	Convention Center	140	76	21
2013	Canby	Grove Conference Ctr	74	67	17

2014	Redmond	Deschutes Cty Fair/Expo	107	69	17
2015	Pendleton	Convention Center	110	62	24
2016	Talent	Middle School	111	67	19
2017	Florence	Event Center	110	64	20
2018	Astoria	Clatsop Cty Fairgrounds	103	61	19
2019	Molalla	High School	108	61	19
2020	Klamath Falls	Klamath Cty Fairgrounds	76	47	16
2021	Enterprise	Wallowa Cty Fairgrounds	101	51	18
2022	Talent	Middle School	82	47	13
2023	Rickreall	Polk Cty Fairgrounds	102	44	

*Delegate names, Granges, and counties were not recorded in the Proceedings.

WHEN SESSIONS WERE HELD AND POMONA DELEGATES

The first four Sessions were held in September. Also, the 2020 Session was postponed from June to September due to COVID. From 1877 to 1919 Sessions were held in May. Since 1924 the State Grange By-Laws specify that the Session will be held in the third week in June, but the Executive Committee can set the date one week earlier to two weeks later.

Most Sessions were four days. In 1937 the State Grange conducted a vote by mail to which 221 Granges responded. The majority voted to increase the number of days of the State Session to five. Apparently, some felt that five days was too long because in 1949 an Interim Committee on the Session Program was appointed. The committee was to conduct hearings and make recommendations for a more efficient and shorter Session. The following year they recommended that there should be no more than 15 guests, each of which should be escorted to the Master's station only once. Also, officer reports, except for those of the Master, Secretary, Treasurer, Juvenile and Youth chairmen, should be shorter. Their recommendations were adopted but may not have fixed the problem.

From 1877 to 1889 Pomona Masters and their wives were voting delegates at State Sessions. It is not clear why Pomonas lost voting rights. In 1912 delegates voted down a resolution that would have given Pomona Masters and their wives the vote. Four years later that decision was reversed. In 1917 Pomona Masters and their spouses were able to vote again.

Year	City	Dates	Delegates	Pomonas
1873	Salem	9/24-27		
1874	Salem	9/15-19		
1875	Portland	9/28-10/1		
1876	Albany	9/26-30		
1877	Salem	5/22-26	3	3
1878	Salem	5/28-6/1	4	2
1879	Salem	5/27-30	7	4
1880	Salem	5/25-27	3	2
1881	Salem	5/24-26	7	4
1882	Salem	5/23-25	7	4
1883	Salem	5/22-24	5	3
1884	Salem	5/27-29	6	3
1885	Salem	5/26-28	9	4
1886	Salem	5/25-27	9	3
1887	Salem	5/24-26	10	5
1888	Salem	5/22-24	7	4
1889	Salem	5/28-31	18	8
1890	Salem	5/27-30		
1891	Hillsboro	5/26-29		
1892	Albany	5/24-27		
1893	The Dalles	5/23-26		
1894	Eugene	5/22-24		
1895	Oregon City	5/28-31		

1896	McMinnville	5/26-28		
1897	Corvallis	5/25-28		
1898	Forest Grove	5/24-26		
1899	Portland	5/23-25		
1900	Independence	5/22-24		
1901	Albany	5/28-30		
1902	Salem	5/27-29		
1903	Oregon City	5/26-28		
1904	Corvallis	5/24-27		
1905	Forest Grove	5/23-26		
1906	Albany	5/22-25		
1907	Hood River	5/28-31		
1908	Eugene	5/12-15		
1909	McMinnville	5/11-14		
1910	Oregon City	5/10-13		
1911	Corvallis	5/9-12		
1912	Roseburg	5/14-17		
1913	Albany	5/13-16		
1914	Monmouth	5/19-22		
1915	Tillamook	5/11-14		
1916	Grants Pass	5/9-12		
1917	Astoria	6/12-15		
1918	Salem	6/5-7	26	15
1919	Hillsboro	5/20-23	28	15
1920	Bend	6/1-4	16	11
1921	Eugene	5/31-6/3	26	17
1922	McMinnville	6/6-9	17	10
1923	Newport	6/5-8	24	15
1924	The Dalles	6/3-6	25	16
1925	Dallas	6/2-5	21	16

1926	Baker	6/1-4	23	15
1927	Corvallis	6/14-17	31	21
1928	Rainier	6/5-8	25	19
1929	Myrtle Point	6/11-14	27	20
1930	Redmond	6/10-13	38	26
1931	Medford	6/9-12	50	27
1932	Silverton	6/14-17	51	29
1933	Pendleton	6/13-16	50	30
1934	Roseburg	6/12-15	54	31
1935	McMinnville	6/11-14	49	30
1936	Lebanon	6/9-12	52	33
1937	The Dalles	6/7-11	44	27
1938	Klamath Falls	6/13-17	55	33
1939	Corvallis	6/12-16	41	30
1940	Salem	6/10-14	52	32
1941	Newport	6/16-20	52	32
1942	Milwaukie	6/15-19	43	28
1943	Eugene	6/7-11	39	26
1944	Grants Pass	6/12-16	46	28
1945	**No Session due to WWII**			
1946	Baker	6/3-7	47	28
1947	Bend	6/2-6	53	34
1948	Astoria	6/7-11	48	29
1949	Coos Bay	6/13-17	58	33
1950	Ontario	6/12-16	56	33
1951	Portland	6/11-15	56	34
1952	La Grande	6/9-13	56	35
1953	Medford	6/8-12	55	33
1954	Albany	6/14-18	60	35
1955	Klamath Falls	6/6-10	53	32

1956	Pendleton	6/4-8	55	34
1957	Bend	6/10-14	51	30
1958	Eugene	6/9-13	54	31
1959	Baker	6/1-5	51	31
1960	Roseburg	6/13-17	52	31
1961	Beaverton	6/12-16	46	28
1962	Grants Pass	6/12-16	49	29
1963	Oregon City	6/10-14	45	29
1964	Eugene	6/15-19	48	30
1965	Pendleton	6/14-18	54	31
1966	Silverton	6/13-17	56	31
1967	North Bend	6/12-16	47	27
1968	Gresham	6/17-21	52	30
1969	Ashland	6/9-13	44	26
1970	Hood River	6/15-19	52	30
1971	Roseburg	6/14-18	52	30
1972	Beaverton	6/12-16	53	31
1973	Grants Pass	6/10-15	51	31
1974	Oregon City	6/9-14	54	31
1975	Klamath Falls	6/16-20	54	27
1976	The Dalles	6/14-18	54	33
1977	Grants Pass	6/13-17	48	30
1978	Eugene	6/12-16	49	33
1979	Gresham	6/18-22	53	31
1980	Woodburn	6/16-20	42	30
1981	North Bend	6/15-19	50	29
1982	Rainier	6/14-18	44	27
1983	Ashland	6/20-24	46	27
1984	Newport	6/25-29	48	27
1985	Canby	6/17-21	45	27

1986	Albany	6/16-20	49	28
1987	Hermiston	6/15-19	59	27
1988	Roseburg	6/20-24	47	26
1989	Enterprise	6/19-23	49	26
1990	Ontario	6/18-22	47	28
1991	Eugene	6/17-21	49	27
1992	North Bend	6/15-19	46	23
1993	Pilot Rock	6/21-25	39	22
1994	McMinnville	6/20-24	40	23
1995	Clatskanie	6/19-23	43	24
1996	Independence	6/23-28	42	26
1997	Sutherlin	6/16-20	42	24
1998	West Linn	6/22-26	41	24
1999	Redmond	6/21-26	41	23
2000	Grants Pass	6/26-30	41	23
2001	Baker City	6/18-22	39	23
2002	Eugene	6/24-28	40	23
2003	Phoenix	6/23-27	33	20
2004	Joseph	6/21-25	33	*
2005	Reedsport	6/20-24	33	18
2006	Molalla	6/19-23	24	14
2007	Jefferson	6/18-22	27	*
2008	Prineville	6/16-20	29	*
2009	Pendleton	6/29-7/3	30	*
2010	Roseburg	6/19-25	29	18
2011	Corvallis	6/19-24	31	19
2012	Seaside	6/10-15	19	17
2013	Canby	6/15-21	18	16
2014	Redmond	6/23-27	19	13
2015	Pendleton	6/28-7/3	21	13

2016	Talent	6/18-23	17	11
2017	Florence	6/24-29	17	11
2018	Astoria	6/23-28	21	13
2019	Molalla	6/22-27	18	11
2020	Klamath Falls	9/17-20	12	8
2021	Enterprise	6/19-24	16	9
2022	Talent	6/18-23	20	10
2023	Rickreall	6/17-22	13	8

HOW DID DELEGATES GET TO THE SESSION?

Probably one of the reasons that most of the early Sessions were held in Salem was because it was easy to get to by train. Although the Grange fought the railroads on freight rates and passenger fares, they had no problem accepting a free ride. In 1878, delegates asked the President of the Oregon and California Railroad to extend the time they could return home for free. Delegates paid full fare to Salem and got a discounted or free return trip.

The first time most delegates saw the east side of the Cascades was in 1920 when the Session was held in Bend. Most delegates took the train and arrived as scheduled. Those traveling by car were late because it had rained, and roads were slippery.

Travel by car from one end of the state to the other was a two-day trip until the mid-1950s. Those going from the coast to Baker City or Ontario or vice versa stayed night in Portland or the Bend-Redmond area.

WHERE DID DELEGATES STAY?

Until the mid-1970s the host committee had a lodging subcommittee who booked hotel or auto court rooms for those who requested help. A coupon in the *Grange Bulletin* asked how many were in the group and how many beds were needed? Did they prefer a hotel, auto court, or rooms in a home? Did they want a kitchen? A deposit for the first night was requested. In 1946 the suggested deposit was $3.

Many towns, including Bend, did not have enough hotel or motel rooms for 200 delegates. Residents near the venue were encouraged to rent their spare bedroom.

For the Silverton Session in 1932, 150 tents were erected in the city park. A State Deputy was named the Mayor of this tent city. He made sure that delegate's belongings stayed in their tent and trash was picked up.

In 1967 the Resolution of Thanks included the North Bend Police for use of their 10-acre fenced training field where 40 campers and trailers were parked. This may not have been the first year that delegates traveled in their motorhomes and RVs, but it definitely became a common mode of travel and housing.

Today many delegates rent vacation homes from Airbnb or similar agencies.

WHERE DID DELEGATES EAT?

In 1920 when delegates arrived in Bend, they were tired and hungry. After they found their rooms and stowed their suitcases, they looked for a cafe or restaurant. Apparently, the operators of these businesses did not know how many Grangers were coming. They ran out of food. However, they called Portland and ordered more brought down on the night train.

Families often brought food with them to prepare meals in the kitchen of the motel rooms. They not only brought eggs and bread for breakfast, but meat and produce for dinner. This assumed that the oven in the motel's stove worked the same way as the one at home. A charred roast was a problem.

When Sessions were held in schools, the host committee prepared meals that attendees could purchase. There was usually a choice of entrée for lunch and dinner. The State Home Economics committee hosted a banquet or breakfast. The Youth committee and others may have had fundraising dinners. The Kickoff Banquet was introduced in 2003. Other banquets soon followed. In 2012 when banquets that had to be catered were too expensive, they became luncheons.

RESOLUTIONS

In 1875 delegates voted that all resolutions "be reduced to writing and handed to the Secretary to be read." It sounds as though some delegates wrote resolutions on their way to Session that had not been adopted by their Grange.

A roll call of counties was introduced in 1888. A delegate from each county read the titles of the resolutions they brought. Then the Division of Labor Committee assigned them to committees based on their title. Currently resolutions must be submitted 60 days before the Session and the Executive Committee acts as the Division of Labor committee.

In 1915 delegates adopted a resolution calling for all resolutions be sent to the State Secretary two weeks before the Session so she could "multigraph them and provide each delegate with a copy on the first day of the Session."

It was not until 1992 that delegates received a packet of resolutions during registration, so they had the opportunity to read through them before their committee meeting and floor discussion.

Old timers often recall years when there were 200 resolutions. In fact, the most submitted in any year was 158 in 1960. The fewest was 16 in 2013.

The number of resolutions submitted is not the only indicator of the health of the organization. The State Overseer in 1994 challenged members to send resolutions to the next Session that dealt with the real work of the Grange: Farm, family, and community. This chart shows the number that set Grange policy versus the number that dealt with internal housekeeping issues. In the 1990s and early 2000s, the number of internal resolutions exceeded or matched the number of external resolutions.

Prior to 1919 not all resolutions were numbered.

Year	Total	Policy	Internal
1919	25	18	7
1920	39	21	18
1921	42	31	11
1922	51	38	13
1923	71	65	6
1924	57	42	15
1925	74	48	26
1926	45	33	12
1927	69	51	18
1928	33	21	12
1929	55	39	16
1930	51	32	19
1931	77	55	22
1932	70	54	16
1933	51	31	20
1934	65	50	15
1935	57	43	14
1936	99	78	21
1937	63	46	17
1938	88	67	21
1939	70	55	15
1940	90	71	19
1941	71	60	11
1942	85	67	18
1943	64	57	7
1944	131	111	20
1945	No Session		
1946	150	121	29
1947	69	40	29
1948	98	81	17
1949	66	57	9
1950	106	85	21
1951	65	54	11

Year	Total	Policy	Internal
1952	81	59	22
1953	67	50	17
1954	77	64	13
1955	93	75	18
1956	73	60	13
1957	55	47	8
1958	73	57	16
1959	44	32	12
1960	146	123	23
1961	81	57	24
1962	98	77	21
1963	79	55	24
1964	93	76	17
1965	74	56	18
1966	81	69	12
1967	88	75	13
1968	67	57	10
1969	94	86	8
1970	84	70	14
1971	86	69	17
1972	83	65	18
1973	76	69	7
1974	84	68	16
1975	80	57	23
1976	75	55	20
1977	74	59	15
1978	100	74	26
1979	102	64	38
1980	87	67	20
1981	96	76	20
1982	122	100	22
1983	111	85	26
1984	81	44	36

Year	Total	Policy	Internal
1985	84	64	20
1986	105	75	30
1987	85	50	35
1988	78	56	22
1989	130	79	51
1990	95	56	39
1991	79	45	34
1992	101	63	38
1993	119	52	67
1994	92	39	53
1995	76	44	32
1996	77	18	59
1997	66	34	32
1998	93	67	26
1999	79	39	40
2000	68	24	44
2001	120	55	65
2002	62	34	28
2003	89	41	48
2004	71	40	31

Year	Total	Policy	Internal
2005	43	29	14
2006	71	51	20
2007	42	28	14
2008	45	21	24
2009	59	41	18
2010	44	27	17
2011	61	38	23
2012	36	18	18
2013	16	9	7
2014	53	35	18
2015	39	24	15
2016	43	25	18
2017	80	63	17
2018	45	35	10
2019	72	56	16
2020	49	35	14
2021	22	17	5
2022	23	11	12
2023	28	20	8

SESSION COMMITTEES

Session committees review resolutions referred to them. They can also write resolutions pertaining to their subject.

At the 1874 Session, State Master Daniel Clark appointed six Session committees: By-Laws, Finance, Good of the Order, Cooperation & Transportation, Legislation, and Appeals. Their purpose was to report "Favorable" or "Unfavorable" on the resolutions referred to them. If the committee agreed with the intent of the resolution, but thought it needed to be improved, they wrote a new resolution, which was called a "substitute." Today if committees rewrite resolutions, they report "Favorable as amended."

When no resolutions were submitted or if committees felt that assigned resolutions did not cover their concerns, they wrote a report that included their policy recommendations. Delegates then adopted or rejected their report.

The names and number of committees have changed over time reflecting the subject matter of the resolutions submitted. In 1881, an Education Committee was appointed, and the following year Agriculture was added. Women's Work was added in 1889. In 1903 the list was expanded to include Assessment & Taxation, Pure Foods, Dormant Granges, and Good Roads.

The Session committee list grew to include these committees for policy resolutions: Banking & Taxation, Cooperatives & Marketing, Environment & Ecology, Foreign Affairs, Forestry, Health & Welfare, Law Enforcement, Natural Resources, Post War, Reclamation & Irrigation, Roads & Highways, Social Welfare, Temperance & Morals, Utilities, and Wildlife.

These Session committees considered resolutions on internal issues: Athletics & Picnics, Community Efforts, Finances & Auditing, Grange Fairs, Juveniles/Juniors, Music, Pomonas, Publicity & News, Ritual & Conferences, and Youth.

Today's By-Laws specify "The State Session Committees shall be Agriculture, Budget, By-Laws, Credentials, Conservation, Education & Health, Financial Affairs & Insurance, Good of the Order, Grange Elections, Grange Programs & Bulletin, Legislation, Progress, Transportation & Utilities, Veterans, and such other committees as the State Master may deem necessary."

The Progress committee was first appointed in 1943. As the number of resolutions submitted increased, someone needed to make sure that Session committees acted on all those assigned, and that none were overlooked. At the end of the 1943 Session, the Progress committee recommended that mimeographed instructions be attached to each committee's folder. The information should include how to organize (who can vote, what's a quorum, keeping records, etc.), what action the committee could take, and a copy of each resolution for each committee member. They also requested an outline of a properly written resolution.

In 1957 the Progress Committee requested that they have access to a telephone either in their room or just outside it. Who they needed to call was not stated. But later the committee requested internet access so that committees could research resolutions if members had questions. Of course, today most delegates bring internet access with them.

In the mid-2000s, the Progress Committees began retyping resolutions when Session Committees made substantial amendments. Delegates had trouble hearing and following when the reader directed them to insert words or sentences and strike other words. It was easier for the Gatekeeper and Deputies to hand out updated copies of amended resolutions so that everyone was clear on what they were voting on. The updates were printed on a different color of paper.

In 1931 members of the same committee were seated together in the Session, so they could get to know each other before their deliberations.

To give committees time to work, in 1908 it was agreed to begin morning sessions at 9:30 a.m., afternoons at 2:30 p.m., and evenings at 8 p.m. Before COVID, committees met on the afternoon of the first day of the Session and then anytime except when the State Grange was in session.

Due to COVID in 2020, committees met prior to Session via video conferencing. Many delegates liked this because they had time to study the assigned resolutions and do research before their meeting. As a result, virtual meetings before the Session have continued. However, some committees still need to meet during Session because sections of the State Master's Address and Good of the Order Address are referred to them. Also delegates often accept a few late resolutions which need consideration, and committees can write new resolutions.

WHO WERE OFFICERS?

Granges at all levels elect at least 16 officers. At the organizing Session, Masters and their wives as well as Past Masters and their wives were eligible to be elected to state offices. The By-Laws specified "All elections shall be by ballot, and it shall require a majority of all the votes cast to elect." All officers elected at the organizing Session were elected for a one-year term.

In 1910 election of officers was "without nominations." The National Grange used this method until recently. The Master announced the office to be filled and each delegate wrote the name of a member on a blank piece of paper. Typically, several members received multiple votes while many received just one. Voting continued until one candidate received a majority of the votes cast.

Delegates changed the voting method in 1917. Nominations were made from the floor at 11 a.m. on the second day. Any member could be nominated. Voting was between 7:30 and 8:30 p.m. with printed ballots that provided that gave voters their first, second, and third choice. If no candidate received a majority, the top two would be voted on at 9:30 a.m. the next day. The results were announced at 10:30 a.m. on the third day. Installation was at 1:40 p.m. on the last day, "unless the proceedings of the Session shall make it convenient to hold such installation earlier."

Allowing Grange members to vote for selected offices was implemented in 1920. Nominations for Master, Overseer, Lecturer, Secretary, and Executive Committee were made at each Grange's August meeting. A primary election was held at the first meeting in October. The three highest vote getters were published in the *Grange Bulletin* and then voted on at the first meeting in December. Sealed envelopes of ballots were held until the Session and counted by the Session Election committee. Other officers were elected during the Session with nominations from the floor. A special committee was appointed to canvas Granges in 1927 to determine whether to continue this method of voting for State Officers. It was upheld by a vote of 1,978 to 1,566.

In 1931 the By-Laws were changed to have Subordinate Granges nominate and elect all state officers, not just Master, Overseer, Lecturer, Secretary, and Executive Committee. Three nominations for the same office were required for a member's name to appear on the ballot.

Oregon's election method did not conform to the National Grange Digest. An Interim By-Laws committee submitted a resolution in 1951 to rectify this by adding "subject to confirmation by vote of the delegates." They also allowed additional nominations to be made from the floor if agreed to by a 2/3s vote of the delegates. The By-Laws were changed in 1987 to allow nominations from the floor only in the case of a death or resignation.

In his 1952 Good of the Order Address, Elmer McClure recommended a By-Laws change to allow candidates for state office to publish in the *Grange Bulletin* their photo with a brief history of their Grange work taking up no more one-third of a column. Delegates agreed. Ten years later delegates specified that candidates' photos must have been taken within one year prior to the election.

In 1992 State Master Wayne Johnson reported that many certified election reports were not counted because Granges did not follow the By-Laws. He claimed that there were enough to have changed the results. He wondered about only 4,000 members voting when there were nearly 27,000 members. Many resolutions have been introduced over the years to have delegates nominate and elect officers at the Session like other State Granges. All have been voted down.

In 2014 the By-Laws were changed to eliminate the preferential primary because few members were nominated or accepted nomination.

Today any Fourth Degree member can be nominated and elected a state officer. However, the member must take the Sixth Degree before being installed.

The By-Laws Committee at the 2023 Session once again reported unfavorable on a resolution to elect officers during State Session like the National Grange and other State Granges do. Their report was adopted by delegates and the resolution was rejected.

MASTER

Twenty-eight Brothers and two Sisters have held the office of Master of the Oregon State Grange. Charles Spence of Central #276 (now Beavercreek) in Clackamas County served as Master for 13 years. Elmer McClure of Harding #122 in Clackamas County served 12 years. Ray Gill of Russellville #353 in Multnomah County, W. C. Harris of Elmira #523 in Lane County, and Susan Noah of Mohawk-McKenzie #747 in Lane County each served ten years.

The initial By-Laws listed only one duty, which was "to open and preside at all meetings." Other sections of the By-Laws required the Master to appoint one deputy per county to organize new Granges, see that there was no discord in the organization, and be paid traveling expenses.

The 2022 By-Laws specify these duties: "1.13.1 Master– It shall be the duty of the State Master to preside at all meetings of the Oregon State Grange; to see that the officers and members of the committees perform their respective duties; to see that the Constitution of the National Grange, the By-Laws of the Oregon State Grange and the rules and regulations of the Order are obeyed; and to sign all drafts on the treasury. The State Master shall appoint the committees provided for in these By-Laws and send to each member so appointed a notice of the committee upon which he/she is to serve; and perform such other duties as pertain to the office or are required by the By-Laws and the usages of the Order."

The State Master is also expected to set a good example in performing the opening and closing ceremonies and the Master's part in the Sixth Degree. The Master needs to have a command of parliamentary procedure and to write and deliver a Master's Address. Since 1935, most Masters have delivered a Good of the Order Address, which informs members of the condition of the Grange and of progress made since the last Session. The Good of the Order Address is not for external publication.

Following the 2020 Session, then Master Susan Noah in response to concern over the term Master, began using the previously approved alternative title of President.

Master	Grange	County	Years
Daniel Clark	Salem #17	Marion	1873-76
William Cyrus	Santiam #37	Linn	1876-78
A. R. Shipley	Oswego #175	Clackamas	1878-80
R. P. Boise	Salem #17	Marion	1880-88 1892-94
H. E. Hayes	Tualatin #111	Clackamas	1888-92
Jacob Voorhees	Woodburn #79	Marion	1894-96
William M. Hilleary	Turner #18	Marion	1896-00
B. G. Leedy	Butte #148	Washington	1900-06
Austin T. Buxton	Gale #282	Washington	1906-10
C. E. Spence	Central #276	Clackamas	1910-23
George A. Palmiter	Park #501	Hood River	1923-30
C. C. Hulet	Myrtle #289	Coos	1930-32
M. C. Glover	Eagle Creek #297	Clackamas	1932
Ray W. Gill	Russellville #353	Multnomah	1932-42
Morton Tompkins	McMinnville #31	Yamhill	1942-50
Elmer McClure	Harding #122	Clackamas	1950-62
Allen P. Wheeler	Goshen #561	Lane	1962-70
Ted Sims	Lake Creek #818	Linn	1970-74
W. C. Harris	Elmira #532	Lane	1974-84
Morton V. Wolverton	Columbia #867	Umatilla	1984-88
Wayne Johnson	Winema #948	Klamath	1988-92
Dale W. Morris	Irving #377	Lane	1992-96
Edward L. Luttrell	Boring-Damascus #260	Clackamas	1996-00
Mike Stewart	Rickreall #671	Polk	2000-02
John M. Fine	Evergreen #460	Douglas	2002-06
Phyllis Wilson	Greenacres #834	Coos	2006-10
Larry Rea	Fern Hill #592	Columbia	2010-11
Mark Noah	Mohawk-McKenzie #747	Lane	2012

Susan Noah	Mohawk-McKenzie #747	Lane	2012-22
Jay Sexton	Willamette #52	Benton	2022-24

Note: Names in this chapter were those used when the member was elected. If a female member married and changed her name during her term, her new surname has been added.

For many years, the town in the officer's mailing address was listed rather than their Grange. Every effort has been made to identify their Grange. If an officer changed Granges after serving, that change is not included.

OVERSEER

The duty of the Overseer has always been to assist the Master in preserving order and preside in his or her absence. In 1956 the Overseer became an ex-officio member of the Executive Committee but was not given a vote until the 1980s. The Overseer usually delivers a response to a welcome given by the mayor or other official of the host city.

The current By-Laws also say: "1.13.2 Overseer–In case the office of the State Master shall be vacant, the State Overseer shall automatically become State Master and be duly installed. It shall be the duty of the State Overseer to attend all State Executive Committee meetings and he/she shall have a voice and vote in all matters discussed."

Thirty-one Brothers and six Sisters have held the office of Overseer. Matt Glover of Eagle Creek #297 in Clackamas County and John Fine of North Douglas #936 and Evergreen #460 in Douglas County each served 12 years. Eleven Overseers were subsequently elected Master. Three were thrust into the position due to a resignation.

Overseer	Grange	County	Years
William Cyrus	Santiam #37	Linn	1873-76
A. R. Shipley	Oswego #175	Clackamas	1876-78

D. S. K. Buick	Umpqua #28	Douglas	1878-84
A. Luelling	Milwaukie #200	Clackamas	1884-88
Jacob Voorhees	Woodburn #79	Marion	1888-92
John Medler	Bigelow Springs #208	Sherman	1892-94
A. S. Roberts	Summit #232	Wasco	1894-96
B. G. Leedy	Butte #148	Washington	1896-98
Mary Edelman	Mayville #203	Gilliam	1898-00
Mary H. Whitby	Willamette #52	Benton	1900-02
Clara H. Waldo	Macleay #293	Marion	1902-04
Jacob Clem		Umatilla	1904-06
C. L. Shaw	Grand Prairie #10	Linn	1906-08
A. T. Shoemake	Deer Creek #371	Josephine	1908-10
J. H. Scott	Tangent #7	Linn	1910-12
T. D. Lee	Rescue #402	Douglas	1912-14
C. D. Huffman	Blue Mountain #345	Union	1914-20
Chas H. Hays	Sherwood #272	Washington	1920-22
M C. Glover	Eagle Creek #297	Clackamas	1922-34
Morton Tompkins	McMinnville #31	Yamhill	1934-42
Elmer McClure	Harding #122	Clackamas	1942-50
William G. Howes	Gold Hill #534	Jackson	1950-58
H. E. Henrickson	Winona #271	Washington	1958-62
Roscoe Roberts	Roxy Ann #792	Jackson	1962-64
Ted Sims	Western Star #309	Linn	1964-70
W. C. Harris	Elmira #532	Lane	1970-74
William Taggert	Rogue River Valley #469	Josephine	1974-78
Wayne Johnson	Rogue River Valley #469	Josephine	1978-80
John Fine	North Douglas #936 Evergreen #460	Douglas Douglas	1980-88 1998-02
Dusty Rhoades	Sunnyridge #898	Lincoln	1988-92
Ben Boswell	South Fork #605	Wallowa	1992-98

Phyllis Wilson	Greenacres #834	Coos	2002-06
Mark Noah	Mohawk-McKenzie #747	Lane	2006-12
Claudia Boswell	South Fork #605	Wallowa	2012-12
Celia Luttrell	Boring-Damascus #260	Clackamas	2012-18
Jay Sexton	Marys River #685	Benton	2018-22
Steve Kroeker	Crow #450	Lane	2022-24

LECTURER

Fourteen Brothers and twenty-six Sisters have held the office of Lecturer. Brothers held the office with one exception until 1914. Since there have been only two male Lecturers. Minnie Bond of Irving Grange #377 in Lane County served 16 years. Four Lecturers were elected to non-consecutive terms: H. E. Hayes of Tualatin #111 (now Frogpond) in Clackamas County, Marie Thiessen of Milwaukie #268 in Clackamas County, Alta Faye Rogers of Santa Clara #746 in Lane County, and Susan Noah of Mohawk-McKenzie #747 in Lane County.

The 1873 By-Laws said that the duties of the Lecturer were those of the Subordinate Lecturer. In other words, the Lecturer was responsible for literary programs and the educational work of the Grange. However, State Master Daniel Clark had a different idea. He proposed that the State Lecturer be a deputy. Between 1884 and 1897 the Lecturer spent from 57 to 201 days per year traveling great distances to visit Granges, organize new Granges, and reorganize dormant Granges.

In 1899 State Lecturer J. S. Casto reported that his eldest son volunteered for the army, so Brother Casto was forced to take charge of the farm or suffer great financial loss. However, according to the Executive Committee minutes, the Brother wanted $1.25 more per day for expenses than they were willing to pay.

Between 1901 and 1923, the State Lecturer served as Editor of the Grange newspaper. In 1915 Sister Bond reported her frustration with publishing the first issues of the *Oregon Grange Bulletin*, especially problems creating a mailing list and getting advertising.

Lecturer Clara Waldo reported in 1906 that she sent out nearly 100,000 pieces of printed matter, including report blanks, leaflets on various topics, and book lists. She also gave 63 public addresses in one year.

During the 1909 State Session, the Lecturer conducted a conference that was "very instructive and profitable." In 1927, the Lecturer led a three-day Lecturer's School. In 1948, 175 attended the Corvallis school and 90 the one in Pendleton. In 1988 the Lecturer held a retreat for Lecturers.

In 1923 the State Lecturer published a book of "Helps for Lecturers." In the late 1930s, the Lecturer established a Lending Library, which proved popular and helpful.

At the 1915 Session a Lecturer's Hour was held at the Tillamook Commercial Club with two speakers from Oregon Agricultural College and music provided by the Tillamook Orchestra. This subsequently became the Lecturer's Program, one evening of the Session that featured entertainment and education. It was coordinated by the Pomona Lecturer of the host county who provided musical numbers, skits, and readings from local Granges and Junior Granges. The last Lecturer's Program was held at the 2001 Session.

In 1927 the State Lecturer bemoaned, "A Lecturer has problems today which were not thought of in the early days of the Grange, for there is such an upheaval of customs and habits in our present-day trend of living, that the new is only for a day and rarely ever creates more than a ripple of excitement, then people are looking for something else out of the ordinary." If that was true in 1927, it's even more so today.

The Lecturer's Program typically featured a speaker. In 1951 the U. S. Atomic Energy Commissioner's title was "Atomic Energy Takes to the Farm." In 1967 Senator Mark Hatfield was scheduled to be the speaker, but he was called to Washington for an important vote. His wife Antoinette tried to deliver his speech. The Senator's staff explained price supports to her using grocery shopping examples. These were a bit elementary for her audience. What they remembered the day after her speech was how much she paid to get the lawn mowed at their new home in Washington, D. C. The Senator was too busy and the kids too young, so she had to pay someone $25. That's what everyone talked about the next day.

After the Lecturer's program, there was often a grand march followed by dancing. In 1959 the Lecturer's program had an Oregon Centennial theme and concluded with a street dance.

In 1928 the State Lecturer broadcast a Grange Lecturer's Hour every Wednesday from September to spring over KOAC, the Agricultural College's broadcast station.

The 1932 Lecturer's Program featured a spelling bee between Wasco County Pomona and Clackamas County Pomona, the finalists in a statewide contest. From then on, the Lecturer oversaw a wide variety of contests: Essay, Booster Night, play, skit writing, quartet, art, photography, and talent.

The current By-Laws say "1.13.3 Lecturer – It shall be the duty of the State Lecturer in addition to the duties prescribed by the Ritual, to have charge, subject to the approval of the State Master, of the educational and literary work of the Order, to be carried on through the Subordinate/Community and Pomona Lecturers of the State."

Over the years Lecturers have made the office a big job. The Lecturer is the only officer who has a standing committee to provide support and assistance. The Executive Committee approved the Lecturer's committee in 1985.

Note: WT stands for Washington Territory.

Lecturer	Grange	County	Years
George Hunter	Dayton #2	Walla Walla, WT	1873
E. L. Smith	Olympia #10	Thurston, WT	1874-76
Mrs. E. N. Hunt	Rock Point #48	Marion	1876-78
W. B. Thomas	Blue Mountain #3	Walla Walla, WT	1878-80
A. R. Shipley	Oswego #175	Clackamas	1880-82

H. E. Hayes	Tualatin #111	Clackamas	1882-88 1892-94
John Simpson	Siuslaw #54	Lane	1888-90
Wm. Holder	Grass Valley #229	Sherman	1890-92
A. F. Miller	Lents #352	Multnomah	1894-96
Dr. J. S. Casto	Warner #117	Clackamas	1896-00
Austin T. Buxton	Gale #282	Washington	1900-04
Mrs. Clara H. Waldo	Macleay #293	Marion	1904-08
J. J. Johnson	Evening Star #27	Multnomah	1908-10
H. A. Darnall	Lents #351	Multnomah	1910-14
Mrs. Minnie Bond	Irving #377	Lane	1914-30
Marie Flint McCall	Brush College #586	Polk	1930-34
Alice Goff	Melrose #434	Douglas	1934-36
Mrs. G. W. Theissen	Milwaukie #268	Clackamas	1936-42 1944-45
Blanche Pickering	Pacific #413	Clatsop	1942-44
Garnet Ruckman	Pleasant Grove #475	Union	1945-48
Mrs. Beulah Moore	Albernethy #346	Clackamas	1948-54
Delta Johnson	Rufus #826	Sherman	1954-58
Mrs. Mary Arne	Dorena #835	Lane	1958-59
Victor Croxton	Sams Valley #666	Jackson	1959-62
Audrey Johnston	Pleasant Grove #475	Union	1962-66
Alta Faye Rogers	Santa Clara #746	Lane	1966-68 1974-76
Margaret Rice	Beaverton #324	Washington	1968-74
Ruth Evans	Myrtle #289	Coos	1976-79
Marie Ireland	Bellview #759	Jackson	1979-82
Glenabell Lewis	Wingville #650	Baker	1982-86
Kay Fine	South Deer Creek #440	Douglas	1986-92
Arlene Force	Central #360	Lane	1992-96

Carmelita Coats	Milwaukie #268	Clackamas	1995-96
Susan Noah	Mohawk-McKenzie #747	Lane	1996-04 2010-12
Nine Stables	The Sandy #392	Clackamas	2004-08
Myrna Colvin	Terrebonne #663	Deschutes	2008-10
Kendell Phillips	Illinois Valley #370	Josephine	2012-13
Jeanie Force	Sunnyside #842	Clackamas	2013-16
Linda Helm	Phoenix #779	Jackson	2016-18
Cookie Trupp	Spencer Creek #855	Lane	2018-24

STEWARD

The 1873 and current By-Laws say that the Steward has charge of the inner gate. In addition, the Steward is responsible for the setup of the hall and the care of Grange property including sashes and implements. The Steward also announces guests.

Thirty-six members have held this office. Roscoe Roberts of Roxy Ann #792 in Jackson County served the longest, which was 20 years. Phil Van Buren, the current Steward, has served non-consecutive terms.

Steward	Grange	County	Years
R. P. Olds	Waitsburg #1	Walla Walla, WT	1873
Wm. M. Shelton	Walla Walla #4	Walla Walla, WT	1874-76
W. B. Thomas	Blue Mountain #3	Walla Walla, WT	1876-78 1882-86
Wm. Hilleary	Turner #18	Marion	1878-82
J. W. Cook	McMinnville #31	Yamhill	1886-90
J. D. Chitwood	Pleasant Valley #201	Polk	1890-94
J. H. Scott	Tangent #7	Linn	1894-96
G. W. Weeks	North Howell #274	Marion	1896-98
W. B. Hawley	Siuslaw #54	Lane	1898-00

H. B. Chapman	Gresham #270	Multnomah	1900-02
C. L. Shaw	Grand Prairie #10	Linn	1902-06
W. A. Young	Cedar Grove #320	Columbia	1906-10
E. C. Huffman	Lorane #54	Lane	1910-12
Robert Grant	Waverly #468	Harney	1912-14
M. P. Young	Cedar Grove #320	Columbia	1914-18
M. C. Glover	Eagle Creek #297	Clackamas	1918-22
Frank Fluke	Kinton #562	Washington	1922-26
W. R. Gekeler	Blue Mountain #345	Union	1926-28
Clarence Davies	Eagle Point #664	Jackson	1928-32
S. J. Howard	Service Creek #675	Wheeler	1932-34
Warren Young	Clatskanie #321	Columbia	1934-36
O. L. Lundell	Willows #672	Morrow	1936-38
Roscoe Roberts	Roxy Ann #792	Jackson	1938-58
Howard Cracroft	Fair Oaks #684	Douglas	1958-62
Roy Means	Redmond #812	Deschutes	1962-64
Millard Martin	Ada #570	West Coast	1964-70
Neil Cullison	Central #276	Clackamas	1970-74
Morton Wolverton	Columbia #867	Umatilla	1974-76
Wayne Johnson	Rogue River Valley #469	Josephine	1976-78
Bob Ludi	The Sandy #392	Clackamas	1978-80
Herman Pendergraft	Lost River #846	Klamath	1980-88
Don Force	Sunnyside #842	Clackamas	1988-96
Wayne Johnston	Keizer #785	Marion	1996-04
Phil Van Buren	Midland #781	Klamath	2004-12 2018-24
Wayne Cabler	Central Point #698	Jackson	2012-16
Alexa Suing	Crow #450	Lane	2016-18

ASSISTANT STEWARD

The Assistant Stewards help the Steward. They escort guests and candidates, and count votes when a division of the house is called. Forty-two Brothers have served as Assistant Steward though the office can be held by either gender. George Murphy of Pine Forest #632 in Deschutes County held the office for ten years.

Assistant Steward	Grange	County	Dates
W. M. Powers	Shedd #9	Linn	1873-76
G. W. Riddle	Canyonville #109	Douglas	1876-78
M. L. Nicholas	Beaverton #324	Washington	1878-80
J. W. Kirkland	Rickreall #671	Polk	1880-82
Wm. Hilleary	Turner #18	Marion	1882-84
F. C. Yeomans	Washougal #32	Clark, WT	1884-86
J. Voorhees	Woodburn #79	Marion	1886-88
W. A. Sample	Juniper #212	Umatilla	1888-92
G. R. Stephenson	Oswego #175	Clackamas	1892-96
Frank Wilson	Harding #122	Clackamas	1896-98
A. T. Buxton	Gale #282	Washington	1898-00
C. L. Shaw	Grand Prairie #10	Linn	1900-02
J. W. Edwards	Mayville #203	Gilliam	1902-04
W. A. Young	Cedar Grove #320	Columbia	1904-06
S. N. Warfield	Hope #269	Benton	1906-08
E. W. Staats	Mono #25	Polk	1908-10
F. E. Griffith	Klamath Falls #402	Klamath	1910-12
Charles H. Hays	Sherwood #272	Washington	1912-20
J. C. Leedy	Kinton #562	Washington	1920-22
George Palmiter	Park #501	Hood River	1922-23
H. B. Davis	Garfield #317	Clackamas	1923-28
Warren Young	Clatskanie #321	Columbia	1928-32

Henry Gustafson	North Bayside #691	Coos	1932-40
Allen Wheeler	Goshen #561	Lane	1940-44
George Murphy	Pine Forest #632	Deschutes	1944-54
Arnold Tarbell	Warren #536	Columbia	1954-58
Joe Guttridge	Springwater #263	Clackamas	1958-62
Wayne Johnson	Rogue River Valley #469	Josephine	1962-68
William Taggert	Rogue River Valley #469	Josephine	1968-74
John Fine	North Douglas #936 Riversdale #731	Douglas Douglas	1974-80 2023
Sam Jones	Gold Hill #534	Jackson	1980-82
Bob Ludi	Sunnyside #842	Clackamas	1982-86
Don Cook	Griffin Creek #848	Jackson	1986-90
Mark Noah	Mohawk-McKenzie #747	Lane	1990-96
Malcolm Trupp	Spencer Creek #855	Lane	1996-04
Keith Colvin	Terrebonne #663	Deschutes	2004-08
Steve Kroeker	Crow #450	Lane	2008-12
Phil Van Buren	Midland #781	Klamath	2012-18
Tim Dehne	Willamette #52	Benton	2018-20
Wayne Cabler	Central Point #698	Jackson	2020-22
Austin VanHouten	Riversdale #731	Douglas	2022-23
Jim J. Dumolt	Clarkes #261	Clackamas	2023-24

LADY ASSISTANT STEWARD

In 1944 the By-Laws were changed to elect the Lady Assistant Steward after the Assistant Steward rather than after the graces. Forty Sisters have been Lady Assistant Steward. Susan Noah of Mohawk-McKenzie #747 in Lane County held the office for ten years.

Lady Assistant	Grange	County	Dates
Chloe Olds	Waitsburg #1	Walla Walla, WT	1873
L. S. Folsom	Junction City #43	Lane	1874-76
Georgia Smith	East Hood River #250	Wasco	1876-78
Irene Hilleary	Turner #18	Marion	1878-86
Lydia Brooks Lydia Leabo	Salem #17	Marion	1886-88 1890-92
M. M. White	Oak Grove #198	Polk	1888-90
Mary Cooley	Cold Springs #801	Umatilla	1892-94
Mary E. Tull	Barlow #262	Clackamas	1894-96
May A. Waldron	Warner #17	Clackamas	1896-88
Clara Swank	Sand Ridge #57	Linn	1898-00
Mrs. A. E. Tilton	Winona #271	Washington	1900-02
Mrs. Bertha Hibbs	McMinnville #31	Yamhill	1902-04
Ida Thorp	Rockwood #323	Multnomah	1904-06
Ollie M. Mason	Pine Grove #356	Hood River	1906-08
Ethel Kelty Brown	Cloverdale #355	Tillamook	1908-10
Mrs. A. V. Davidson	Salem #17	Marion	1910-12
Mrs. E. R. Allen	Tangent #7	Linn	1912-18
Miss Dorothy Byrom	Winona #271	Washington	1918-20
Mrs. Jessie Millar	Fairview #344	Multnomah	1920-24
Mrs. R. W. Gill	Russellville #353	Multnomah	1924-28
Mrs. James Kelly	Evening Star #27	Multnomah	1928-32

Alice Goff	Melrose #434	Douglas	1932-34
Dorothy Perkins Kipling	Wingville #650	Baker	1934-40
Mrs. Lucy Woodward	Wild Horse #797	Umatilla	1940-46
Roma Johnson	Rockwood #323	Multnomah	1946-52
Elsie Wheaton	Coquille #396	Coos	1952-58
Mrs. Amy Cloud	East Side #583	Lake	1958-62
Della Johnson	Rogue River Valley #469	Josephine	1962-68
Winifred Taggert	Rogue River Valley #469	Josephine	1968-74
Kay Fine	North Douglas #936	Douglas	1974-80
Sandi Ludi	Sunnyside #842	Clackamas	1980-86
Susan Noah	Mohawk-McKenzie #747	Lane	1986-96
Cookie Trupp	Spencer Creek #855	Lane	1996-04
Myrna Colvin	Terrebonne #663	Deschutes	2004-08
Susie Kroeker	Crow #450	Lane	2008-12
Louise Holst	Midland #781	Klamath	2012-18
Maggie Schwartzendruber	Riversdale #731	Douglas	2018-20
Connie Suing	Crow #450	Lane	2020-22
Auriana VanHouten	Riversdale #731	Douglas	2022-23
Stacy Brown	Forest Grove #282	Washington	2023-24

CHAPLAIN

The Chaplain recites a prayer during the opening and closing ceremonies and is often called upon to say grace before meals. In 1926 a Memorial Service was added to honor Sixth Degree members who had passed in the prior year. In recent years the Memorial Service honors past state officers, committee directors, and delegates. From 1964 to 2015, the Chaplain led a Worship Service on Sunday evening. In recent years Chaplains have circulated cards for members to sign for those whose health or situation made them unable to attend a Session.

Sixteen Brothers and sixteen Sisters have served as Chaplain. Cyrus Walker of Grand Prairie #10 in Linn County, J. D. Chitwood of Damascus #260 in Clackamas County, and Sharon Mahan of Vale #696 in Malheur County served as Chaplain for ten years each.

Chaplain	Grange	County	Dates
Anthony Simpson	Locke #15	Benton	1873
Martin Peterson	Jacksonville #88	Jackson	1874-76
W. H. Gray	Young's River #172	Clatsop	1876-84
A. Shumway	Charity #15	Idaho Territory	1884-86
A. F. Miller	Lents #352	Multnomah	1886-88
David Eby	Goshen #561	Lane	1888-94
J. C. White	Oak Grove #198	Polk	1894-96
J. W. Messenger	Milbra #228	Sherman	1896-98
Louisa H. Clarke	Multnomah #71	Multnomah	1898-00
Oscar Eaton	Oswego #175	Clackamas	1900-10
Cyrus Walker	Grand Prairie #10	Linn	1910-20
T. R. A. Sellwood	Milwaukie #268	Clackamas	1920-24
J. D. Chitwood	Damascus #260	Clackamas	1924-34
Edyth Tozier Weatherred	Oswego #175	Clackamas	1934-40
Mrs. Blanche Pickering	Pacific #413	Clatsop	1940-42
Arthur Brown	West Salem #885	Polk	1942-48
John Crow	White Eagle #386	Umatilla	1948-50
Florence Tarbell	Yankton #301	Columbia	1950-56
Mrs. Susie Wells	Pine Grove #356	Hood River	1956-58
Florence Hammer	Willakenzie #498	Lane	1958-64
Martha Wright Hopkins	Rockwood #323	Multnomah	1964-70
Margaret Pease	Kilchis #800	Tillamook	1970-74

Ivy Webster	Chetco #765	Curry	1974-78
Allen Wheeler	Goshen #561	Lane	1978-82
Margaret Harris	Pleasant Valley #348	Multnomah	1982-86
Grace Stork	Midland #781	Klamath	1986-90
Sharon Mahan	Vale #696	Malheur	1990-00
Gail Wilson	White Eagle #683	Umatilla	2000-08
Dan LeBrun	Eagle Creek #297	Clackamas	2008-12
Peggy Fine	Riversdale #731	Douglas	2012-20
Randy Embree	Macleay #293	Marion	2020-21
Paula Herrick	Walterville #416	Lane	2021-24

TREASURER

The 1873 By-Laws said that the Treasurer was to receive money, issue receipts, keep accurate accounts, pay on order of the Master with consent of the Grange, and give a full accounting at each Session. At that time the Treasurer worked from home. Now Grange office staff print checks, make deposits, and provide the Executive Committee with financial reports on dues and loan repayments.

In 1875 the Treasurer's report showed a balance of $144.45. One hundred years later, the reported total of all accounts was $223,740. In many years, the State Grange struggled to pay its bills. Delegates had to weigh whether to raise dues or cut programs.

In 1966 the State Grange set up a budget for the first time and stuck to it. The Treasurer usually chairs the Budget Committee. Fortunately, due to careful money management and wise investments, the organization today is in a good financial position.

Twenty-one Brothers and seven Sisters have held the office of Treasurer. H. Hirschberg, a banker from Independence in Polk County, held the office for 25 years. When he passed, his chair at the 1925 Session was appropriately decorated.

Treasurer	Grange	County	Dates
B. A. Witzel	Turner #18	Marion	1873
S. P. Lee	Damascus #260	Clackamas	1874-77
David Smith	Lebanon #21	Linn	1878-82
B. F. Burch	Mono #25	Polk	1882-86
E. Strong	Salem #17	Marion	1886-89
J. B. Stump	Suver #253	Marion	1890-98
J. C. White	Oak Grove #198	Polk	1898-00
H. Hirschberg	Monmouth #476	Polk	1900-25
B. K. Denney	Beaverton #324	Washington	1925-32
R. M. Nedrow	Pine Forest #623	Deschutes	1932-37
Glen Adams	Brush College #586	Polk	1937-58
Mrs. Bonifay Yancey	Shasta View #830	Klamath	1958-62
Pearl Dental	Maplewood #662	Clackamas	1962-66
Curt Weber	Central #276	Clackamas	1966-69
Lester Hess	Maplewood #662	Clackamas	1969-72
Walter Holten	Silverton #748	Marion	1972-76
Herb Steiner	Beavercreek #276	Clackamas	1976-83
Ralph Fenton	Friendly #897	Multnomah	1983-88
John Cameron	Western Star #309	Linn	1988-94
Celia Luttrell	Boring Damascus #260	Clackamas	1994-96
Suzanne Kroeker	Scio #923	Linn	1996-97
Gordon Lucas	Buell #637	Polk	1997-00
Joyce Ramm	Colton-Foothills #831	Clackamas	2000-02
Roger Neff	Ada #570	West Coast	2002-06
Joe Canady	Crow #450	Lane	2006-12
Sarah Kingsborough	Warner #117	Clackamas	2012-16
Paula Herrick	Walterville #416	Lane	2016-20
Sonny Hays-Ebert	Marys River #685	Benton	2020-24

SECRETARY

The 1873 By-Laws said that the Secretary shall keep an accurate record of proceedings, make necessary payments to the National Grange, pay once quarterly to the Treasurer all moneys received, and keep a register of numbers and names of Subordinates and the names and addresses of their Masters and Secretaries.

The duties of the Secretary increased over time. The Secretary was expected to sell supplies, multigraph resolutions, send and receive quarterly reports, mail election ballots to Granges, maintain the *Grange Bulletin* mailing list, and award pennants for prompt payment of dues. In 1922 the Secretary became an ex-officio member of the Executive Committee so that she could record minutes of their meetings. In 1936 the Secretary was given a vote.

In 1901 the Good of the Order committee recommended that the hardworking State Secretary be furnished a typewriter. However, the committee's report was not adopted until the typewriter was stricken. There is no record of when the first typewriter was purchased, but in 1973 the State Grange bought an IBM electric. In 1988 the first computer was purchased.

State Secretaries were paid, though not nearly enough. In 1880 the State Grange was still recovering from its early cooperative buying and selling disasters. Delegates felt they had to cut the Secretary's annual salary from $300 to $100 per year. However, the salary climbed steadily to $23,000 in 2004. Insurance benefits were provided.

In 2004, the State Secretary became an honorary position. The current By-Laws say "1.13.5 The State Secretary shall make and keep an accurate record of all proceedings of the meetings of the Oregon State Grange, the State Executive Committee and provide aid and instruction to Community Grange Secretaries. It shall be the duty of the State Secretary to attend all State Executive Committee meetings and he/she shall have a voice and vote in all matters discussed." An office secretary with computer and general accounting skills was hired.

Fifteen of the 21 Secretaries have been Sisters. Bertha Beck of Calamette #543 in Linn County and later Friendly #897 in Multnomah served 32 years. Mary Howard of Molalla #310 in Clackamas County and Mildred Norman of Friendly #897 in Multnomah each served 22 years.

Secretary	Grange	County	Dates
John H. Smith	Harrisburg #11	Linn	1873-76
T. L. Davidson	Salem #17	Marion	1876-77
N. W. Randall	Warner #117	Clackamas	1877-82
Mrs. M. J. Train	Harrisburg #11	Linn	1882-90
W. M. Hilleary	Turner #18	Marion	1890-96
J. H. Scott	Tangent #7	Linn	1996-98
Mary S. Howard	Molalla #310	Clackamas	1898-20
Bertha Beck	Calamette #543 Friendly #897	Linn Multnomah	1920-52
Mildred Norman	Friendly #897	Multnomah	1952-74
Faye Tarbell	Warren #536	Columbia	1974-78
Kathy Fox Hekking	Winona #271	Washington	1978-83
Celia Luttrell	Eagle Creek #297	Clackamas	1983-93
Gayle Alton	Friendly #897	Multnomah	1993-97
Susanne Kroeker	Scio #923	Linn	1997-99
Cheri Drake	McMinnville #31	Yamhill	1999
Mike Stewart	Rickreall #671	Polk	1999-00
Catherine Johnston	Keizer #785	Marion	2000-04
Susan Noah	Mohawk-McKenzie #747	Lane	2004-10
Phyllis Wilson	Greenacres #834	Coos	2010-15
Alice Nowicki	London #937	Lane	2015-16
Sarah Kingsborough Jenkins	Sandlake #546	Tillamook	2016-24

GATEKEEPER

The current By-Laws say that it shall be the duty of the State Gatekeeper to see that the gates are properly guarded. The Gatekeeper takes the password and distributes copies of the previous day's journal and any amended resolutions.

Forty-two Brothers have served as Gatekeeper. Lennie Haldorson of Central #360 in Lane County held the office for ten years. John Simpson of Siuslaw #54 and C. C. Borland of Oswego #175 served non-consecutive terms. Orrin Schnetzky of Tigard #148 was elected to non-consecutive terms but did not serve during his second term.

Gatekeeper	Grange	County	Dates
Frank Shelton	Walla Walla #4	Walla Walla, WT	1873
E. E. Fanning	Tangent #7	Linn	1873-74
A. A. Mathews	Looking Glass #420	Douglas	1974-76
H. Graham	Mill Plain #24	Clark, WT	1876-77
Daniel Clark	Salem #17	Marion	1877-78
C. N. Wait	Canby #135	Clackamas	1878-80
Thomas Smith	Wingville #150	Baker	1880-84
John Simpson	Siuslaw #54	Lane	1884-88 1894-96
S. A. Dawson	Harmony #23	Linn	1888-92
J. M. Kees	Fair View #131	Morrow	1892-94
J. R. Booth	McMinnville #31	Yamhill	1896-98
J. Clem	Harmony #23	Linn	1898-00
H. C. Wheeler	Pleasant Hill #284	Lane	1900-02
S. G. Schoonover	Vernonia #305	Columbia	1902-04
S. N. Warfield	Hope #269	Benton	1904-06
E. C. Huffman	Russellville #353	Multnomah	1906-08
L. S. Lambert	Stayton #340	Marion	1908-10

J. K. Hansen	Gravel Ford #304	Coos	1910-12
C. C. Borland	Oswego #175	Clackamas	1912-20 1924-30
C. S. Dow	Netel #410	Clatsop	1920-24
L. F. Bailey	Missouri Flat #612	Baker	1930-36
Max Kligel	Multnomah #71	Multnomah	1936-42
Arthur Hahn	Poison Creek #776	Harney	1942-46
Frank Wooden	Jewell #876	Clatsop	1946-48
Lennie Haldorson	Central #360	Lane	1948-58
Roy Means	Redmond #812	Deschutes	1958-62
Rolland Johnson	Rufus #826	Sherman	1962-68
Berl Akers	Willows#672	Morrow	1968-76
George Durand	Sams Valley #666	Jackson	1976-78
Ken Nelson	Mohawk #922	Lane	1978-82
Charles Cramer	Mohawk-McKenzie #747	Lane	1982-88
Ed Luttrell	Boring-Damascus #260	Clackamas	1988-92
Dean High	Midland #781	Klamath	1992-94
Scot Jacobson	Fort Union #953	Union	1994-98
Wayne Gorbett	White Eagle #683	Umatilla	1998-00
Don Sether	Molalla #310	Clackamas	2000-06
Derrell Witty	Hurricane Creek #308	Wallowa	2006-08
Vernon Herrick	Walterville #416	Lane	2008-12
Orrin Schnetzky	Tigard #148	Washington	2012-14 2020-22
Jesse O'Dell	Santiam Valley #828	Linn	2014-16
James Clute	Forest Grove #282	Washington	2016-20
David McBride	Hurricane Creek #608	Wallowa	2022-24

CERES

Forty-seven Sisters have served as the Goddess of Grain. Connie Burch Suing of Crow #450 held the office for a total of fourteen years. Carrie French of Corvallis #242 and Connie Burch Suing served non-consecutive terms.

Ceres	Grange	County	Dates
Jane Cyrus	Santiam #37	Linn	1873-76
B. A. Miller	Jacksonville #88	Jackson	1876-78
M. J. Train	Harrisburg #11	Linn	1878-82
E. B. Heath	Butte #148	Washington	1882-84
Harriet Cooper	Oakland #86	Douglas	1884-86
Annie Simpson	Siuslaw #54	Lane	1886-88
S. L. Dawson	Harmony #23	Linn	1888-90
Hattie Heninger	Howell Prairie #80	Marion	1890-92
Carrie French	Corvallis #242	Benton	1892-94 1898-99
Sarah J. Edwards	Mayville #203	Gilliam	1894-96
Louisa H. Clark	Multnomah #71	Multnomah	1896-98
Isabelle Horner	Corvallis #242	Benton	1899-00
Mrs. N. E. Olin	Tangent #7	Linn	1900-02
Mrs. C. H. Winecoff	Coast Fork #243	Lane	1902-04
Mrs. Ruby Boyd	Beaverton #324	Washington	1904-06
Mary Griesenthwaite	Central #276	Clackamas	1906-08
Mrs. Cora Legg	Vail #294	Columbia	1908-10
Mrs. Sadie Hawley	Bellefountain #277	Benton	1910-12
Mrs. Laura McMorris	Condon #225	Gilliam	1912-14
Mrs. Vinnie M. Reed	Spring Bank #409	Linn	1914-16
Mrs. Lizzie Withee	Unionvale #407	Yamhill	1916-18
Mrs. Carrie Sale	Netel #410	Clatsop	1918-22

Mrs. Lillian Pierson	McMinnville #31	Yamhill	1922-24
Mrs. Esther Warren	Morning Star #311	Linn	1924-26
Maud Mills	Deer Island #334	Columbia	1926-28
Mrs. Elmer Cook	Brush College #586	Polk	1928-30
Mrs. Mary E. Jones	Hudson Bay #361	Umatilla	1930-32
Alice Hamilton	Fort Rock #758	Lake	1932-36
Mary Knowles Kingley	Mapleton #584	Lane	1936-40
Ruth Potter	Igo #315	Gilliam	1940-44
Hazel Lewis	Stateline #693	Umatilla	1944-56
Rosa Meeker	Lost River #846	Klamath	1956-60
Helen Cooper	Valley Falls #930	Lake	1960-64
Ethel Huffman	Hudson Bay #361	Umatilla	1964-72
Sue Walters	Lost River #846	Klamath	1972-74
Shirley Dunten Beaubein	Drewsey #738	Harney	1974-76
Karen Larsen	Tigard #148	Washington	1976-82
Karen Wheeler	Russellville #353	Multnomah	1982-86
Arlawene Silvester	Phoenix #779	Jackson	1986-88
Connie Burch Suing	Crow #450	Lane	1988-94 1996-04
Susie Marshall Jones	Clarkes #261	Clackamas	1994-96
Shirley Naylor	Crooked River Ranch #955	Jefferson	2004-08
Paula Herrick	Walterville #416	Lane	2008-12
Beverly Doescher	Azalea #768	Douglas	2012-16
Elizabeth "Liz" Dehne	Walterville #415	Lane	2016-20
Linda Pugh	Ada #570	Lane	2020-22
Jessie Jo Guttridge	Springwater #263	Clackamas	2022-24

POMONA

Fifty-four Sisters have served as the Goddess of Fruit. Paulina Ross of Vale #696 in Malheur County held the office for ten years. Vickie High of Midland #781 served non-consecutive terms.

Pomona	Grange	County	Dates
M. A. Powers	Shedd #9	Linn	1873-76
S. D. Durham	McMinnville #31	Yamhill	1876-78
C. E. Shipley	Oswego #175	Clackamas	1878-80
S. L. Hayes	Tualatin #111	Clackamas	1880-82
M. J. Harris	Willamette #52	Benton	1882-86
S. M. Cook	McMinnville #31	Yamhill	1886-88
E. A. Boise	Salem #17	Marion	1888-90
M. J. Train	Harrisburg #11	Linn	1890-92
Lillie J. Searcy	Mayville #203	Gilliam	1892-94
Emma D. Spores	Mohawk #147	Lane	1894-96
Millie McConnell	Mayville #203	Gilliam	1896-98
Ofa Wiesner	North Howell #274	Marion	1898-00
Mrs. E. A. Niblin	Evening Star #27	Multnomah	1900-02
Jennie R. Miller	Lents #351	Multnomah	1902-04
Mrs. Anna Crasswell	Multnomah #71	Multnomah	1904-06
Mrs. Bertha M. Durbin	Tangent #7	Linn	1906-08
Mrs. Lulu Miller	Western Star #309 Friendly #897	Linn Multnomah	1908-12
Mrs. F. L. Buker	Waldport #425	Lincoln	1912-14
Mrs. Ruth Mihills	Rogue River Valley #469	Josephine	1914-18
Miss Golda Combs	Grand Prairie #10	Linn	1918-20
Mrs. Kathryn M. Randall	Warner #117	Clackamas	1920-22
Mrs. Jessie Kirk	Hudson Bay #361	Umatilla	1922-24

Mrs. Maud Mills	Deer Island #334	Columbia	1924-26
Florence Robinson	Chenowith #591	Wasco	1926-28
Olive K. Davis	Yankton #301	Columbia	1928-30
Marjorie Kingsley	Elmira #532	Lane	1930-32
Dorothea Mack	Henley #708	Klamath	1932-34
Lillian Loder	Milwaukie #268	Clackamas	1934-36
Eleanor Rich	Cove Orchard #545	Yamhill	1936-40
Mrs. Mable Hughes	Shan Creek #794	Josephine	1940-44
Paulina Ross	Vale #696	Malheur	1944-54
Ruby Pope	Nehalem Valley #804	Clatsop	1954-56
Mona Rydell	Sunnydale #877	Douglas	1956-58
Mrs. Priscilla Mast	McKinley #289	Coos	1958-62
Ila Clark	Chetco #765	Curry	1962-64
Glenabell Morin	Wingville #650	Baker	1964-66
Cecelia Kee Palm	Shady Cove #931	Jackson	1966-70
Linda Dorland	Washington #313	Washington	1970-78
Nelda Bryant Jensen	Myrtle Creek #442	Douglas	1978-82
Marsha Snook	Lacomb #907	Linn	1982-84
Carol Hales	Warren #536	Columbia	1984-88
Karen Wheeler	Russellville #353	Multnomah	1988-90
Vickie High	Midland #781	Klamath	1990-94 1996-98
Debra Dumolt Hood	Beavercreek #276	Clackamas	1994-96
Betty Huff	Ada #570	West Coast	1998-02
Jeanne Trudeau	Triangle #533	Lane	2002-04
Beverly Smith	Liberty #613	Wallowa	2004-06
Roberta Sellars	Goldson #868	Lane	2006-08
Kim Schettig	Beavercreek #276	Clackamas	2006-12
Qiana Helm	Phoenix #779	Jackson	2012-14
Eva Frost	Warren #536	Columbia	2014-16

Mikela Heimuller	Warren #536	Columbia	2016-20
Linda Helm	Phoenix #779	Jackson	2020-24

FLORA

The State Grange and the Sixth Degree are the domain of the Goddess of Flowers. In Oregon, Flora presents and retires the U. S. Flag. Oregon adopted a flag presentation ceremony in 1927 and approved the National Grange ceremony in 1960. In some other states, Flora presents the flag when Grange opens in the Sixth Degree on the first day of the Session and before exemplifying the Sixth Degree. Ceres presents the flag when Grange is at work in the Fourth Degree.

Currently Flora is responsible for purchasing flowers, making corsages and boutonnieres, and decorating the stage for the Sixth Degree. Forty-two Sisters have served as Flora. Louise Holst of Midland #781 in Klamath County and Cookie Trupp of Spencer Creek #855 in Lane County each held the office for eight years. Four Sisters had non-consecutive terms.

Flora	Grange	County	Date
Mrs. L. C. Reid	McMinnville #31	Yamhill	1973-76
E. A. Kelley	Evening Star #27	Multnomah	1976-78
S. C. Durham	McMinnville #31	Yamhill	1878-80
E. B. Heath	Butte #148	Washington	1880-82
Harriet Cooper	Oakland #86	Douglas	1882-84
Jennie R. Miller	Lents #351	Multnomah	1884-86
E. Russell	Washougal #32	Clark, WT	1886-88
S. M. Cook	McMinnville #31	Yamhill	1888-90
Isabel J. Gibson		Umatilla	1890-92
Annie Lacey	Springwater #263	Clackamas	1892-94 1898-00

Electa J. Phillips	Fairmount #252	Benton	1994-96
Carrie M. French	Corvallis #242	Benton	1896-98
Clara Swank	Sand Ridge #57	Linn	1900-02
Mrs. Louie Bond	Charity #103	Linn	1902-04
Miss L. Lucille West	Scappoose #303	Columbia	1904-06
Mrs. Rosa M. Littlepage	Columbia #267	Multnomah	1906-08
Mrs. Susie Wells	Igo #315	Gilliam	1908-12
Mrs. R. S. Goff		Crook	1912-14
Mrs. Inez Sargent	Locust Grove #505	Sherman	1914-16
Mrs. Hester Coovert	Lincoln #395	Lincoln	1916-18
Mrs. Mildred Leedy	Kinton #562	Washington	1918-20
Grace Harris McTimmonds	Crowfoot #314	Linn	1920-24
Mrs. C. W. Craft	Riverside #526	Washington	1924-26 1928-30
Mrs. J. H. King	Missouri Flat #612	Baker	1926-28
Mrs. Arthur Brown	West Salem #885	Polk	1930-32
Mildred Crow	White Eagle #683	Umatilla	1932-38
Mrs. L'Rena Slack	Bonanza #772	Klamath	1938-40
Mrs. Bertha Hanscom	Cold Spring #801	Umatilla	1940-46
Myrtle Potter	Igo #315	Gilliam	1946-50
Helen Henrickson	Winona #271	Washington	1950-56
Jean Kizer	Charity #103	Linn	1956-60
Alta Faye Rogers	Santa Clara #746	Lane	1960-66
Glenabell Morin Lewis	Wingville #650	Baker	1966-72
Nadina Evans Niles	Myrtle #289	Coos	1972-76
Sandra Furgason Sandi Ludi	Winona #271 Sunnyside #842	Washington Clackamas	1976-80 2020-24
Kay Fine	North Douglas #936	Douglas	1980-86
Joanne Stark	Kinton #562	Washington	1986-88

Janet Naylor Kelly	Clarkes #261	Clackamas	1988-90
Louise Holst	Midland #781	Klamath	1990-98 2002-08
Kris Fine	Mid Valley "O" #960 Evergreen #460	Benton	1998-02
Cookie Trupp	Spencer Creek #855	Lane	2008-16
Eva Frost	Warren #536	Columbia	2016-20

EXECUTIVE COMMITTEE

According to the 1873 By-Laws the Executive Committee consisted of the Master and six members, three to be elected for two years and three for one year. In 1876 the By-Laws were changed, and the committee was the Master and two members.

The Executive had authority to act on all matters of interest to the Order when not in Session; they provided for the welfare in business matters and were to report their acts in detail to the State Grange on the first day of the next Session.

The State Secretary became an ex-officio member in 1922 and was given a vote in 1936. In 1956, the State Overseer became an ex-officio member; in the 1980s was given a vote.

In 1978 delegates voted that the state be divided into three districts and an Executive Committee member elected from each district. The Master was designated the chairman. The committee holds as many meetings as they deemed necessary.

Duties include to audit and pay claims against the Oregon State Grange; to supervise the preparation and circulation of petitions and referendums of such legislation as may be ordered between Sessions of the Oregon State Grange; to pass upon all official bonds of the State Officers; to make a detailed report of its actions to the State Session; and to submit the financial part of such report to the Budget Committee previous to the State Session. They also have responsibilities for most of the tasks that the State Secretary previously performed: quarterly reports, annual roster, Session proceedings, updating By-Laws, and remitting dues to Pomonas.

Sixty Brothers and two Sisters served on the Executive Committee before 1980 when the state was divided into three districts. Eleven were past State Masters or later became State Master.

E. C. Member	Grange	County	Dates
R. A. Gurney	Umpqua #28	Douglas	1873
Orlay Hull	Blue Mountain #3	Walla Walla, WT	1873-75
G. A. Wells	Buena Vista #4	Polk	1873
Thomas Munkers	Scio #36	Linn	1873
A. B. Henry	Lafayette #32	Yamhill	1873
H. N. Hill	Grand Prairie #10	Lane	1873-76
S. W. Brown	Vancouver	Clark, WT	1874-76
Chas. E. Moore	Corvallis #242	Benton	1874-76
E. Forbes	Eagle Creek #297	Clackamas	1874-76
M. Fisk	Salem #17	Marion	1874-75
A. W. Stanard	Brownsville #19	Linn	1875-76
C. C. Crane	Walla Walla #4	Walla Walla, WT	1875-76
Robert Clow	Dallas #39	Polk	1875-77
E. L. Smith	Olympia #10	Thurston, WT	1876-78
A. Holder	Willamette #52	Benton	1877-80
A. Warner	Warner #117	Clackamas	1879-82
Daniel Clark	Salem #17	Marion	1980-82
William Cyrus	Santiam #37	Linn	1882-86
John Minto	Salem #17	Marion	1982-88
A. R. Shipley	Oswego #175	Clackamas	1985-87
J. G. Powell	Harmony #23 Coast Fork #243	Linn Lane	1887-92 1896-98
B. P. Boise	Salem #17	Marion	1888-92

J. C. White	Oak Grove #198	Polk	1892-94
W. J. Edwards	Mayville #203	Gilliam	1893-96
S. A. Dawson	Harmony #23	Linn	1894-96
O. P. Lent	Evening Star #27	Multnomah	1895-99
J. R. Booth	McMinnville #31	Yamhill	1898-00
G. R. Stephenson	Oswego #175	Clackamas	1899-06
J. Clem	Harmony #23	Linn	1900-02
Thomas Paulsen	Butte #148	Washington	1902-04
Austin T. Buxton	Gale #282	Washington	1904-06
C. E. Spence	Central #276	Clackamas	1905-10 1924-28
B. G. Leedy	Butte #148	Washington	1906-08 1912-23
Eugene Palmer	Harmony #23	Linn	1908-10
A. I. Mason	Pine Grove #356	Hood River	1910-12
C. L. Shaw	Grand Prairie #10	Linn	1910-22
C. H. Bailey	South Deer Creek #440	Douglas	1922-32
M. C. Glover	Eagle Creek #297	Clackamas	1923-24
F. M. Gill	Pinecrest #504	Wasco	1924-26
Ray W. Gill	Russellville #353	Multnomah	1926-32 1942-63
H. E. Keeney	Haystack #495	Jefferson	1927-28
W. R. Gekeler	Blue Mountain #345	Union	1928-30
Walter M. Pierce	Blue Mountain #345	Union	1930-34
George A. Palmiter	Milwaukie #268	Clackamas	1932-37
A. Slaughter	Salem #17	Marion	1932-36
Peter Zimmerman	Cove Orchard #545	Yamhill	1934-50
Fred A. Goff	Melrose #434	Douglas	1936-42
W. A. Johnson	Rogue River Valley #469	Josephine	1938-42
Henry Gustafson	North Bayside #691	Coos	1942-44

Allen Wheeler	Goshen #561	Lane	1944-48 1974-78
Charles Wicklander	Russellville #353	Multnomah	1948-54
Luke Reif	Powell Butte #629	Crook	1951-52
Bertha Beck	Friendly #897	Multnomah	1952-58
William G. Ross	Vale #696	Malheur	1954-63
William G. Howes	Friendly #897	Jackson	1958-60
Robert Schmidt	Morning Star #311	Linn	1960-62 1963-70
Elmer McClure	Harding #122	Clackamas	1962-66
Chris Wyckoff	Wallowa #603	Wallowa	1964-72
Clarence Brooks	Sixes #856	Curry	1966-70
Fred Heard	Midland #781	Klamath	1970-74
Earle Johnson	Brush College #586	Polk	1970-74
Earl Moore	Pine Grove #356	Hood River	1972-74
Mildred Norman	Friendly #897	Multnomah	1974-78
Ted Sims	Lake Creek #818	Linn	1974-80
Bill Taggert	Rogue River Valley #469	Josephine	1978-80
Berl Akers	Willows #672	Morrow	1978-80

POSITION 1

Seven Brothers and one Sister have been elected to Position 1 of the Executive Committee. Four served as State Master before or after their terms.

Member	Grange	County	Dates
William Taggert	Rogue River Valley #469	Josephine	1980-84
Dale Morris	Irving #377	Lane	1984-88
John Fine	North Umpqua #947 Evergreen #460 Riversdale #731	Douglas	1988-94 2006-08 2018-22

John Cameron	Western Star #309	Linn	1994-96
Mark Noah	Mohawk-McKenzie #747	Lane	1996-06
Malcolm Trupp	Spencer Creek #855	Lane	2008-16
Jeff Dehne	Walterville #416	Lane	2016-18
Susan Noah	Mohawk-McKenzie #747	Lane	2022-24

POSITION 2

Seven Brothers and two Sisters have been elected to Position 2. One later was elected State Master.

Member	Grange	County	Dates
Wesley Simmons	Pleasant Valley #537	Tillamook	1980-84
Neil Cullison	Beavercreek #276	Clackamas	1984-88
Bob Ludi	Sunnyside #842	Clackamas	1988-98
Don MacKinnon	Springwater #263	Clackamas	1998-00
Carol Everman	Beaver Valley #306	Columbia	2000-06
Larry Rea	Fernhill #582	Columbia	2006-07
Don Sether	Molalla #310	Clackamas	2007-18
Sam Keator	Winona #271	Washington	2018-22
Celia Fox	Boring-Damascus #260	Clackamas	2022-24

POSITION 3

Six Brothers and three Sisters have been elected to Position 3. One was a past State Master.

Member	Grange	County	Dates
Berl Akers	Willows #672	Morrow	1980-82
Eleanor Grant	Poe Valley #710	Klamath	1982-88

Morton Wolverton	Columbia #867	Umatilla	1988-93
Glenabell Lewis	Wingville #650	Baker	1993-98
Phil Van Buren	Midland #781	Klamath	1998-04
Ken Naylor	Crooked River Ranch #955	Jefferson	2004-08
Derrell Witty	Hurricane Creek #608	Wallowa	2008-12
Roger Wilson	White Eagle #683	Umatilla	2012-18
Louise Holst	Midland #781	Klamath	2018-23

MUSICIAN

The Musician is appointed by the State Master. Many were from a Grange in the host county and served only one year. Linda Wetzell of Goshen #561 has been installed. Elizabeth Royal of Winona Grange #271 Washington County served as Musician for 11 years.

RITUAL

Oregon State Grange officers pride themselves on the precision with which they perform their seating drill, open and close the Grange, and present the flag and guests. Visitors from National Grange and other State Granges always complement the officers on their performance.

The first evening of the organizing Session in 1873 was devoted to the unwritten work. This was probably an explanation and demonstration of the signal, password, sign, and salutation of the first four degrees. Unwritten work was on the agenda many Sessions thereafter. The State Master, Lecturer, or Deputy usually presented it.

FIFTH DEGREE

On another evening of the 1873 Session, National Grange Deputy N. W. Garretson "informally conferred" the Fifth Degree, which was the state level degree at that time. He and others probably read officer parts from the manual while he explained how the degree, which is like a play, was to be staged.

The 1874 Proceedings say, "All took the Fifth Degree." The state officers probably conferred it. The following year, according to the *Proceedings*, "three delegates were appointed to procure paraphernalia for the Fifth Degree." This would have been sashes, candles, and a cornucopia.

The 1899 Session was held in Portland and Multnomah Pomona exemplified the Fifth Degree. This began the tradition of the host Pomona exemplifying the degree, though team members were not necessarily current Pomona officers. In 1956 all members of the team from Morrow County were members of Rhea Creek #669 and the following year team members from Harney County were all from Poison Creek #776. Drewsey #738 provided the music. The two Granges were too far apart to meet for practices. In 1967, the team from West Coast District Pomona was all female. In 2009 the Fifth Degree was put on by G.R.O.W. Club members and other volunteers.

At the 1879 Session, delegates voted to change the By-Laws to set the minimum fee for the Fifth Degree to $2 for men and $1 for women. Today the fee is $2 for both. Inflation. What inflation?

The Fifth Degree can be exemplified by any Pomona Grange; delegates and members attending a Session usually have taken it. Therefore, the highest number of candidates was 153 in 1907 at Hood River. The fewest was 9 in 2015 at Pendleton. Today, only Clackamas and Lane Pomonas exemplify the Fifth Degree regularly.

1873	33	1883	12	1893	24
1874	115	1884	22	1894	25
1875	61	1885	33	1895	47
1876	51	1886	39	1896	23
1877	29	1887	37	1897	41
1878	16	1888	29	1898	33
1879	13	1889	86	1899	16
1880	16	1890	27	1900	31
1881	13	1891	55	1901	35
1882	17	1892	150	1902	22

1903	62
1904	80
1905	43
1906	64
1907	153
1908	55
1909	82
1910	75
1911	67
1912	48
1913	38
1914	35
1915	67
1916	28
1917	55
1918	42
1919	26
1920	68
1921	52
1922	33
1923	50
1924	60
1925	37
1926	97
1927	84
1928	25
1929	70
1930	45
1931	37
1932	34
1933	27
1934	34
1935	33
1936	53
1937	35
1938	85
1939	28
1940	44
1941	38
1942	52
1943	107
1944	85
1945	No Session
1946	111
1947	95
1948	35
1949	115
1950	147
1951	124
1952	35
1953	12
1954	58
1955	19
1956	16
1957	38
1958	33
1959	43
1960	32
1961	55
1962	28
1963	69
1964	26
1965	16
1966	38
1967	43
1968	33
1969	40
1970	60
1971	38
1972	43
1973	49
1974	37
1975	45
1976	48
1977	38
1978	61
1979	28
1980	36
1981	91
1982	29
1983	59
1984	26
1985	65
1986	16
1987	20
1988	33
1989	22
1990	21
1991	48
1992	27
1993	27
1994	62
1995	44
1996	32
1997	20
1998	36
1999	34
2000	19
2001	18
2002	21
2003	10
2004	12
2005	16
2006	30
2007	17
2008	10
2009	16
2010	22
2011	26
2012	38
2013	34
2014	17
2015	9
2016	24
2017	24
2018	10
2019	22
2020	Not given
2021	21
2022	15
2023	16

SIXTH DEGREE

The first time the Sixth Degree was exemplified in Oregon was at the 1889 Session. Both the Fifth and Sixth Degrees were conferred in the Good Templar Hall, because the Senate Chamber where the Session was held could not be secured.

The symbol of the Sixth Degree is the rosebud. In 1930 roses were ordered but misplaced. At the last minute, six rose buds were purchased for the marching candidates. In 1933 there were more than enough roses. “Two hundred rosebuds were donated by members who were in the floral business and 250 were furnished at one cent each.” There were plenty of roses for the 248 candidates.

The first mention of a rosebud drill was in 1933. The Session was held in Pendleton, but the drill team was from Fruitvale #379, which is in Grants Pass. The Proceedings say, “This was a very beautiful addition to the degree work.” Over the years a number of rosebud drills were memorable, none more so than in 2019 when Clackamas Pomona had a total of 26 marchers representing three generations.

The first mention of a soloist singing “Only a Rose” was 1953.

The 1939 Proceedings reports, “Formal gowns in pastel shades, colorful tableaus, impressive music, lovely flowers, and letter-perfect charges all contributed in making the exemplification of both degrees as an impressive demonstration of the beautiful ritualistic work of the Order.” In Oregon state officers take pride in dressing appropriately for the degrees. In other states, each Sister may wear her best dress, which means they are different lengths, styles, and colors. At a California State Session, female officers were told to wear a pink dress. Who knew there were so many shades of pink, from salmon, coral, and peach to mauve, fuchsia, and magenta? In Oregon a difficult decision is made on what dress to order given the range of ages and body types of the current officers. When the dresses arrive, some always require alteration. But traditionalists argue that Sisters wearing matching dresses and Brothers wearing tuxedos contributes to their performance.

2013 Oregon State Grange officers dressed appropriately to exemplify the Sixth Degree.

Officers are expected to memorize their speaking parts. Those who speak when the room is dark have a greater challenge. But for all the problem is that the degrees were written before 1873. Word choice and sentence structure is not the way we speak today.

After the Sixth Degree, Grange is closed and then Flora and the State Master lead a grand march into the dining room. In 1892 the Fifth and Sixth Degrees began at 8 p.m. Afterward, likely around 10:30 p.m., "a banquet" was served. In 1906 the refreshment was ice cream and cake. The following year strawberries, cream, and cake were served. Cookies and ice cream were the treat in 1917. In 1936 the Lebanon Chamber of Commerce served strawberry shortcake to 1,000 at the close of the Sixth degree. When the tradition began of having Dixie Cups is not recorded. They are becoming hard to find.

Prior to hosting a National Session, state officers have conferred the Sixth Degree so more members were prepared to take the Seventh Degree. For example, 28 conferrals were held around the state in 1938 with 1,843 members taking the Fifth and Sixth. Before hosting in 1946, twelve conferences were held around the state and the Sixth degree conferred that evening. A total of 2,890 members took the degree.

The Sixth Degree is only given by a State Grange. The highest number of candidates taking the degree at a State Session was 805 in 1951 in Portland and the fewest was 14 in 2015 at Pendleton.

A line without a date indicates a special conferral prior to a National Session.

1889	88
1890	57
1891	89
1892	150
1893	30
1894	31
1895	77
1896	39
1897	45
1898	55
1899	80
1900	38
1901	47
1902	44
1903	181
1904	113
	300
1905	59
1906	83
1907	168
1908	78
1909	97
1910	163
1911	100
1912	90
1913	118
1914	84
1915	179
1916	162
1917	118
1918	104
1919	156
1920	117
1921	238
	577
1922	126
1923	149
1924	234
1925	256
1926	510
1927	178
1928	242
1929	287
1930	257
1931	232
1932	157
1933	248
1934	191
1935	284
1936	218
	44
1937	217
1938	381
	1,843
1939	127
1940	113
1941	200
1942	254
1943	305
1944	499
1945	No Session
1946	578
	2,890
1947	216
1948	153
1949	341
1950	371
1951	805
1952	242
1953	457
1954	705
1955	192
1956	174
1957	186
1958	413
1959	156
1960	296
1961	383
1962	287
1963	749
	506
1964	121
1965	137
1966	209
1967	287
1968	277
1969	286
1970	322
1971	213
1972	295
1973	307
1974	341
1975	169
1976	276
1977	315
1978	410
1979	299
1980	325
1981	296
1982	205
1983	279
1984	245
1985	346
1986	65
1987	104

1988	165	2000	60	2012	59
1989	104	2001	61	2013	47
1990	72	2002	93	2014	19
1991	220	2003	23	2015	14
1992	114	2004	25	2016	40
1993	68	2005	30	2017	30
1994	150	2006	46	2018	18
1995	144	2007	21	2019	28
1996	101	2008	17	2020	Not given
1997	73	2009	24	2021	22
1998	92	2010	43	2022	19
1999	94	2011	29	2023	25

FIRST FOUR DEGREES

The founders planned that new members would receive the First and Second Degrees at one meeting and the Third and Fourth Degrees at the next. These degrees are based on the seasons of the year and teach the lessons of faith, hope, charity, and fidelity. Winona #271 followed that plan. Organized in 1895, officers conferred the degrees 34 times in the first ten years. When key officers were not present, there was too much other business, or there was only one candidate, Winona administered the Obligation Ceremony as a temporary measure. In 1979 the By-Laws were changed to allow Degree Days when all four degrees were conferred.

In 2005 delegates adopted a resolution that required new members who took the Welcoming Ceremony to take the first four degrees within one year. Today there is no such requirement. Between 2013 and 2019 the first four degrees were exemplified on Sunday afternoon during State Session. Clackamas Pomona exemplifies these degrees twice a year. G.R.O.W. Club exemplifies them upon request.

Some Granges have been following the National Grange Heirloom Program, which presents a quotation from a degree for discussion at each meeting. Even members who oppose the ritual as old fashioned have found wisdom in these selected passages.

COMMUNITY GRANGE MEETINGS

In this 1935 Good of the Order Address, State Master Ray Gill reported that more Granges were using officer seating drills, which resulted in better attendance and opening meetings on time. In 2010 State Master Larry Rea was surprised when the officers of Springwater #263 lined up for their seating drill. Unfortunately, the fire siren sounded, and all who were volunteer firemen left immediately.

In his 1999 Good of the Order Address, State Master Ed Luttrell raised the question whether the annual password was still relevant. The National Grange authorized Action Granges in 2001. Ada #570 was one of the first Action Granges in Oregon. Ada reported that they set up their hall like a traditional Grange, "but don't take up the password or give the salutation."

At State Session the Gatekeeper and his deputies require passwords for a member's first entry into the hall. They place a colored dot on the member's name tag to indicate the password they have given. Few Granges use the password, but it is required to log onto the members-only sections of the State and National Grange websites.

Many halls have steep stairs that are a barrier for some members, so those Granges meet around a table downstairs. A legal meeting requires the flag and a Bible. Officers may wear their sashes. The 2013 Subordinate Grange Manual contains the Alternative Opening and Closing ceremonies, which use more contemporary language.

Most Granges follow the order of business to ensure that members focus on one topic of business at a time. Some observe *Parliamentary Procedures for Grange Members*, which is based on Roberts' Rules.

In 2022 State Membership Director David McBride advised, "I would strongly suggest that at least occasionally the meeting should be conducted using the full Grange ritual, if your Grange does not currently do so. I feel that without the Grange's traditions and founding symbolism, we could, over time, become just another social club. We could lose track of the precepts and philosophy that is at the core of our Grange organization."

GUESTS

The Oregon State Grange has welcomed to its Sessions a long list of guests. Whether they are Grange members or not, the State Steward announces them, and with the aid of his Assistant Stewards, presents them to the Master's Station. Members stand and clap to the beat of the march played by the Musician because non-members typically are not in step. Except during COVID, the Master greets the guest with a handshake. State Flora pins a corsage or boutonniere on their lapel. Since 1970, at the conclusion of the guest's speech the State Master has presented non-members with an application to join the Grange before they are escorted from the hall.

The first recorded guest was Governor W. W. Thayer in 1872. The Governor reportedly gave a welcoming address, but no text exists because it was described as "an off-hand talk." Thayer was the first of 16 Governors to address delegates.

The most noteworthy was Charles H. Martin, who was invited to address the Session in 1935. The Grange and the Governor differed on several issues, but the biggest battle came on the Governor's ruling to make the county unit school system mandatory. Four hundred farmers, mostly Grangers, protested outside the Capitol. The Governor told them to return to their plows. Apparently, Martin thought farmers could have opinions on agricultural issues, but not on other topics.

Governor Martin's speech was held in the McMinnville High School gymnasium, which was filled its capacity of 1,400. However, before the Governor spoke, National Grange Master Louis Taber was escorted to the Master's Station and addressed the delegates. Then the Oregon State Treasurer, Secretary of State, and Director of Agriculture were presented and introduced as Brothers because all were Grange members. Each was given an opportunity to speak while the Governor was kept waiting. Newspapers anticipated that the Governor would be subjected to heckling, but the *Oregon Statesman's* headline was "Martin Heard in Silence by Grange Crowd." Members criticized Martin for reading from a manuscript. His speech was not included in the *Proceedings*.

The following year Governor Martin was again invited to speak. In his hour-long speech, the Governor avoided controversial topics and spoke from notes. This time he was even cheered when he praised Oregon prunes and highways. However, in 1937 a motion to invite the Governor was voted down.

The most famous guest was Supreme Court Justice William O. Douglas. In 1942 he was the featured speaker at a Session held at Milwaukie High School. His talk was open to the public and broadcast over KEX. He was in the area to deliver the keynote speech at the Oregon Publishers Association three days later. Douglas was considered a Westerner, although he was born in Minnesota and lived in Connecticut. He attended Whitman College in Walla Walla, taught in Yakima, and often vacationed in the area because he was an avid fly fisherman. In his speech, Douglas noted that the "magnificent strength awakened in America by this war" must be used to ensure world-wide freedom. "What men can do to defend freedom, they can also do to make freedom live."

Other guests included:

- National Masters Wilson, Lowell, Taber, Goss, Newsom, Scott, Andersen, Barrow, Richardson, Luttrell, Huber
- High Priests of Demeter Bean, Davis, Tucker, Valentine, Croucher
- Priest Analyst Snyder
- Washington State Masters Russell, Goss, Carstensen, Nelson, Joy, Silvers, Hill, Hamp, Gwin
- Idaho State Masters Deal, Taylor, Hersley, Adams, Jerome, Kistler, Tate, Deweese, Don Johnson, Mary Johnson, Cheney, Weaver, Heikkila, Javaux
- California State Masters Schlmeyer, Quinn, Deaver, Koster, Austin, Bergeron, Clouse, Fletcher, Felder, Stefenoni, Westwood
- Governors Thayer, Moody, Pennoyer, Geer, West, Withycombe, Pierce, Martin, Sprague, Snell, McKay, Patterson, Smith, Holmes, Hatfield, McCall. Atiyeh
- Senators Morse, Hatfield
- Oregon Agriculture College President Arnold, deans and professors

- Oregon State University President Strand
- OSU Deans of Agriculture
- OSU Dean of Women
- University of Oregon President Campbell, Wilson
- Eastern Oregon College of Education President
- Oregon Directors of Agriculture
- Oregon Secretaries of State
- Oregon State Treasurers
- Oregon Superintendents of Public Schools and Public Instruction
- Oregon Farm Bureau Presidents
- Oregon Farmers' Union Presidents
- Women in Agriculture President
- Cattlemen's Association President
- Grain Growers President
- FFA State Presidents and winners of the prepared public speaking contest
- American Federation of Labor and CIO Presidents
- American Bankers Association officers
- Local Mayors and Chamber of Commerce Presidents
- Agricultural Attaché of the Israel Embassy
- Sears, Roebuck Foundation Vice President
- Coos Bay Pirates, Grants Pass Cavemen, Pendleton Main Street Cowboys
- Oregon Dairy Princesses, Timber Carnival Princesses, Red Raspberry Princesses, Apple Blossom Princesses, Northwest Cherry Growers Sweetheart, Molalla Rodeo Queen
- Chairman of the March of Dimes
- Representative of Oregon Fair Share
- Director of Northwest Irrigation Utilities
- Legal Counsel for Oregonians in Action

TOURS AND ENTERTAINMENT

The 1873 organizing Session was all business. However, that has not always been the case.

Delegates accepted invitations to visit the Oregon Penitentiary, Willamette University, and public buildings in Salem, but turned down an invitation to visit the "insane asylum." Salem #17 regularly entertained delegates one evening with a program of entertainment, music, and refreshments. State Master Boise and his wife hosted delegates in their home.

When the State Grange met in Hillsboro in 1891, delegates were led by the Hillsboro Cornet Band as they marched to the Washington County Courthouse for a program followed by State Master H. E. Hayes' annual Address. Since many delegates had never been to that area, Hillsboro Grange invited them to take a carriage ride around the surrounding country the following afternoon.

In subsequent years delegates visited the Oregon Agricultural College campus and the Monmouth State Normal College (now Western Oregon University). When the Session met in Oregon City, delegates took a ride on the Willamette Falls Railway and from Hood River, they rode the train to O'Dell, eleven miles up the Hood River Valley. On the return trip, the train stopped at Van Horn so that those who wanted could climb the butte to view the surrounding orchards and farms.

In Tillamook some took a 15-mile auto ride to two cheese factories. On the second day "450 Grangers in machines furnished by the community" were taken to Seaside. "The weather was ideal, and all enjoyed the trip greatly." Lunch was clam chowder with crackers. The U. S. Navy provided free transportation to the mouth of the Columbia "(where there is no bar)."

Josephine County Patrons and the Commercial Club served a sumptuous banquet for 600 in the old Dreamland Rink building. The original plan was for a basket picnic in Riverside Park, but heavy rains prevented that. Dinner was accompanied by a band and amusing toasts.

In Bend in 1920 delegates and visitors assembled on the banks of the Deschutes River for a Trout Barbecue provided by the Bend Rod and Gun Club and the Bend Commercial Club. Four hundred pounds of trout that were caught in the previous two days were cooked and served on wooden plates. On the afternoon of the third day, the Commercial Club took members on a tour of sawmills and ice caves, ending at the hall of Eastern Star #482 for a delicious spread.

When Lane County hosted in 1921, the meeting recessed at 11 a.m. to view a mile-long parade of the livestock, farm products, automobiles, trucks, and floats provided by Lane County Granges.

From Newport in 1923 delegates traveled to Siletz for a barbeque dinner and Feather Dance by Indians in costume. On the way back they stopped in Toledo to see the spruce mill.

In 1929 Session goers traveled in a 183-automobile caravan from Myrtle Point to Bandon. The Chamber of Commerce served 1,500 in a city park. An enjoyable program followed. "All adjourned to the beach, many taking advantage of a swim in the large natatorium."

Some delegates made the trip from Silverton to Silver Falls in 1932 which began at 5 a.m. with a stop for breakfast at a Grange hall, and arriving back in time for the Session opening at 8 a.m.

In 1938 some delegates went to the Tule Lake district, likely their first trip into California.

It was all business from then until 1950 when 20 buses transported 700 Session attendees to the Amalgamated Sugar Company in Nyssa for a tour and box supper. In 1956 a tour of the Pendleton Woolen Mills was offered one morning. The following year, an open house was held at Skyline Lodge, the Juvenile Grange camp site on arrival day. Tours were available to Eberhart Creamery, the State Tree Farm, Shevlin Park, the *Bend Bulletin*, and Peterson Rock Gardens. During registration, delegates exchanged larger bills for $2 bills, which were seldom seen in circulation, to call the community's attention to the amount of business Grangers brought in.

The now popular Ag Tour started in 1989 in Enterprise. That tour was to a horse logging operation. Those who did not have to rush home toured a tree farm on the day after the Session concluded. In 1996 the Energy committee organized a tour from Independence to a methane gas plant at the Coffin Butte Landfill.

DEPUTIES

The 1873 By-Laws gave the State Master authority to appoint current or past Masters as deputies to organize new Granges, install officers, and report any discord in Granges to the State Master.

STATE OFFICERS AS DEPUTIES

In his 1876 Master's Address, Daniel Clark proposed having the State Lecturer be in the field to encourage Granges. However, three of the first five Lecturers were from the Washington territory. The first State Lecturer to serve as an Oregon Deputy was H. E. Hayes from 1882 to 1888 and 1892 to 1894. Other Lecturers, who functioned as state deputies, were William Hilleary, A. F. Miller, Dr. J. S. Casto, Austin Buxton, Clara Waldo, and Minnie Bond.

Lecturers were not the only state officers to serve as deputies. State Chaplain Cyrus Walker reported in 1911 on how he used various forms of transportation to organize six Granges in Lincoln County in just under two months.

> Leaving Albany, September 8, 1910, I had the pleasure of taking in the last day of the Lincoln County Fair at Toledo, Sept 9, and was surprised at the excellence of the various products on exhibition there.

From Toledo I went to the thriving settlement on Beaver Creek, where among the hills is situation Ona Grange hall. It had been the purpose to dedicate the hall at this time but owing to circumstances that had retarded the work of completion, the exercises were postponed.

Gaining courage for the work of organizing that was before me by the hearty welcome accorded me beneath the hospitable roof of Brother John A. Coovert, County Deputy, and his cheering words, I passed on to Alsea Bay and across to Waldport, where I decided to begin work in the southern part of the county.

A ten-mile ride down the beach in a farmer's wagon to the mouth of the Yachats River and up the same seven miles brought me to the home of S. G. Ackerson, where in his parlor, after a week's canvassing, Yachats Grange was organized with 30 members. Then on by wagon over a high mountain dividing Yachats and Five Rivers Valley. After a few days canvassing Five Rivers Grange was organized with 42 members. Another week and Mountain Dell Grange in Lobster Creek Valley was added with 23 members.

Passing through the beautiful Alsea Valley the home of Hope Grange and of County Deputy S. N. Warfield, whom I met in his pleasant home and gathered fresh inspiration, I journeyed on by a chance team and by a tramp of ten miles to wide water, from there to Waldport by gasoline launch, and by the end of that week Waldport Grange, with 26 members, was organized. Then by stage along the beach to Yaquina Bay and across to Newport; from there to Toledo, where I took over a week to organize Toledo Grange with 25 members, then to Eddyville, where on November 1, Eddyville Grange was organized with 22 members. This completed the work in Lincoln County. Six new Granges and 168 members.

APPOINTED STATE DEPUTIES

In 1914 State Deputies A. P. Davis and C. D. Huffman both of Blue Mountain #345 in Union County reported they worked 111 days. They traveled 4,223 miles by rail, 373 by livery or stage, and walked 100 miles. They also mailed 1,400 letters. Such dedication.

W. R. Gekeler, also of Blue Mountain #345, reported in 1927 that he attended 59 meetings, drove 8,000 miles, organized nine Granges, reorganized one, saved another, and organized one Juvenile Grange.

In 1929 the State Executive Committee provided a Chevrolet for a State Deputy. Minnie Bond, C. H. Bailey, A. C. Miller, M. C. Glover, Bertha Beck, and Ray Gill were all deputies that year. Which one got to drive the Chevrolet? By 1932 three full-time district deputies were paid salaries and provided a car. But due to a reduction in dues, the following year the number was reduced to two.

Some State Masters appointed several State Deputies and others named one or two. Some deputies were assigned a section of the state while others were sent wherever the need was greatest. Some made their own schedule and itinerary and others went when and where the State Master sent them.

Arthur Brown, called Papa Brown, retired in 1942. He organized 75 to 80 Granges, of which 67 were still active. This was significant because many Granges lasted only a couple of years. He also organized six Pomonas and eight Juvenile Granges.

In the 2000s the focus of deputies was reorganizing Granges and securing the halls of Granges that had closed. John Knox, Forest Grove #282, reported that he traveled 13,298 miles between the 2008 and 2009 State Sessions. Derrell Witty and his wife Clarann, Hurricane Creek #608, traveled about 50,000 miles in four years from Elgin to Lakeview and from Sherman to Malheur Counties.

State Deputies who served ten years or more years were:

Mary S. Howard	Molalla #310	Clackamas	1904-13 1918-21
B. G. Leedy	Butte #148	Washington	1907-13 1915-23
Minnie Bond	Irving #377	Lane	1918-30
Charles Wicklander	Russellville #353	Multnomah	1930-35 1938-39 1943-48
Robert Coble	Eagle Valley #656	Baker	1964-75

COUNTY DEPUTIES

In the 1880s the State Master appointed three or four Deputy Masters in each county to visit Granges for the purpose of instructing members in the objects and purposes of the Grange, resuscitating dormant Granges, and organizing new Granges. They were expected to pass on to the State Grange information they collected: The number of members in good standing, average meeting attendance, whether officers (especially the Master and Secretary) attended regularly, whether the books were properly kept, whether they owned their own hall and its value, and total receipts for the year.

In 1963 County Deputies and Pomona Masters initiated County Conferences. These meetings typically covered officer duties, floorwork demonstrations, and the roles of standing committees.

CURRENT CHALLENGES

Recently State Masters/Presidents have asked their State Deputy to handle difficult situations. The report of Deputy Carol Everman, Beaver Valley #306, indicates the nature of the challenges she has dealt with.

At last year's convention, I accepted the Worthy Master's invitation to serve as her deputy. Over the last year, some of you have seen me at your meetings or activities. A few of you have seen more of me than you'd like. To quote Rodney King, "Can't we all just get along?" Unfortunately, no. But it would help if everybody used their 'company manners' at Grange...even your own Grange, even if you're related to everyone there.

In the Fourth Degree, we are instructed how to keep our children on the farm. The lesson is the same for how to get and retain new members: If we are to encourage them to love the Grange, we must make its labors cheerful. What a person sees makes the most lasting impression. Is your hall inviting? Are your activities interesting? Are you having a good time? Worker bees will come to sweet bait. Vinegar mostly attracts gnats.

Put a pleasant face on the Grange. It doesn't have to be the Master. Not everyone is cut out for sales; find someone who is, and that's your Membership Chair. And, for pity's sake, quit telling people they need to join or your Grange will collapse. New members can indeed save a faltering Grange, but "savior" shouldn't be in the want ad.

MEMBERSHIP

A total of 962 Subordinate/Community Granges have been organized in Oregon. Washington has Granges with numbers in the 1,100s and Pennsylvania has some with numbers in the 2,100s.

At the time of the organizing Session in 1873 there were 40 Granges in Oregon and five in the Washington Territory. In Oregon, Grange #100 was organized in 1874, #200 in 1885, 300 in 1901, #400 in 1909, #500 in 1913, #600 in 1922, #700 in 1928, #800 in 1932, and #900 in 1941. #962 was organized in 2000.

When some Granges were reorganized, they were assigned a new number. Other reorganized Granges assumed their original number.

The most Granges existing simultaneously was 377 in 1939. There were 300 Granges in Oregon between 1931 and 1968. Then the number of Granges dropped steadily to 200 in 2006. Currently there are 163.

NUMBER OF MEMBERS

In 1875 there were 10,885 members, but then the number quickly fell to 1,241 in 1880. The number reached 10,000 again in 1912. 20,000 was exceeded in 1931 and held until 1946. The peak was 32,069 in 1948. There were 30,000 members again between 1977 and 1981. Then 20,000 until 2000. The most significant drop was from 16,099 in 2002 and 9,754 in 2003. Since 2019 membership has held steady at around 4,500.

Net gain is a measurement often used today. The Oregon State Grange had a net gain in 67 year of its 150 years. However, some years the gain was quite small.

Year	Granges	Members
1873	40	1,000
1874	175	7,292
1875	187	10,885
1876	109	7,101
1877	189	7,567
1878	64	4,195
1879	65	2,477
1880	53	1,241
1881	53	1,440
1882	50	1,549
1883	45	1,848
1884	54	2,189
1885	59	2,291
1886	65	2,597
1887	62	2.541
1888	69	2,512
1889	86	3,049
1890	93	3,000
1891	88	3,040
1892	70	2,993
1893	70	2,692
1894	77	2,223
1895	78	1,860
1896	84	1,862
1897	90	2,046
1898	99	2,082
1899	59	2,340
1900	57	2,228
1901	58	2,470
1902	80	3,786
1903	96	4,897
1904	97	5,260
1905	92	5,393
1906	97	5,632
1907	108	6,465
1908	120	7,609
1909	127	8,085
1910	144	8,288
1911	193	9,712
1912	189	10,288
1913	188	10,182
1914	183	9,478
1915	119	10,323
1916	108	10,036
1917	202	10,010
1918	194	10,259
1919	176	9,258
1920	175	9,233
1921	174	9,984
1922	169	10,226

Year	Granges	Members
1923	181	10,238
1924	201	10,757
1925	218	11,016
1926	225	12,536
1927	229	13,710
1928	237	14,976
1929	256	16,761
1930	282	19,287
1931	316	21,849
1932	332	21,894
1933	330	19,463
1934	334	19,191
1935	338	19,642
1936	353	20,787
1937	370	21,488
1938	373	22,239
1939	377	22,583
1940	371	22,464
1941	368	21,687
1942	360	21,043
1943	351	20,233
1944	341	22,878
1945	341	26,367
1946	354	29,846
1947	355	31,452
1948	358	32,069
1949	354	29,846
1950	354	31,406
1951	351	30,473
1952	343	29,938
1953	341	29,541
1954	341	28,434
1955	339	28,407
1956	337	27,715
1957	336	26,726
1958	330	26,060
1959	331	26,042
1960	328	26,451
1961	324	26,492
1962	322	26,215
1963	318	26,119
1964	316	25,681
1965	312	24,852
1966	311	24,456
1967	306	24,823
1968	303	25,151
1969	298	25,439
1970	294	25,876
1971	290	26,781
1972	288	27,869
1973	284	28,614
1974	282	28,972
1975	277	28,800
1976	277	28,885
1977	276	30,318
1978	274	31,116
1979	274	31,052
1980	271	30,461

Year	Granges	Members
1981	272	30,675
1982	270	29,987
1983	270	28,546
1984	267	27,262
1985	265	26,753
1986	265	26,269
1987	263	25,584
1988	264	25,869
1989	262	25,842
1990	261	26,017
1991	258	26,591
1992	258	26,772
1993	257	26,679
1994	258	26,341
1995	258	25,771
1996	252	25,497
1997	246	24,412
1998	245	24,001
1999	246	22,887
2000	246	20,431
2001	234	17,843

Year	Granges	Members
2002	228	16,099
2003	221	9,754
2004	207	8,168
2005	205	7,644
2006	200	7,243
2007	195	7,035
2008	190	6,526
2009	202	6,500
2010	185	6,345
2011	185	5,872
2012	177	5,541
2013	178	5,392
2014	173	5,105
2015	174	4,984
2016	175	4,746
2017	175	4,722
2018	168	4,719
2019	165	4,587
2020	165	4,663
2021	163	4,458
2022	163	4,587

MEMBERSHIP CONTESTS AND AWARDS

Deputies were responsible for organizing and reorganizing Granges. Recruiting new members was left to each Grange and its members.

The first membership contest was held in 1903. The Executive Committee offered $7.50 to the Grange with the greatest gain in membership and the same to the Grange with the greatest percentage gain. They also awarded $5 to the member who secured the most "accepted applications" between June 1, 1902 and May 1, 1903 and $2.50 to the member with the second most. Today that $5 would be worth $171.50.

In 1938 any member who secured five new members received a free ticket to the Seventh Degree during the National Session in Portland. That was an effective incentive because 233 tickets were awarded.

In 1954 the grand prize for bringing in the most new members was a week's stay for two at Harrison Hot Springs in British Columbia. In 1985 a couple won a trip to Hawaii. In 1987 the Membership Committee gave a mini vacation to the top recruiter and dinner certificates to others.

STANDING MEMBERSHIP COMMITTEE

A State Membership Committee was not appointed until 1968. The new Membership Director reported 853 members were initiated and 731 lost. She started off with a net gain.

1970 was the first time that the State Master presented a guest speaker who was not a member with a membership application. That guest filled it out and wrote a check on the spot.

In 1989 the Membership Director urged Grangers to become salesmen and advertise. Most members were not comfortable assuming that role. It is often claimed that the Grange is the best kept secret. Conferences tried to train members to deliver an elevator speech.

Merchandise: Displaying the Grange name and logo can be effective forms of advertising. In 1941 State Master Ray Gill reported that Grange signs for farms were available for 50 cents each and automobile signs for 25 cents. In 1985 the Membership Committee sold "I'm Proud to be a Granger" license plate holders. The committee has sold Grange T-shirts, jackets, shopping bags, and mugs. Calendars featuring winning photos from the State Grange Photography Contest were not as popular.

The National Grange offers discounts on purchases of health care, insurance, hotels, rental cars, office supplies and other items potential members might buy. In 1989 Oregon tried offering a discount at Lens Crafters.

Slogans: In 1908 a $1.00 prize was given for the best Grange yell sent into the *Grange Bulletin*. The winner was "Farmers, farmers, hear the call, Patrons of Husbandry beats them all." Who yelled and who heard the yell is not known. In 1976 the Membership Committee came up with the slogan "Everyone Bring a Member – Make 1977 A Year to Remember."

Booklets, Brochures, and Ideas: In 1990 the Membership Committee published the pamphlet "People are the Key to a Successful Grange" to give to new members before they were initiated. State and National Granges have created lots of brochures over the years. Since many Granges are reluctant to throw anything away, it is interesting to see the collection of brochures some Granges still have. Some look to have been produced on a Royal upright typewriter.

In 2017 the Membership Committee combined two Idea Booklets with a Community Service Booklet to create "The Endless Sea Filled with Possibilities" booklet. It suggested events and contained information on how to organize each. The State Membership Committee also offers to help Granges with events. Committee members volunteer to serve a meal or ice cream while local members visit with attendees.

Life Memberships: It took the Oregon State Grange seven years to develop a Life Membership plan. The cost of the plan adopted in 1988 was based on the member's age: Ages 14 to 35 paid $325, 36 to 45 paid $300, 46 to 55 paid $250, 56 to 60 paid $200, 61 and over paid $150. The following year, 36 life memberships were purchased. In 1998 the cost was changed to $200 regardless of age. In 2017 delegates voted to raise the Life Membership fee to ten times the annual dues paid to the Oregon State Grange. Today that is $45 per year so a Life Membership costs $450.

At the time the plan was instituted, dues were low and interest rates were high. Granges did not feel a pinch when living Life Members did not pay annual dues. However, there have been years in which Granges lost money on Life Members. Fortunately, in 2021 the State Grange's investments yielded 12%, which meant that Life Memberships paid $71.13

or $26.13 over dues to the State Grange. Granges with many of Life Members paid no dues for one or more quarters.

Business, Family, and E-Memberships: In 2002 associate business memberships were added. Some Granges have recruited local businesses who support the aims of the organization but are not interested in attending meetings. Dues for business members is the same as for voting members, but the Grange passes on less to the State Grange.

In 2003 delegates approved a family membership plan. A family consists of one or more adults and their children, grandchildren, or great-grandchildren between the ages of 14 and 23 who live in the same household or are absent due to illness, education, or military service. Foster, adopted, stepchildren, and other legal dependents are considered part of a legal guardians' family. Dues for a family is the same as for two persons.

Delegates accepted e-memberships in 2009. This member connects electronically and is free to participate in a Community Grange as the member's schedule allows, attending a potluck, helping with a community service project, or participating in a social event.

Awards: In 1991, handmade wall hangings were presented to the two members who secured the most new members; those who brought in ten or more new members received belt buckles. These prizes must have been coveted because ten members brought in 201 new members.

In 1995 the top recruiter brought in 21 new members and received a Life Membership for his efforts. In 2002 members who brought in four or more new members received a denim shirt, likely with a Grange logo.

Granges usually receive certificates or plaques for having a 10% or greater gain in membership. Beginning in 2009, cash prizes of $100, $75, $50, and $25 have been awarded to the four Granges that have the highest percentages of gain.

National Recognition: In 1971 the Membership Committee reported a net gain for the first time since 1947. That year Oregon won a silver platter for membership gain but had to return it to National Grange.

2022 was the first time since 1955 (that's 67 years) that the National Grange had a growth in members. However, it was the fourth year in six that Oregon increased its membership. Sixty-two Oregon Granges were recognized as Honor Granges for having a net gain between July 1, 2021 and June 30, 2022. Oregon ranked second among State Granges in the number of Granges and fourth in number of members.

Ten Sisters and eight Brothers chaired the Membership Committee. Lorimer Ireland served ten years.

Chairman/Director	Grange	County	Years
Dorothy Lucas	Buell #637	Polk	1968
Cecil Kee	Shady Cove #931	Jackson	1971-74
Lorimer Ireland	Bellview #759	Jackson	1974-84
Marie Ireland	Bellview #759	Jackson	1974-84
Jack Preston	Cherry Park #667	Wasco	1984-85
Mary Knapp	Pleasant Valley #348	Multnomah	1985-90
Ruth McKnight	Lacomb #907	Linn	1990-92
Lois McGlothin	Santa Clara #746	Lane	1992-98
Tom Crosby	Forest Grove #282	Washington	1998-00
Gaye Stewart	Rickreall #671	Polk	2000-02
Charlotte Luttrell	Boring-Damascus #260	Clackamas	2002-04
Silas Miller	Charity #103	Linn	2004-06
Malcolm & Cookie Trupp	Spencer Creek #855	Lane	2006-12
Bob & Sandi Ludi	Sunnyside #855	Clackamas	2012-18
David McBride	Hurricane Creek #608	Wallowa	2018-22
Jill Hamm	Fruitdale #379	Josephine	2022-22

JUVENILE AND JUNIOR GRANGES

The first in Oregon was organized at Macleay #293 in 1904. State Lecturer Clara Waldo said, "The parent Grange will derive much benefit from the aid the little ones give in the Lecturer hour, from the better average attendance, and from new members drawn in by the enthusiasm of the children."

A barrier was having at least 13 children between the ages of 5 and 14 and someone to serve as its Matron or Patron. Having a place for them to meet may also have been an issue, although they usually met in the dining room at the same time as the adults held their meeting.

In 1965 the name Juvenile Grange was officially changed to Junior Grange. However, not until 1979 were Junior Matron or Patron replaced with Junior Grange Leader.

GRANGES AND MEMBERSHIP

In 1923 the Good of the Order Committee recommended that the State Overseer become Superintendent or Advisor to Juvenile Granges. M. C. Glover took his assignment seriously. He organized 17 Juvenile Granges in the next seven years.

The number of Juvenile Granges and their membership were not consistently reported. Often the numbers reported by the State Secretary were different from those given by the State Juvenile leader.

The number of Juvenile/Junior Granges organized in each decade varied from 4 to 71.

Before 1909	9
1910s	4
1920s	48
1930s	71
1940s	66
1950s	47
1960s	46
1970s	24
1980s	21
1990s	16
2000s	9

A total of 358 Juvenile/Junior Granges have been organized in Oregon. Many lasted only a few years because the children aged out. Some Juveniles were re-organized multiple times. North Bayside #99 celebrated its 25th anniversary and did not declare dormancy until 1976.

In 1931 there were 38 Juvenile Granges with nearly 1,000 members. In 1948 75 Juvenile Granges had 1,550 members. In 1966, 50 Junior Grangers had a membership of 1,866. In 1984 Oregon had the largest Junior membership in the nation although at that time there were only 21 Junior Granges in Oregon. The following year Oregon gained one Grange and was first place in the nation in membership gain.

Gilliam-Wheeler Pomona Juvenile Grange organized in 1931 was the first Pomona Juvenile Grange in the nation. Coos, Deschutes, and Jackson Counties also had Juvenile or Junior Pomonas.

In 1991 the new Junior Director reported that when she took over there were only three active Junior Granges. But 50 Juniors attended State Session. Twenty-two Junior Granges were organized in the 1990s and 2000s. One new Junior Grange even had 45 members. Today there are no Junior Granges in Oregon, but 45 Granges have 1+ members.

SESSIONS

In 1929 delegates voted to hold a Juvenile Grange Session in conjunction with the annual State Session. The first Session was held in 1931 in St. Mark's Guild Hall in Medford while adults were meeting at the High School. State Matron Lottie Blake reported that the first morning was spent getting acquainted and organized. The afternoon was devoted to recreation. The second day was spent playing games and preparing for degree work. Lake Creek #64 in Jackson County conferred the degree for 18 candidates. A picnic at Lithia Park was enjoyed by 90 children. More than 25 children attended all days of the Session.

In 1944 State Juvenile officers were elected for the first time. Delegates represented 12 Juvenile Granges and 58 members attended. Governor Snell, National Grange Juvenile Superintendent Carstensen, and the Oregon State Lecturer, Secretary, and HEC Chairman visited the Session. Nature and craft classes were held each day. A puppet show and a bird imitator entertained the children.

2014 State Junior Officers who conferred the Junior Degree at State Session in Redmond. Master Austin VanHouten, Overseer Austin Anchetta, Lecturer Elias Utt, Steward Cameron Herrick, Assistant Steward Riley Reynolds, Lady Assistant Steward Payton Miller, Chaplain Audrey VanHouten, Treasurer Owen Anchetta, Secretary Aurianna VanHouten, Gatekeeper Ethan Utt, Ceres Briauna Herrick, Pomona Elizabeth Bence, Flora McKenzie, Executive Committee C. J. Lindler, Jaden Peters, and Ginny Ford.

In 1949 30 Juvenile delegates and 105 members registered. In 1973, there were 62 delegates, 17 officers, 11 Matrons & Patrons, and 12 honorary members.

State Juvenile Grange By-Laws were written in 1951. Children usually read them aloud before they elected officers. Those elected were installed on the last day and served the following Session. But often some were not able to attend to fulfill their duties, so leaders had to find pro tems. Since 1993 Juniors, like the Youth, have applied for the office they want to have. This also saved the time that was spent electing sixteen officers.

Beginning in 1974 Junior leaders provided activities during the Sixth Degree. If the children promised to be very quiet, they are allowed to watch the Rosebud drill.

JUVENILE DEGREE

At the 1919 State Session in Hillsboro, Scholls Juvenile #3 demonstrated "their work in a beautiful manner. The State Grange extended to them a hearty applause."

After a team from Clackamas County exemplified the Juvenile Degree "in a pleasing and efficient manner" at the 1925 Session in Dallas, delegates agreed that it should be made an order of business at future Sessions. In 1942 delegates adopted a resolution that clarified that those who took the Juvenile Degree at Session would become members of a Juvenile Grange within their jurisdiction. If one did not exist, they would be members of the State Juvenile Grange.

State Juvenile Officers began conferring the Juvenile Degree during Session in 1957. Previously a Juvenile Grange in the host county exemplified it. In November 2012 six Oregon Juniors were on a Western States team that exemplified the Junior Degree at the National Session in Boise under the leadership of Oregon's Junior Director.

When there were no Junior Granges and none of the Junior officers had seen the degree, it no longer made sense for officers to learn and perform it at State Session. In 2019 Juniors marched in, opened the Grange, and then the State Master and Assistant Stewards demonstrated the Junior Obligation Ceremony.

TOURS AND FUN

A feature of each Session was a tour and an activity like swimming. In 1942 Juveniles took a field trip to Chase Gardens and held a picnic. When the Session was in Bend in 1947 Juveniles took a bus ride to Peterson's Rock Gardens. The following year at Astoria they enjoyed a whole day at the beach at Seaside and a skating party at a local rink.

Juniors have visited museums, walked to a local bank to see a gold nugget display, toured the Pendleton Woolen Mills, visited the Astor Column, and climbed the State Capitol dome. A caravan of 11 cars transported Juniors and their chaperones in 1966 to Silver Creek Falls. In 1976 a bus load plus seven cars toured The Dalles Dam. Juniors enjoyed the Enchanted Forest in 1980 and 2007.

Juniors attracted media attention when they delivered a donation to the Zoo's family farm.

Dogs for the Deaf demonstrations and visits to a local fire department were always popular. The children loved samples at Dutch Girl Ice Cream and Grandma's Cookies. Their least favorite activity was probably a picnic in the cafeteria due to rain.

Four excursions really stood out.

- In 1983 Juniors visited the Shakespeare Antique Costume Museum where they got to try on velvet robes, crowns, pointed toe shoes, helmets, hats, and veils.
- At the Newport Session in 1984, their bus driver gave them the grand tour. After visiting the Marine Science Center and the Undersea Gardens, they had lunch in the banquet room of Moby

Dick's. Then they toured the *Newport Times*. Energy must have been lagging so they stopped for ice cream before driving to view an oil tanker that broke up on the rocks.

- In 2008 Juniors rode the Crooked River Train. Tickets were bought by 28 Granges.
- When Juniors visited the Oregon Zoo in 2013, they delivered a check for $1,350, which was a donation from delegates to the Zoo's family farm. The press followed the story, a Portland TV station covered the visit, and the Zoo's website featured a photo of the group.

CONTESTS FOR INDIVIDUALS

In 1927 the first of many contests for Juvenile members was an essay contest with two age categories and prizes of $2.50 and $1. A Declamatory contest was held for the first time in 1941. For it, children memorized and recited a monologue, poem, or humorous essay. It was replaced by a talent contest with musical and variety divisions in 1964. Ten years later there were 30 entries in the talent contest.

The White Satin Sugar Canning Contest added a division for those between the ages of 9 and 18 in 1944. The Home Economics Committee offered cooking and cake baking contests for Juniors in the 1960s.

In 1947 the State Juvenile committee selected a theme for contests, which was Birds of Oregon. Scrapbook, poster, and essay entries were built around the year's theme. Other themes were Oregon parks, industries, products, Indians, history, safety, conservation, wildlife, agriculture, and wildflowers. Delegates assigned to the Session Juvenile Committee judged the entries in 1944.

Over the years many contests were added: Wood carving, mobiles, popcorn creations, foam art, patchwork pillows, yarn pictures, tree cone creations, nut and nutshell creations, seed pictures, hand puppets, Halloween masks, macaroni creations, Christmas stockings, bird feeders, painted T-shirts, wall hangings, bead craft, kites, rock paperweights, refrigerator magnets, Christmas ornaments, tray favors, sailboats, bead craft, Junior yell, and the list goes on. The largest number of entries in all contests was 152 in 1976.

National Grange also sponsored contests for Juniors. In 1956 Oregon members won first place in the nation in the soap carving and ping pong game contests. The Something from Nothing contest generated 37 entries in 1971. However, Oregon often did not send entries to National because their timing was set for State Granges that met in the fall.

CONTESTS FOR JUVENILE GRANGES

In 1932 at Silverton, three Juvenile Grange drill teams competed for prize money. Scrapbooks, relief maps, and models were usually group projects. The National Achievement Contest was also. The County Deputy judged how officers opened and closed the Grange and conducted their meeting. The top winner was awarded a banner, altar cloth, or mat. The Achievement Contest was held at least until 1983. Elmira #114 won first prize 17 times. In 1948 the Matron of the Juvenile Grange that receive the highest score was named Outstanding Matron.

CAMP

In 1946 a three-day summer camp for Juvenile Grangers in Coos and West Coast District Pomonas was held at Camp Lawhorn near McKinley. Two years later, a camp was held near Bend so that Juvenile Grangers throughout the state could attend.

In 1952 an Interim Juvenile Camp Committee evaluated three sites and recommended Skyline, 12 miles west of Bend. The annual lease from the U. S. Forest Service was $50 per year. During a work party in July, four sleeping cabins with eight bunks each were built in the girls' area and four in the boys' area. The power plant was repaired. In 1952 Juvenile camp was attended by 98 children and 24 adults. The following year, so many Juveniles registered that two weeks of camp were held, and 25 children were turned away. The following year three weeks were scheduled.

In 1975 the Executive Committee voted not to rent Skyline another year because the Forest Service demanded nearly $10,000 worth of repairs. A 1980 Junior Grange Campsites Committee recommended renting a facility in a different area of the state, just like the State Session moved around. But it was hard to keep momentum when the camp was held at a different location on a different week each year.

In 1992 CENEX provided a $5,000 grant. Camp Co-op had a store and bank to teach campers cooperative buying and selling. The fee was $40 with scholarships available for those who could not afford it. The last Camp in 2003 was shorter because CENEX cut funds. Juniors participated in several weekend camps that were held in conjunction with the State Leadership Camp in Glide.

1+ MEMBERS

In 2013 the National Grange introduced 1+ membership for Juniors. It allows those between the ages of 5 and 14 to become members of their parents' or grandparents' Grange. 1+ members can serve as pro tem officers, help with community service projects, fundraisers, Lecturer's programs, fair booths, and any other activities the Grange sponsors. 1+ members can enter State and National Grange contests. In 2015, 1+ members in Oregon totaled 38. They belonged to 21 Granges. By 2023, that number grew to 107 members of 41 Granges in 19 counties.

When all Junior State Session attendees were 1+ members, the focus of their Session was no longer on exemplifying the Junior Degree. It was on learning to conduct a meeting, make a motion, give reports, sing Grange songs, and understand each officer's role. There were still crafts, tours, and fun. Oregon offers talent, photography, cookie baking, apron sewing, and Minecraft contests. Members can also enter National Grange sponsored community service, quilt block, public speaking, sign-a-song, baseball (trivia), creative art, and creative writing contests.

STATE JUNIOR LEADERS

The first State Juvenile Committee was appointed in 1929. Twenty-four Sisters and five Brothers have served as State Juvenile or Junior Leader. They were called Matron, Superintendent, or Director. Melvina Carver of Forest Grove #282 served 18 years.

Leader	Grange	County	Years
Mrs. Lottie Blake	Mountain View #429	Benton	1928-36
Mrs. Fannie M. McCall	Brush College #586	Polk	1936-38
Mrs. L.'Rena Slack	Bonanza #772	Klamath	1938-43
	Illinois Valley #370	Josephine	
Hilda Reiher	North Bayside #691	Coos	1943-48
Helen Roberts	Smith River #585	West Coast	1949-50
Naomi Clark	Fruitdale #379	Josephine	1951-52
Helen Mast	McKinley #582	Coos	1952-54
Willie McLean	Gold Hill #534	Jackson	1955-56
Lillian Peterson	Elmira #523	Lane	1956-58
Minnie Andrieu	Midland #781	Klamath	1958-60
Clyde Thornton	Warren #536	Columbia	1961-62
Melvina Carver	Forest Grove #282	Washington	1962-80
Wanda Mulholland	Dixie Mountain #860	Washington	1981-90
Bonnie Sims	Midland #781	Klamath	1990-92
Scot Jacobson	White Eagle #386	Umatilla	1992-94
Bill Davis	Elmira #523	Lane	1993
Dixie Thramer	Goshen #561	Lane	1994
Janice Schiedler	Scotts Mills #938	Marion	1995
Brenda Gubrud	Crow #450	Lane	1995-98
Sarah Kingsborough	Warner #117	Clackamas	1998-00
Celia Luttrell	Boring-Damascus #260	Clackamas	2000-04
Sherry Firman	Santa Clara #746	Lane	2004-05
Jeffery Dehne	Walterville #416	Lane	2006-10
Elizabeth Dehne	Walterville #416	Lane	2006-14
Peggy Fine	Evergreen #460	Douglas	2010-12

Charlotte Luttrell	Boring-Damascus #260	Clackamas	2014-16
Elizabeth & Keegan Williams	Fairmount #252	Benton	2016-18
Peggy Jillson	Irving #377	Lane	2018-24

YOUTH

In 1938 delegates adopted a resolution to create a State Youth Department. Klamath Pomona Master L. Alva Lewis and Juvenile Deputy L'Rena Slack came up with the idea of Young Grangers' Auxiliaries (YGAs) for members between the ages of 16 and 30. YGAs spread quickly to Jackson and Marion Counties.

Ten youth were required to form an Auxiliary. Members adopted By-Laws, elected officers, and conducted meetings. Approximately 40% of their time was spent on Grange activities and service projects, and 60% on recreation. Some YGAs sponsored basket socials, picnics, carnivals, plays, and drill teams. Soon 59 Granges and 18 Pomonas had YGAs.

In 1938 20 YGA members traveled in a truck decorated to look like a covered wagon from Klamath Falls to Portland for the National Session. Their vehicle had a "sturdy engine" but was stopped by the State Police for not having an Oregon P.U.C. license. While in Portland members stayed and prepared their meals in Grange halls. Two years later a group drove to the National Grange Session in Peoria, Illinois, traveling through 25 states and meeting as many youth as possible along the way.

While the YGA had the support of the State Master, the name "Auxiliary" bothered some members. At the 1939 session, delegates voted to keep YGA but change the name to Young Grangers of America.

Oregon was one of five states in 1944 to receive a plaque from the National Grange for outstanding service to youth. The Youth Superintendent reported in 1946 that there were over 1,000 members under the age of 20. In 1948, 201 Granges and 34 Pomonas had appointed a youth chairman. YGAs are not mentioned in the State Grange Proceedings after 1943, but some Granges continued them until 1949.

Since the 1950s, when Grange youth have been asked to help, they have been taught to respond "I'd be delighted."

Oregon received national recognition several other times. Oregon's Directors were named State Directors of the Year in 1994, 1997, and 1998. Oregon's entries in the Outstanding Young Couple were national winners in 1960, 1975, 1981, and 1983. Clackamas County's All-Night Scavenger Hunt, a city-wide tour of Portland on public transportation, won first for Most Creative Youth Night Program in 2000.

STATE YOUTH OFFICERS

State Master Ed Luttrell reported in 1997 that twelve of the sixteen Oregon State Grange officers were graduates of the youth program. Many got their training by being state youth officers.

In 1963, youth elected officers on the first day of session. Those officers opened and closed the Grange in the fourth degree on Thursday afternoon. Then they attempted to use the method of the State Juvenile Grange: elect one year and perform the next. Many got jobs and could not return the following year. There were too many pro tem officers. Having youth apply for the office they wanted worked better. Those who wanted the spotlight could apply for a marching or speaking part. In 2010 the Youth Director did not need to urge youth to apply. She received 16 applications and another five expressed interest.

In 1988 delegates voted that youth officers open the session one morning. At 7:30 am each morning, they practice a seating drill, opening the Grange in the Fourth Degree, presenting guests, and a retiring drill even though half of them were still asleep. In 2023 the practices were finally changed to after Grange closed for the night. A much better time for most youth.

State Youth Officers perform impressive seating and retiring drills and remind members how to perform the traditional opening ceremony.

COMMUNITY SERVICE PROJECTS

In the 2000s youth performed a community service project at each State Session. They collectively spent 200 hours cleaning a veterans' cemetery. They volunteered at the Humane Society, a soup kitchen, cleaned a beach, and made and donated skid resistant socks to seniors at an assisted living center.

A youth team installed the State Junior officers. In 2012-2013 youth collected donations for Ash Butte #802 whose hall burned to the ground.

Since 2018, youth have conducted a Keeping Oregon Warm campaign. One year they collected donations from 30 Granges including 472 hats, 316 pairs of gloves, 176 scarves, and 85 pairs of socks. These donations were distributed to those in need in the host district. It seems strange to bring wool clothing to State Session in late June when the temperature is over 100 degrees, but it is for a good cause.

TOURS AND FUN

Youth activities were not all Grange or all serious. They enjoyed barbecues, played miniature golf, and attended a re-enactment of the Great Joseph Bank Robbery. They have toured a nickel mine, tree farm, OSU Experiment Station, the Ore-Ida potato factory, and Pendleton Underground where they found all the buried secrets. They visited the Henry Estate Winery, which they claimed was an agricultural experience.

For the Oregon State Grange's 100th anniversary, Clackamas County Youth had fun putting on a "Thru the Years with Fashion" style show. The bunny hop and line dancing have been added to the Youth Coronation Ball.

Youth bring energy and new ideas to State Sessions. In 2023 youth and others competed in axe throwing during one dinner hour. Who would have guessed that some state officers are so good at this sport?

CONTESTS FOR INDIVIDUALS

Youth held fewer contests than Juniors. A youth division was added to the White Satin Sugar canning contest in 1943. Essay, poster, and declamatory contests were short lived. Public speaking has been offered since the early 1970s. In 1979 youth studied American Sign Language and soon there were entries in the Sign-A-Song contest. In 2000 Hope Gard and Scott Andry from Mid Valley "O" #960 won first prize in Sign-A-Song at National Grange. Currently, youth participate in Grange Baseball, which is a Grange trivia challenge.

CONTESTS FOR TEAMS

A Youth Degree team contest was introduced in 1946. At the 1949 Session, the winning team exemplified the First and Second Degrees. In 1956 six teams competed and an all-star team was named. The all-star Chaplain was an exchange student from Germany.

In the 1950s drill teams were popular. Teams could be composed of members from several Granges in the same county. Installation teams competed in the 1990s and early 2000s. In 1994 four teams entered and the winner had the honor of installing the State Officers.

Sports competitions were popular. Beginning in 1977, a Youth Bowling Contest was the first State Session event. Twenty-three teams competed in 1994. In the 1980s five softball and volleyball teams competed. In 1988 Youth sponsored a golf tournament the Saturday before the Session began. The tournament continued until most participants were way beyond youth age.

CAMPS, CONFERENCES, AND WESTERN REGIONALS

Creating a year-round program was a challenge. The first Youth Camp was held in Tillamook County in 1947. Camps were usually strictly social events with hikes, ballgames, and parties. After the Grange leased Skyline Camp near Bend, a weekend Youth Camp was held nearly every year. In 1976 Youth Camp was the last event held at Skyline.

Spring, fall, and couples' conferences were usually held in Grange halls around the state. They attracted 40-60 attendees over a weekend. Attendees slept on the floor one or two nights. Sometimes the host Grange furnished meals; if not, participants pitched in to make their own. Workshops were presented on topics such as leadership, resolution writing, and parliamentary procedure.

Conferences or workshops have been held during Sessions, often with participants preparing and presenting the content. National Master Betsy Huber attended an early morning workshop on social media led by two youths in 2017. She reported that she established an Instagram account and increased her Facebook friends.

Oregon sends youth to the Western Regional Conference to compete in national contests. Winners represent the Western Region at National Grange. Ambassadors are required to attend Regionals to represent the state at National Grange. In 1995, a caravan with 39 youths traveled to Anaheim. Oregon hosts Western Regionals every four years.

FUNDRAISING

Sending youth to the Western Regionals Conference and to the National Grange is expensive. In 1971 delegates adopted a resolution that a Youth Travel Fund be established, and that youth raise money to pay their own way. Youth have sold flowers, seat cushions, greeting cards, stationery, candles, and jewelry. In 1976 a member donated a beef, and youth sold tickets for a drawing to win a half or quarter of the meat.

Before banquets were scheduled, the youth held one as a fundraiser. The dinner was attended by 130.

In 1988 youth sold tickets on a Treasurer Chest and raised $1,741. This led to Goodie Baskets. Each district filled an actual basket with items and sold tickets for $1. Over time, items "in the basket" became too big to fit: A kayak, tent filled with a BBQ grill and camping equipment, and enough kids' furniture to fill a playhouse. Transporting all these items home may have been a challenge. Tickets were sent to Granges and sold by aggressive youth salespersons during the Session. The drawing became a feature of the Youth Banquet or Luncheon. Youth held a small Junior by the feet, dipped him into a barrel full of tickets, and had him retrieve winning tickets. The first winner got first choice. The last ticket drawn was stuck with what is left. Juniors thought this was great fun! The first year Goodie Basket tickets raised $1,800. In 1999 youth raised $4,300.

Some years youth have had a concession stand at State Session. They have also had a car wash. In the early 2000s, "Penny Wars" pitted one district against another. The district that collected the most pennies got to throw a pie in the face of a deputy or high-ranking officer.

OUTSTANDING YOUNG GRANGERS, ADULTS, COUPLES, AND NATIONAL YOUTH OFFICERS

The State Youth committee named an Outstanding Young Granger in 1943. When National adopted this program, a Prince and a Princess were crowned in each state. Oregon applicants compiled an impressive scrapbook that documented their Grange activities. Today youth between the ages of 16 and 23 apply to be Youth Ambassadors. A total of 85 Oregon youths have been honored.

Between 1993 and 2016 eleven Oregonians between the ages of 22 and 37 have been named Outstanding Young Adults or Young Patrons.

From 1956 to 2001 Outstanding Young Couples, who were between the ages of 22 and 37, were also crowned. National Grange selected one of the state young couples to be the national winner. Oregon had more than their share of national winners: Robert and Sybil Barnes of Waldo Hills #918 in 1960, Jim and Sue Dumolt of Clarkes #261 in 1975, Steve and Joanne Stark of Kinton #582 in 1981, and Bob and Sandi Ludi of Sunnyside #842 in 1983.

From 1970 to present, Oregon youth have been named National Youth Officers. The officers open the National Session one morning. Thirty youths have held 41 national offices, all offices except Assistant Steward and Flora. Ed Luttrell of Eagle Creek #297 served as National Youth Master in 1985 and JC Junkman of Clarkes #261 was National Youth President in 2022.

G. R. O. W. CLUB

Members of G.R.O.W. Club (Go Right on Working) represented Oregon at a National Grange Session as Prince, Princess, Young Couple, Young Patron, or Ambassador. In Oregon, the group has served ice cream socials, put on degrees, and is available to install officers.

STATE YOUTH LEADERS

Twenty-two Brothers and 19 Sisters have served as State Youth Superintendent, Chairman, or Director. It is a challenging job; none have served more than six years.

Leader	Grange	County	Years
Fred A. Lewis	Shasta View #860	Klamath	1939-41
Ben Buisman	Friendly #897	Multnomah	1941-42
May Taylor	Malin #707	Klamath	1942-43
Edyth Bohnert	Central Point #698	Jackson	1943-46
Albert Bohren	Fairview #273	Tillamook	1949
Joe Guttridge	Springwater #263	Clackamas	1950-52
Mable V. Wood	Rockwood #323	Multnomah	1952-53
Henry Henrickson	Winona #271	Washington	1953-58
Charles S. Kizer	Charity #103	Linn	1958-59
Fred Anderegg	Redland #796	Clackamas	1959-62
Gerald Riley	Walterville #416	Lane	1963-63

Neil Cullison	Central #276	Clackamas	1964-66
Shirley Cullison	Central #276	Clackamas	1966-68
Lavina Clack	Myrtle Creek #442	Douglas	1968-71
James Dumolt	Redland #796	Clackamas	1971-73
Beverly Ficek	Crow #450	Lane	1973-74
Tom Walters	Lost River #846	Klamath	1974-76
Harry Coulson	Winona #271	Washington	1976-78
Jeanie Dickson Force	Clarkes #261	Clackamas	1978-82
Steve & Joanne Stark	Kinton #562	Washington	1983-86
Bob & Sandi Ludi	Sunnyside #842	Clackamas	1986-88
Kathy & Paul Dailey	Smith River #585	West Coast	1989-90
Ed Luttrell	Boring-Damascus #260	Clackamas	1990-92
Mike & Gaye Stewart	Rickreall #671	Polk	1992-98
Debbie Hood	Beavercreek #276	Clackamas	1998-00
Bill Hood	Beavercreek #276	Clackamas	1999-00
Steve Kroeker	Scio #923	Linn	2000-02
Ross & Kris VanHouten	Vale #696	Malheur	2002-08
Mark & Julie Schnetzky	Tigard #148	Washington	2008-10
Kitty "Cat" Thomas	Milwaukie #268	Clackamas	2010-14
Scot & Clare Jacobson	Columbia #867	Umatilla	2014-16
Connie Suing	Crow #450	Lane	2016-21
Christy Dumolt	Clarkes #261	Clackamas	2021-24
JC Junkman	Clarkes #261	Clackamas	2021-24

COUNTY COUNCILS AND POMONA GRANGES

The Founders did not include a district-level Grange in their organizational plan. However, members saw a need to organize by county or district. The *States Rights Democrat* (Albany) published an announcement that Linn County Masters were meeting on Tuesday August 12, 1873 at 1 p.m. in room 9 of the St. Charles Hotel to organize an Association of Granges. National Grange Deputy N. W. Garretson arrived in time to meet with the group.

COUNTY COUNCILS

Article XXI. Associations of the By-Laws adopted at the organizing Session of the Oregon State Grange includes this description.

> It shall be lawful for Subordinate Granges to form themselves into associations, to be called Councils, for the purpose of facilitating the transaction of business of buying, selling and shipping, and for such other purposes as may seem for the good of the Order. They shall be governed and the membership decided by such laws as the Council may from time to time make, not in conflict with the Constitution of the National and State Granges.

Other County Councils were organized between 1874 and 1876 in Benton, Clackamas, Jackson, Lane, Marion, Multnomah, Union, Washington, and Yamhill Counties. Although authorized by the State Grange, their By-Laws were not uniform. From newspaper reports most appeared to have these features:

- The purpose was to facilitate mutual business transactions of buying, selling, and shipping.
- Membership was limited to Subordinate Grange Masters and no more than three Fourth Degree members who were elected annually.
- Each Grange paid dues plus dues on each of their representatives.
- Nine members constituted a quorum. Members had to be present to vote.
- Council officers were elected annually. They were President, Vice President, Secretary, Treasurer, and possibly a Chaplain, Gatekeeper, Steward, and Assistant Steward. Female officers were not elected.
- Each Grange elected one of their representatives to be a Trustee. They had authority to hire a business agent and make decisions for the Council between regular meetings.
- Some Councils met monthly.
- Councils conducted open meetings without ritual.

Several County Councils adopted resolutions in favor of the state regulating freight and fares on railroads, rivers, and canals, and against Chinese laborers. Linn County Council pressed for faster development of the Oregon Pacific Railroad to Yaquina Bay Harbor. Some Councils sold and shipped grain or wool. Others bought sacks and twine in bulk. The Linn County Council recommended plows and binders in newspaper advertisements for Osborne Harvest Machinery Company.

POMONA GRANGES

In his 1875 Address, State Master Daniel Clark proposed the formation of Pomona Granges. Some County Councils became Pomonas almost immediately, electing a full slate of Grange officers and exemplifying the Fifth Degree for members who had not taken it at a State Grange Session.

Linn County Council was the hold out. It had functioned effectively for nearly 40 years when Linn County Pomona was organized in 1911. The Pomona met quarterly, and the Council met monthly except in the months the Pomona met. In 1915 the two groups held a joint meeting to adopt resolutions to be sent to State Session. It appears that the Council did not meet again after that.

At the 1877 Session delegates adopted By-Laws for Pomona Granges. Most Pomonas were organized by county. However, some were District Pomonas that included several counties. For example, Multnomah District Pomona included Granges from Clackamas and Washington counties. Jacksonville District Pomona was composed of Granges in Jackson, Josephine, and Lake Counties.

From 1877 to 1889 Pomona Masters and their wives were voting delegates at State Sessions. It is not clear why Pomonas lost voting rights. In 1912 delegates voted down a resolution that would have given Pomona Masters and their wives the vote. Four years later that decision was reversed. In 1917 Pomona Masters and their spouses could again vote.

Pomonas typically held day and evening meetings. They began mid-morning with reports and routine business, recessed for dinner, and resumed at 1:30 to discuss and vote on resolutions. After a break for supper, they conferred the Fifth Degree. A Lecturer's program followed. Clackamas Pomona's Lecturer's hour in July 1902 listed 22 recitations, poems, and essays interspersed with musical numbers, which would have taken far more than one hour. The *Oregon City Courier-Herald* reported "A dance followed, which lasted until daylight."

Clackamas Pomona discussed building their own hall. The idea was quickly rejected because the building would have been used only four times a year. But few halls were large enough to accommodate the 200 or more attendees. This was not just a problem in Clackamas County, Pomonas in Columbia, Deschutes, Hood River, Marion, Morrow, Multnomah, and Washington Counties also reported these numbers. Providing two meals became a burden for some host Granges. Attendees were encouraged to bring a "basket supper."

Some Pomonas fulfilled the function of County Councils by transacting the businesses of buying, selling, and shipping. Multnomah, Lane, and Douglas established public markets. Lane formed a cooperative livestock shipping association that did over $450,000 worth of business in two years. Washington and Hood River Pomonas purchased feed, lime, and plaster in bulk. Umatilla ordered two carloads of plows, harrows, wagons, and hacks. Josephine marketed surplus produce in Northern California and Klamath Falls.

In addition, Pomonas sponsored picnics, visitations, contests, and conferences. In the 1930s some Pomonas held a different kind of "County Council" meeting. These roundtable discussions for the Master, Overseer, and Lecturer of each Grange plus the Agriculture, Legislative, and Home Economics chairs. The exchange of ideas was meant to strengthen the Granges that participated.

In August 1916, Hood River Pomona sponsored an Encampment attended by 500 members who pitched their tents in the fir grove next to the Parkdale train station. They participated in sports, enjoyed dancing, and listened to speeches by Oregon Agricultural College and extension staff and State Grange officers. Each of the five Granges in the county provided a program of music and entertainment. The Pomona drill team performed. A highlight was a debate on the single tax between W. S. Uren, the father of the Initiative and Referendum, and a Portland attorney. All looked forward to returning the next year, but the event was not repeated.

In 1939 State Master Ray Gill reported that 14 Pomona had adopted the Pennsylvania Plan. Rather than Pomonas collecting dues, the Oregon State Grange sent the Pomonas 20 cents of each member's dues. By 1942 all 37 Pomonas had adopted the plan.

In the 1950s the State Grange Executive Committee paid Pomonas 25¢ for each member who took the Fifth Degree and gave $50, $30, and $20 prizes to Pomonas that had the highest percentage of net gain in membership. State Master Elmer McClure suggested projects for Pomonas like participating in the Federal Highway Building program and establishing a credit union. He urged Pomonas to adopt a program to correct voters' impression that cooperatives were farmer's attempts to avoid taxation rather than the only way small farmers could stay in business.

In his 1981 Good of the Order Address, State Master W. C. Harris reported that many Pomonas were failing. His successor Morton Wolverton claimed, "Far too many of our Pomonas have become nothing more than a social gathering, without goals other than a potluck dinner." In the 1990s State Master Ed Luttrell held visioning conferences and encouraged Pomona Masters to share their vision statements during State Session.

State Master Susan Noah held a school for County Deputies and Pomona Masters in 2013. At that time there were 20 Pomonas in the state. Susan was surprised when nearly 40 attended. Her training filled a need but did not fix the problem. She held a series of meetings to discuss the purposes of Pomona Granges, the barriers that keep them from accomplishing their purposes, and ways to overcome the barriers. Weather and other issues prevented the group from completing its assignment.

During the 2022 State Session, National Grange Executive Committee member Leroy Watson presented a talk on Pomona Granges via video conferencing. His talk inspired some conversation but has not resolved issues with this weakest link.

Bold indicates that the Pomona is currently active. When multiple dates are listed, the Pomona was reorganized several times. For example, Clackamas County District Pomona has been active since 1887. Washington County Pomona was organized in 1897 and its name was changed to Washington-Yamhill Pomona when Yamhill County Pomona consolidated with it in 1980. Polk County Pomona was organized in 1892 and reorganized in 1901 and 1913.

#	Pomona	Organized	Dormant
1	**Clackamas County District**	1887	
2	Washington County	1897	
	Washington-Yamhill	1980	
3	**Polk County**	1892, 1901, 1913	
4	Marion County	1877, 1890, 1900	2018
5	Yamhill County	1909	1980
6	Union County	1910	2006
7	Gilliam County	1911	
	Gilliam-Wheeler Counties	1922	1979
8	Hood River County	1915	2006
9	**Tillamook County**	1897, 1914	
10	**Lincoln County**	1916	
11	Wasco County	1920	2005
12	Linn County	1911	
	Linn-Benton County	1921	
	Linn County	1935	
13	**Douglas County**	1911	
14	**Lane County**	1878, 1896, 1909, 1921	
15	Multnomah County	1877	2015
18	**Columbia County**	1902	
19	Clatsop County	1913, 1918	1999

20	**Josephine County**	1911	
22	**Wallowa County**	1923	
23	Grant County	1924	1991
24	**Baker County**	1924	
25	**Deschutes County**	1925	
26	Umatilla District	1925	
	Umatilla-Morrow	2013	2022
27	Jackson County	1925	2022
28	Crook County	1926	1983
29	Morrow County	1926	1980
	Wheatland	1980	2009
30	Coos County	1912, 1920	
	Coos-Curry Counties	2002	
	Coos-Curry-West Coast	2013	2017
31	Sherman County	1928	1980
32	Jefferson County	1928	1983
33	Malheur County	1928, 1940	2007
34	Klamath County	1929	2012
35	Lake County	1920, 1931	2004
36	**Benton County**	1935, 2009	
37	Curry County	1936	2000
38	Harney County	1937	
	Harney-Grant	1992	2005
39	West Coast District	1940	2011
40	South Malheur	1940	1952
42	Crooked River	1982	2007

OREGON STATE GRANGE BULLETIN

At the organizing Session in 1873, members were urged to subscribe to the *Willamette Farmer.* The first editor of that weekly published in Salem was John Minto, a charter member of Salem #17, its long-time Secretary, and a member of the State Executive Committee from 1882 to 1888.

The "Proceedings of the Oregon State Grange Patrons of Husbandry" took up two and a half columns on the frontpage of the October 4, 1873 issue. That November the paper published Daniel Clark's report of his visit to the California State Session in San Jose. The paper often published a listing of Granges, their officers, and meeting dates.

In 1885 *The Pacific Rural Press* published in San Francisco and then *The Northwest Pacific Farmer* were named Oregon State Grange official publications.

STATE LECTURERS

In his final Master's Address, Daniel Clark proposed that the State Grange publish its own newspaper. It was not until 1901 that State Lecturer Austin Buxton published the *Oregon State Grange Quarterly Bulletin.*

The following year it became a monthly and soon had a circulation of 1,700.

In 1909, the Oregon and Washington State Granges agreed to publish the *Pacific Grange Bulletin*. State Lecturer J. J. Johnson became editor of the Oregon department. By 1911 the paper had a circulation of 16,500 families in Oregon, Washington, California, and Idaho. But two years later, the Washington State Grange withdrew from the publication. Oregon continued to publish it. Some said it was then a better paper.

The State Lecturer Minnie Bond published the *Oregon Grange Bulletin* from 1915 to 1923. She reported problems, not with writing and editing, but with maintaining a mailing list and getting advertising.

DR. C. H. BAILEY

Sister Bond did not seem happy when State Master George Palmiter hired Dr. C. H. Bailey to be Bulletin Editor in 1923. C. H. was the first Master of South Deer Creek #440. He was also Master of Douglas County Pomona. He was a State Deputy from 1918 to 1935 and was elected to the State Executive Committee in 1922.

When C. H. settled in Douglas County, he raised sheep and chickens. Then he was named county fruit inspector and helped organize the Umpqua Valley Fruit Union before being elected President of the Oregon Horticulture Society. C. H. introduced broccoli to Douglas County and was its champion. He grew it, wrote about, and gave talks on it.

Dr. C. H. Bailey was Bulletin Editor for 17 years. He was called "Doctor" because he had been a dentist in Michigan. Why he gave up his practice and moved to Oregon is not known.

At that time, the *Grange Bulletin* had as many advertisers as the law allowed and more articles than could be printed given its size and frequency of publication.

URSEL NARVER

In 1924 delegates adopted a resolution to accept political advertising in the *Grange Bulletin*. The *Bulletin* position was spelled out in 1973: The Grange did not endorse candidates but did sell ads that carried a notice of who placed the ad. An attempt was made to give the opposing candidate equal space. For example, the *Bulletin* ran a four-page ad for McGovern for President, for which the candidate paid $600. The Advertising Manager attempted to get a similar ad for Nixon, but Oregon Farmers for Nixon was not interested. The *Bulletin* did not accept advertising for measures that opposed the Grange position but did accept ads for measures on which the Grange did not have a position.

The Bulletin was published twice a month beginning in 1925. Advertising from businesses in cities where there were Granges financed the additional issues. The print run was 8,000 copies.

During the depression, the Bulletin lost money because many advertisers did not renew their contracts. In 1933 Advertising Manager Ursel Narver introduced the Sales Slip Program. A member sold two- or three-line ads to local businesses. Members saved their sales slips for purchases from those advertisers. Each Grange turned them in and was paid $1 for every $2,000 worth of slips. By 1957 the Sales Slip Program made a profit of $111,154. The program continued until 1982.

Ursel worked for the Grange Bulletin for over 50 years. Before he took the job, he was Student Body President of Oregon College of Agriculture, Editor of the *Beaver*, and a member of the forensics team. After graduation he became President of the Alumni Association and later President of the OSU Dad's Club. He served 12 years on the Oregon State Fair Commission, five as Chairman.

Beginning in 1959 the *Grange Bulletin* made a profit thanks to advertising Grange tours to Hawaii, Canada, New England, and National Sessions. The tours were not limited to Grange members. In 1962 State Master Elmer McClure reported that the *Grange Bulletin* had advertising revenue of $64,000.

BEN BUISMAN

Ben Buisman was hired as Editor in 1940. After graduating from Washington State College, Ben taught journalism and print shop at Gresham High School. He was Bulletin Editor for 21 years. He also edited *The Timberman* and *Pacific Retail Lumberman*. State Master Elmer McClure reported that "Editors of newspapers around the state often quote the *Grange Bulletin*." Ben was Master of Friendly #897 when he passed in 1965.

In 1946, the *Grange Bulletin* faced a paper shortage and the threat of a strike that would have affected the printing facility. The *Bulletin* survived thanks to full-page ads run by Oregon Grange Wholesale.

The *Pacific Grange Farmer*, a color supplement published by the Grange papers of Oregon, Washington, Idaho, and California, was inserted once a quarter beginning in 1951. Readers and advertisers liked it. In 1955 it became a monthly.

KEN FITZGERALD

Ken Fitzgerald was hired to be Grange Bulletin Editor in 1967. After graduating from the University of Oregon journalism school, he was publicity director for the Anti-Sales Tax Federation. When he returned from serving in the U. S. Army in World War II, he worked as a copy chief and public relations director for two Portland advertising agencies.

Ken took a two-year break but edited the Bulletin for a total of 23 years. The Portland Club of Printing House Craftsmen named him Craftsman of the Year in 1970. In 1985 the National Grange presented him with a certificate of excellence as "Dean of Grange Editors." He was also President of the Consumer Power League and the Oregon Shores Conservation Coalition. He operated his own advertising agency. The Clackamas County Fair was one of his accounts.

CHALLENGES

The *Grange Bulletin* was printed by Grange Cooperative Printing Association in Seattle from 1935 to 1977. Printing out of state was criticized, but the co-op used Oregon-made newsprint, employees were unionized, and it was a cooperative. However, when the *Gresham Outlook* offered a savings of $9,000 a year, the Executive Committee jumped at the chance to change printers.

In 1981 due to inflation, the Executive Committee faced the decision whether to raise dues, cut programs, or reduce the size or frequency of publishing the *Grange Bulletin*. They chose the *Bulletin*. Beginning Aug 1, 1982, it became a monthly publication.

During the first 92 years, three editors served for 17 or more years. Ten Editors have held the position in the last 30 years. Some had little experience with the Grange or with the job. Budgets were cut sharply when postal rates increased rapidly. Sorting zip codes down to the carrier and eliminating advertising helped reduce mailing costs.

In 2003 the Bulletin's publication schedule changed to every other month. Starting in 2015 two issues contain four-color pages (back, front, and middle section). Stories from 100 Granges were published each year. Beginning in 2016, a special election issue was published in even years with each candidate's photo and statement.

GRANGE BULLETIN EDITORS

Twelve Brothers and eight Sisters have edited the Grange Bulletin. Ben Buisman and Kenneth Fitzgerald edited the paper for 21 years and Dr. C. H. Bailey for 17.

Editor	Grange	County	Years
Austin Buxton	Gale #282	Washington	1900-04
Clara H. Waldo	Macleay #293	Marion	1904-08

J. J. Johnson	Evening Star #27	Multnomah	1908-10
H. A. Darnall	Lents #351	Multnomah	1910-14
Mrs. Minnie E. Bond	Irving #377	Lane	1914-23
Dr. C. H. Bailey	South Deer Creek #440	Douglas	1923-40
Ben Buisman	Friendly #897	Multnomah	1940-61
Olga Wilson Nelson	Friendly #897	Multnomah	1961-62 1976-78
Loren Milliman	Friendly #897	Multnomah	1962-67
Kenneth Fitzgerald	Friendly #897	Multnomah	1967-76 1978-92
Ed Luttrell	Boring-Damascus #260	Clackamas	1992-96
Ruth Hawkins	Rickreall #671	Polk	1996-98
Ellen Alsever		Marion	1998-99
Aaron Hill	Capitol #959	Marion	1999-00
Eddie Dirickson	Capitol #959	Marion	2000-01
Cliff Engle		Klamath	2002
Jan Jackson	Fernhill #582	Columbia	2002-03
Charlotte Luttrell	Boring-Damascus #260	Clackamas	2003-04
Chris Rea	Fernhill #582	Columbia	2004-13
Suzy Ramm	Springwater #263	Clackamas	2013-23

STANDING COMMITTEES

Legislative bodies and Robert's Rules of Order describe a standing committee as "permanent," appointed to deal with a specific subject or fulfill certain duties all year long. The State Grange Master/President appoints standing committees to study a subject, provide members information, organize events, and/or conduct contests between State Sessions. Although their responsibilities differ, all are expected to report their activities at the next State Session. The names of standing committee members are called during roll call and those present stand.

Section 15 of the By-Laws lists these Standing Committees: Agriculture, Budget, Community Service/Involvement, Deaf Awareness/Family Health, Division of Labor, Education, Grange Workers', Junior, Lecturer's, Legislative, Legislative Lobbying Team, Membership, Veterans, and Youth.

The By-Laws go on to say, "All Standing Committees except Budget, Division of Labor and Legislative Lobbying Team consist of at least six members, including the chairman, to be appointed by the State Master. One member shall be appointed from each of the five districts and the committee director to be from the state at large."

These committees are listed in the order they were initiated. Juniors, Youth, and Membership are standing committees but are covered in separate chapters.

LEGISLATIVE COMMITTEE

State Master William Cyrus appointed the first Legislative Committee in 1878. The committee's focus was on tariffs, transportation, assessment laws, efficient roads, completion of wagon roads across the Cascades, reduced interest rates, and the creation of a state bureau of agriculture. The committee was expected to work with legislators to write bills.

Between 1893 and 1930, delegates elected two members to the Legislative committee. One member was to be from east of the Cascades. The State Master chaired the committee. Regardless of who served on the committee, resolutions adopted by delegates at annual State Sessions determined their priorities.

Success was not always quick. In 1899 delegates passed a resolution to allow property taxes to be paid semi-annually. The committee got a bill introduced in the legislature. It finally passed in 1915.

Each new legislative session had fewer friends of agriculture. In 1921, 28 of the 90 legislators were farmers. By 1969 fewer than 25% of the legislators were farmers and the House Agriculture Committee had only one member who was a farmer. The Legislative Committee spent more time trying to kill legislation that would be harmful to agriculture than promoting legislation that would be beneficial.

By 1917 the committee was so active that the Commissioner of Labor made an office available to them. In 1931 the committee was assigned an information booth on the first floor of the Capitol for the convenience of Patrons. They also got seats at the press tables of both houses. In 1989 the State Grange rented an office in Salem during the legislative session. One of the reasons for moving the State Grange office to Salem was to be close to the legislature.

The State Grange established a research department in 1947. The organization was lucky to hire Ray Kell, a Harvard Law School graduate and BPA legal staff member, as part-time director. He was invaluable in gathering information and getting copies of bills passed or considered in other states. Today the website of the Portland law firm Kell, Alterman & Runstein, L.L.P. acknowledges their early Grange connection.

State Master McClure reported in 1960 that some Legislators were commuting from their homes, but Legislative Committee members could not do that. One committee member parked his motorhome in the closest park and walked to the Capitol and back each day from 1975 to 1984.

In addition to the committee's column in the *Grange Bulletin,* members issued a weekly Legislative Report during the legislative session. In 1985 the first Legislative Policy Handbook was published. Despite the availability of this information, State Master W. C. Harris expressed frustration that Granges did not know State Grange policy. Legislators contacted the state office because they received conflicting reports.

The 1995 Legislative Committee report made these points: "The Grange is a unique organization. No other group has an active presence in every county in Oregon." Members needed to use that influence. "We have the power to be heard without buying them gifts or paying for favors." Resolutions like the one in 1957 to exempt non-profit organizations from food licensing requirements were sent not only to every legislator but also to every candidate for the office.

The Legislative committee's report in 1975 included this statement, "The idea of grassroots involvement must, however, go beyond writing of resolutions and voting them either up or down in convention. Every Granger must be a committee of one to write letters when so advised supporting the Grange position on legislation matters."

During the January to June legislative session held in odd years, the State Legislative Committee usually held a Grange Day at the Capitol. Legislators and lobbyists from similar groups were featured speakers. Time was allocated to watch floor debate and visit the Senators and Representatives offices.

In 1998 the Legislative Committee introduced their strategic plan with a purpose, goals, calendar, and action plan. The purpose was to "advanced the interests of members and raise the profile of the Grange by influencing the law-making process in the community, the state, and the nation by carrying on the legislative tradition of the Grange." The next

Director reiterated the strategic plan with two additions. He proposed a CLOUT Experiment in which each Grange would send ten postcards per meeting. He was disappointed when only eight Granges participated and sent a total of 146 postcards.

In 2000 the Legislative Director stated, "You worked hard to draft a good resolution that could solve a problem, you worked hard to get it passed through the Subordinate and Pomona Granges and through State Session. SUCCESS! Now you can rest on your laurels, content in a job well done, right? WRONG! Contrary to most Granger's belief, there is no individual, committee, or resources to implement your resolution. If you're lucky, some other organization will submit an initiative or introduce legislation that corresponds to your resolution..."

In 1977 the Legislative Committee recommended hiring a full-time lobbyist. In 2004 a part-time lobbyist was hired.

Currently, the Legislative committee sponsors a monthly virtual internet meeting on petitions, measures, and bills the committee is following. They answer questions about resolution writing and the procedure for submitting resolutions to the State Grange. These virtual meetings are open to all members and typically attract 10 to 30 members.

Between 1894 and 1930 twenty-two Brothers were elected to the Legislative committee. The State Master chaired the committee. A. R. Shumway served 15 years.

Members	Grange	County	Years
W. O. Warren	Cold Springs #801	Umatilla	1894-95
H. E. Hayes	Tualatin #111	Clackamas	1894-98
Jacob Voorhees	Woodburn #79	Marion	1986-04
P. W. Haley	Highland #287	Polk	1998-00
J. W. Maxwell	Fairview #273	Tillamook	1898-00
W. M. Hilleary	Turner #18	Marion	1900-06
	Surprise #233		
Thomas Paulsen	Butte #148	Washington	1904-08

C. J. Quinn	Mayville #203	Gilliam	1906-08
A. I. Mason	Pine Grove #356	Hood River	1908-10
F. M. Gill	Garfield #317	Clackamas	1908-12
	Pinecrest #504s	Wasco	
C. D. Huffman	Blue Mountain #345	Union	1910-14
E. A. Bond	Irving #377	Lane	1912-16
M. M. Burtner	Ramsey Park #352	Wasco	1916-26
James A. Stewart	Butte Creek #224	Wheeler	1916-18
A. R. Shumway	Fork City #681	Umatilla	1916-31
R. W. Gill	Russellville #353	Multnomah	1918-20
H. C. Wheeler	Pleasant Hill #284	Lane	1920-22
			1926-28
A. J. French	Carlton #391	Yamhill	1922-24
J. D. Mickle		Washington	1924
R. V. Stockton	Sheridan #595	Yamhill	1925-26
L. F. Bailey	Missouri Flat #612	Baker	1928-30
M. S. Schrock	Milwaukie #268	Clackamas	1930-32

Since 1930 thirty-nine Brothers and five Sisters have served as Legislative chairmen, directors, or lobbyists. Jim Welsh was a lobbyist for 14 years and Clarence Carter was chairman for ten.

Chairman/Lobbyist	Grange	County	Years
Fred Tooze	Lents #351	Multnomah	1931
Morton Tompkins	McMinnville #31	Yamhill	1932-40
John W. Crow	White Eagle #683	Umatilla	1932-34
Vern Livesay	Plainview #624	Deschutes	1935 & 49
C. A. Schooling	Junction City #744	Lane	1936-42 & 53
Blanch Pickering	Pacific #413	Clatsop	1941-43
Elmer McClure	Harding #122	Clackamas	1941

			1973-74
Clarence Carter	Blue Mountain #345	Union	1943-53
William Howes	Gold Hill #534	Jackson	1947-48 1959
Earl Mason	Morning Star #311	Linn	1950-51
Olga Wilson	Friendly #897	Multnomah	1953-61
Peter de Laubenfels	Willamette #52	Benton	1955
Fred Adams	Ophir #767	Curry	1957
Henry Henrickson	Winona #271	Washington	1960-61 1974-76 1980-84
Clarence Brooks	Sixes #856	Curry	1962-65
Glenn Simmons	Sunset #941	Washington	1962
Earl Moore	Pine Grove #346	Hood River	1967-72
Bob Schmidt	Morning Star #311	Linn	1967-68
W. C. Harris	Elmira #523	Lane	1971-74 1984-88
George Stevens	Coquille #396	Coos	1975-84
Herbert Steiner	Beavercreek #276	Clackamas	1977-78
Victor Herrick	Greenacres #834	Coos	1978-79
William Taggert	Rogue River Valley #469	Josephine	1980-82
George Starr		Multnomah	1981-82
Thurman Smith	Santiam Valley #828	Linn	1983-92
Art Laubach	Natal #302	Columbia	1989-92
K. C. Van Natta	Natal #302	Columbia	1989-90
Eugene Lasater	Siletz Valley #558	Lincoln	1992-94
Ruby Ringsdorf	Irving #377	Lane	1993
Quintin Borba	Nestucca #503	Tillamook	1993
Tonya Rice	Roxy Ann #792	Jackson	1993

Ray Swinhart	Irving #377	Lane	1993-99 2001-02
Ben Boswell	Lostine #605	Wallowa	1996-98 2008-10
Joanne Van Natta	Natal #302	Columbia	1996-99
Jerry George	Gresham #170	Multnomah	1998-99
John Shank	Greenacres #834	Coos	1999-06
Jeff Van Natta	Natal #302	Columbia	2006-08
Jim Welsh	Elmira #523	Lane	2001-15
Roger Wilson	White Eagle #683	Umatilla	2010-12
Dean High	Midland #781	Klamath	2012-16
Ed Luttrell	Boring-Damascus #260	Clackamas	1998 2016
Mark Noah	Mohawk-McK-enzie #747	Lane	2016-24
Craig Loughridge	Clarkes #261	Clackamas	2017
John DeHaas	Springwater #263	Clackamas	2018-24

GRANGE WORKERS' ACTIVITIES COMMITTEE

The first Session committee on "Women's Work" was appointed in 1889. The committee reported "that as a rule, the Sisters are more prompt than the Brothers in attending Grange." Two years later the committee recommended that Granges observe Arbor Day, designate one meeting in June as Flora's Day, support the building of a Temple to Ceres in Washington, D. C., and devote one meeting a quarter to children so that Juvenile Granges could be organized.

In 1892 the committee wrote a resolution that women should be able to serve on school boards. They wrote another that the Legislature should give suffrage to women who were age 21 and over. Both were adopted.

In 1910 the Session committee recommended that the State Master appoint a three-member State Grange Women's Work Committee. He did and by the following Session, twenty Granges had established Women's Work Committees.

Women's Work was renamed Home Economics in 1919. HEC was used until 1968 when the name was changed to Committee on Women's Activities (CWA). In 1986 CWA was changed to Grange Women's Activities (GWA) to avoid confusion with Christian Women Clubs. Then to not discriminate against Brothers, in 2008 delegates voted to change GWA to Grange Workers' Activities.

Clubs: Oregon was the first Grange state to organize Home Economics Clubs. In the 1930s the State Home Economics Committee suggested By-Laws for clubs and compiled a handbook. Most clubs met once a month usually in members' homes. Husbands and school-aged children may have been included during summer meetings. Some clubs worked on sewing projects while they planned the next Grange fundraiser. In 1933, 317 of 330 Granges had clubs. In 1962, there were still 279 clubs (322 Granges) with 5,000 members.

The State Home Economics Committee's report in 1929 raised, but did not answer, a difficult question: "The money question so often causes discord: 'Who shall keep it?' Shall the HEC earn the money and the Grange spend it, without regard to the wishes of the HEC and the purpose they had in mind when earning the money?" The amount raised by clubs was not insignificant. In 1960 the State HEC chair estimated the amount to be over $60,000 a year.

Clubs were encouraged in the 1930s to plant trees around their hall in honor of the first National Grange Master William Saunders and post their Grange name on their hall. During World War II clubs purchased war bonds and stamps totaling over $10,000.

Contests: The first Home Economics Committee sponsored contest in 1931 was called an Efficiency Contest. Granges earned points for decorating their hall for each meeting, doing charity or community work, giving a report at each Grange meeting, and reporting to their district chairperson.

In 1940 the Amalgamated Sugar Company of Nyssa announced the Oregon Grange - White Satin Sugar Canning Contest. Over the next 29 years, thousands of members (women, men, and children) entered jars of home canned fruit, berries, and jelly. In 1956 there were 2,500 entries from every county in Oregon. The top prize in each division was a major electric appliance. Electricity reached farms in the 1940s so an electric refrigerator, range, or washing machine was a highly desired prize. Later top prizes were freezers, dryers, dishwashers, and TVs. Second through sixth place prizes were smaller appliances like radios, mixers, toasters, and coffee makers. During World War II all prizes were war bonds or sugar. County winners received sacks of sugar, a total of 10,800 pounds.

Winning entries in each county were sent to the State Grange office in Portland for judging by the food editors of the *Oregonian* and *Oregon Journal* and the director of the Oregon State College Extension Service.

Judging 2,500 canning contest entries took all day because the judges tasted every jar, something not always done by 4-H and county fair judges.

Between 1940 and 1980, the National Grange offered needlework and sewing contests. In 1966 Oregon won five prizes in the National needlework contest. But for years, Oregon struggled to reach its sewing quota. Finally in 1971, 847 entries exceeded the goal of 750, which meant the next year's goal increased. In 1978, Oregon had 1,965 entries. The following year delegates adopted a resolution opposing quotas for sewing and other CWA contests.

The purpose of some contests is to preserve traditional homemaking skills. In the 1960s the State HEC added contests for aprons, cookies, pillowcases, handicrafts, and quilts. In the 1970s they added beach and tote bags, tatting, dressed dolls, and stuffed toys. Doll and toy entries were donated after judging to Doernbecher Hospital, the Children's Farm Home, or the Ronald McDonald House. Bread baking contests were co-sponsored by the Oregon Wheat League and winners were awarded silver trays.

In the 1980s contests for quilt blocks, afghans, decorative centerpieces, woodworking, candy, and decorated sweatshirts were added. In the 1990s diabetic divisions were introduced along with baby quilts, embroidery, crochet, counted cross stitch, tole painting and creative recycling. In the 2000s muffins, pickles and relishes, hot dish covers, and potholders were new. Offering prize money, even $5 for 1st place, $4 for 2nd place, and $3 for 3rd place, became expensive. In 2005 the Director got members to sponsor contests and donate prize money.

Cookbooks: Compiling, publishing, and selling cookbooks raised lots of money. In 1940 the State Home Economics Committee requested recipes for its first cookbook. "Many more recipes came in than we could possibly use." That cookbook included recipes for mincemeat, head cheese, potato cake, salmon pie, and suet pudding. Five pages of recipes were for quantity cooking for 50 or 100 servings. That cookbook was revised in 1950.

In 1966 the HEC gathered cookie recipes and published a 70-page Cookie Book. Proceeds paid for a chair for the State Master's office, a paper cutter, and a $500 donation to the State Grange Headquarters debt retirement. Sales also funded a scholarship for a member majoring in home economics.

The National Grange Bicentennial Year Cookbook was published in 1976. Each State Grange was expected to sell copies. Oregon's CWA was recognized by National Grange for selling the most Bicentennial Cookbooks.

For the 125th anniversary of the Oregon State Grange in 1998, the GWA gathered recipes and printed another cookbook. The Director typed the recipes on her computer and saved the files to disc so that the book could be printed outside the state office. The process was more complicated than expected. But the first 200 copies sold in 30 minutes during the annual GWA Breakfast. Another 150 were sold before that Session ended and 1,000 were printed and sold by July 4. Proceeds from that cookbook went to the State Grange's debt retirement fund.

Donations: An HEC project in 1939 was to donate items to the National Grange Building in Washington, D. C. Oregon sent tea towels, dishes, and draperies. In 1948 Oregon clubs raised money to buy a chair for the conference room.

The HEC gave a Bible to each newly organized Juvenile Grange. They also supplied items needed for Grange Camp: An 18 cubic foot refrigerator-freezer, electric food mixer, electric roaster, large baking pans, 50 dessert dishes, a record player, and a duplicating machine.

Clubs donated over $25,000 to organizations that searched for a cure for muscular dystrophy, Parkinson's disease, and cancer. They sent money to CARE in a different South American country each year.

Clubs collected items to give to various agencies. For example, they gave handicraft supplies to the VA Hospital. They provided food, cleaning supplies, sheets, razors, hair dryers, toothbrushes, and shampoo to the Ronald McDonald House. In 1992 they filled seven large garbage bags with used pantyhose to be turned into pressure pillows for cancer patients.

Clubs made and donated 533 pillowcases to the New Horizons Boys Ranch in Bly, 186 baby blankets to a teen parent program, and 1,900 comfort pillows and turbans, 500 bibs, as well as lap robes and wheelchair bags to Home Away from Home who distributed them to nursing homes and veterans' hospitals. In 2005 they made quillows and donated them to

Oregon Foster Parents Association and gave 30 twin-sized quilts to Hurricane Katrina victims who relocated to Oregon.

Members collected glasses and cases for Eyes for the Needy. Used hearing aid batteries were recycled to raise money for other projects. The same with pull tabs from soda cans, which GWA has recycled since 1993. The proceeds have been donated to abused children, the National Kidney Association, and Make-A-Wish Foundation.

Scholarships: In 1931 delegates passed a resolution that each Grange donate $1 per year to the Spence Memorial Fund. In most Granges, the HEC fulfilled this promise, some donating more than a $1. Over the years, loans were made to members who needed financial help furthering their education. Unfortunately, the State Grange had trouble collecting repayments. In 1957, the $200 that remained in Spence Fund was given to the HEC to award a scholarship. They received 53 applications and drew the winner's name during their annual breakfast. This began an annual project of raising money for a $200 scholarship for one member in each of the six districts. There was so much anticipation during this drawing because at that time $200 nearly covered tuition for one term at a state school. In 1962 a seventh at-large scholarship winner was drawn.

Deaf Awareness: When the National Grange began a program for the deaf in the early 1970s, the CWA donated $1,200 to the fund. They also donated equipment to schools for the deaf, gave scholarships to members' children who had impairments, and donated $10,000 to Dogs for the Deaf. The CWA Director was not happy when a Deaf Activities Director was appointed. In 1985 the CWA Chairman announced in her report, "I am the Deaf Awareness Chairman."

Before a State Grange Membership committee was appointed, the Executive Committee turned over the membership gain contest to the HEC. Sisters had a history of performance, organizing contests, raising funds, feeding crowds, and showing up. When roll was called in Session each morning, every member of the committee was present. That was not true for other committees.

In 1971 the CWA hosted an officers and delegates reception after the church service on Sunday evening. That tradition continued until the Kickoff Banquet was instituted. In 1998 the GWA made aprons, pouches, and sashes for the 64 team members who exemplified the first four degrees as they were done in 1873.

Today, the GWA sponsors 80 contests for baked goods, candies, preserved foods, crafts, and textiles at State Session. In addition, members and non-members can enter the National Grange quilt block contest. Entries in Bailey's Good Dog Gift Package and Here Kitty Gift Bag are donated to the local Humane Society for dogs and felines awaiting adoption. The committee holds a luncheon and gives everyone who attends a door prize, which is most likely a bag of White Satin Sugar. GWA awards a $1,000 scholarship to a Grange member who has completed at least one year of college, business school, nurses training, or vocational education. Pull tabs are recycled and the money raised ($90 in 2021) is donated to a charity in the host district.

Thirty-six Sisters chaired this committee. Josie Cross and Irene Homolka served eight years and Eleanor Grant and Margaret Clute served seven.

Chairman/Director	Grange	County	Years
Orla Buxton	Gale #282	Washington	1910-15
Florence Dickenson	Oswego #175	Clackamas	1915-18
Ann Welling	Gresham #270	Multnomah	1918-19
Mrs. C. H. Bailey	South Deer Creek #440	Douglas	1919-22
Mary Jones	Hudson Bay #361	Umatilla	1922-28
Jessie Millar	Fairview #344	Multnomah	1928-30
Mrs. F. B. Harlow	Willakenzie #498	Lane	1930-32
Mrs. Chas. Hook	South Fork #605	Wallowa	1932-33
Mrs. G. A. Palmiter	Milwaukie #268	Clackamas	1934-35
Mary Lundell	Willows #672	Morrow	1936-38
Mrs. Kathryn Wilcox	Mosier #234	Wasco	1938-40

Inez Langdon	Chapman #788	Columbia	1940-42
Mrs. Mildred Norman	Deer Creek #371	Josephine	1942-44
Gladys Hinrichs	Rockford #501	Hood River	1944-46
Agnes Flint	Mt. View #429	Benton	1946-48
Ethel Lathrop	Central Point #698	Jackson	1948-50
Lucy Case Gruetzmacher	Mt. View #429	Benton	1950-52
Eva Stone	Fairview #344	Multnomah	1952-55
Pearl Dental	Maplewood #662	Clackamas	1956-60
Leona Krenz	Union Hill #728	Marion	1960-64
Josie Cross	Mud Springs #619	Jefferson	1964-72
Eleanor Grant	Poe Valley #710	Klamath	1972-79
Irene Homolka	Thurston #853	Lane	1980-88
Doris Reid	Columbia #867	Umatilla	1989-92
Betty Huff	Ada #570	West Coast	1992-98
Rosella Tooker	Macleay #293	Marion	1998-99
Debby Fawver	Siletz Valley #558	Lincoln	1999-00
Jean Beaver	Myrtle #289	Coos	2000-03
Sharon Wilson	North Douglas #936	Douglas	2003-04
Maxine Smith	Lacomb #907	Linn	2004-06
Beverly Doescher	Azalea #768	Douglas	2006-12
Mary Parrott	Parkdale #500	Hood River	2012-14
Margaret Clute	Forest Grove #282	Washington	2014-21
Joanne McBride	Hurricane Creek #608	Wallowa	2021-22
Rose Jacobs	Central #360	Lane	2022
Susan Noah	Mohawk-McKenzie #747	Lane	2022-24

AGRICULTURE COMMITTEE

In 1930 State Master George Palmiter appointed the Agriculture Committee. This may seem late, but the Oregon Department of Agriculture was not established until the following year. Palmiter's vision was for the Agriculture Committee to be a connecting link between Grange committees, the Extension Service, and the U. S. Department of Agriculture.

The committee got off to a strong start, holding conferences in 26 counties. As a result, many Granges created buy and sell lists: members listed on a blackboard or paper what they wanted to buy and what they had to sell. This activity led to connections and substantial savings. Other committees created marketing pools, developed weed, rodent, or predatory animal control programs, or sponsored 4-H or boys' and girls' clubs.

The State Grange began sponsoring the Future Farmers of America's Prepared Public Speaking contest in 1931. Most winners attend the State Grange Session and deliver their winning speech. Some topics have been the dilemma of cholesterol and how it affects agricultural products and practices, alternative fuels from waste products such as straw and manure, and non-dairy milks vs. animal milk.

State Master Allen Wheeler presents awards to FFA Prepared Public Speaking contest winners.

In 1950 the Agriculture Committee together with the Santiam Soil Conservation District held a Willamette Soil Conservation Field Day on a farm in Marion County. Speakers at their State Session Agricultural Conference in 1966 were the Presidents of the Oregon Farm Bureau, Oregon-Washington Farmers Union, and the Assistant Director of Agricultural Experiment Stations. The State Director of Agriculture, who had been a Grange member since 1927, spoke to the 1969 Session. He reported that only five percent of Oregon's population lived on a farm, but four in ten were employed by agriculture. He said milk was safer to drink than water, and pesticides were the farmer's best hired man.

Master Allen Wheeler urged members to tell the story of agriculture's importance and Granges to initiate a rural-urban activity to improve communication between farmers and consumers. The committee developed a pamphlet on Grange Agricultural policy.

In 1997 the committee served an Agricultural Awareness Lunch at the State Capitol for 250 legislators and their staff members. The purpose was to educate them on the small return the farmer receives for his products. A pamphlet compared the cost of the meal in a restaurant and the price of the ingredients in the supermarket with what a farmer would be paid.

The following year the committee had two booths at Ag Fest at the State Fairgrounds. One was for children with a computer to play the Farm City game. Children were given corn seed, tree seedlings, and balloons. The other booth, for parents, highlighted eleven Grange programs. Today the State Grange has a very popular booth with volunteers helping children transplant a tomato or marigold they can take home.

Agriculture Director Vernon Herrick holds a plant while this girl fills her pot with soil.

The popular State Session Ag Tour began in 1989. It was held on Wednesday afternoon while the state officers practiced the Sixth Degree. Since 2002 the tour has been on Saturday morning. A school bus transports participants to two or three sites that are unique to the host county.

The most popular Agriculture Conferences in recent years have dealt with wolves.

The committee has named an Agriculturalist of the Year from those nominated by their Grange. A garden design contest was new in 2023.

Twenty-nine Brothers and two Sisters served as Agriculture chairmen and directors. Fred Goff and Morton Tompkins served the longer, each serving for six years.

Chairman/Director	Grange	County	Years
Fred A. Goff	Melrose #434	Douglas	1930-36
Morton Tompkins	McMinnville #31	Yamhill	1936-42
Ralph Laird	Jasper #532	Lane	1942-45
O. W. Cutsforth	Lexington #726	Morrow	1946
Roy Perry	East Side #583	Lake	1946
Oscar Loe	Silverton Hills #743	Marion	1948-49
Robert Schmidt	Morning Star #311	Linn	1949-50

Oscar Peterson	Willows #672 Friendly #897	Morrow Multnomah	1950-55
Ralph Witcher	Junction City #744	Lane	1956-58
Earl Moore	Pine Grove #356	Hood River	1959-60
David Macpherson	Western Star #309	Linn	1961-62
Glenn Simmons	Sunset #941	Washington	1963-64
C. H. Brooks	Sixes #856	Curry	1965-67
Kay C. Van Natta	Fernhill #582	Columbia	1967-68
Allen Moore	Pine Grove #356	Hood River	1968-70
George Jenkins	Coquille #396	Coos	1971-76
Wayne Gilbert	Macleay #293	Marion	1976-80
Barton Clark	Rhea Creek #669	Morrow	1981-82
Ray Hughes	Mill Creek #590	Wasco	1983-84
Raymond Simms	Valley Falls #930	Lake	1984-88
Don Logan	Dixie Mountain #860	Washington	1988-89
Chris Rebmann	Scio #923	Linn	1989-92 2001-02
Gerald George	Cold Spring #801	Umatilla	1992-96
Don Sether	Molalla #310	Clackamas	1996-99
John Knox	Forest Grove #282	Washington	1999-01
Gerald Freeman	Oak Grove #198	Polk	2002-06
Vernon & Paula Herrick	Walterville #416	Lane	2006-10
John Fine	Evergreen #460	Douglas	2010-14
Jay Sexton	Marys River #685	Benton	2014-18
June Colony	South Fork #605	Wallowa	2018-24

EDUCATION COMMITTEE

A Session Education Committee was first appointed in 1880. Since then, the State Grange has had policy on school funding, consolidations, facilities, curriculum, and higher education.

The first standing State Education Committee was appointed in 1959. Their duty is to study issues pertaining to education and submit a report of recommendations at each State Session. The committee's initial report recommended that a State Board of Education be elected and that the Board appoint the Superintendent.

The committee has supported vocational education, the teaching of civics, and financial literacy. The committee urges Granges and members to support Agriculture in the Classroom, which uses agricultural-based content to teach science, social studies, language arts, and math.

Eleven Brothers and Eight Sisters have chaired the Education Committee. Victor Berger served a total of 11 years.

Chairman/Director	Grange	County	Years
Minnie McFarland	North Lincoln #861	Lincoln	1959-60
Eugene Fisher	Kellogg #811	Douglas	1961-62
Nadie Strayer		Baker	1963
Harold Densmore	Melrose #434	Douglas	1964-68
Cecil Kee	Shady Cove #931	Jackson	1969-70
Victor Berger	Olney #793	Clatsop	1971-78 1984-88
Dale Riddle	Crow #450	Lane	1978-80
Thurman & Olene Smith	Santiam Valley #828	Linn	1980-84
Carol Everman	Beaver Valley #306	Columbia	1988-96
John Fine	Evergreen #460	Douglas	1996-98
Judy Fitzgerald	Crooked River Ranch #955	Jefferson	1998-99
Robert & Irma Lee Smith	Woodburn #79	Marion	2001-02
Dan LeBrun	Eagle Creek #297	Clackamas	2002-04 2006-12
Roy Whitman		Yamhill	2004-06

Jane Netboy	Pleasant Valley #348	Multnomah	2010-12
Lyle Utt	Fairmount #252	Benton	2012-18 2022-24
Paula Herrick	Walterville #416	Lane	2018-22

PUBLIC POWER, UTILITIES, ENERGY COMMITTEE

From 1963 to 2014 the State Grange had a committee that was first named Public Power, then Power, then Utilities, and finally Energy. The committee's first report identified why the state of Washington had 22 Public Utility Districts and Oregon had only four. In Oregon a vote was required to establish a P.U.D. and another to raise revenue for it. That gave private power companies two chances to defeat a P.U.D.

The committee's primary purpose was to report their research. In the first five years committee members wrote and published 40 articles in the *Grange Bulletin*. Their State Session reports and conferences covered many forms of energy including nuclear, thermal, natural gas, methane, electric cars, and gasohol. They sponsored tours to the Ogden Martin Waste to Energy plant in Brooks and the methane gas plant at the Coffin Butte Landfill.

The committee wrote one resolution, recommended that members teach non-Grangers how to organize a P.U.D., and urged members to send an "avalanche of letters" in opposition to overturning the Preference Clause, which would have given private power companies equal access to BPA power.

Nine Brothers and one Sister chaired the committee. Walter Wells served 13 years. In 2014 delegates voted to remove the Energy Committee from the By-Laws.

Chairman/Director	Grange	County	Years
Walter Wells	Pine Grove #356	Hood River	1963-76
Charles Means	Warner #117	Clackamas	1976-78

Victor Berger	Olney #793	Clatsop	1978-84
Tom Alton	Friendly #897	Multnomah	1984-92
Bill Taggert	Fruitdale #379	Josephine	1992-96
Jim Gray	Willamette #52	Benton	1996-98
Ken Phillips	Illinois Valley #370	Josephine	1998-00
Joe Canaday	Crow #450	Lane	2000-06
Tom Surface	Columbia #867	Umatilla	2006-10
Carol Everman	Beaver Valley 306	Columbia	2010-14

DEAF AWARENESS AND FAMILY HEALTH COMMITTEE

A Deaf Activities Committee was appointed in 1983. However, the State Grange supported the hearing impaired long before. In 1981 Sue Dumolt served one year as Dogs for the Deaf Chairman.

In the early 1970s the National Grange began programs for the deaf. Oregon's Committee on Women's Activities (CWA) donated $1,200 to the National Grange Deaf Fund. CWA also donated to schools for the deaf. They collected and recycled 4,000 used hearing aid batteries. CWA had several speakers at their Session breakfasts, including an audiologist who spoke on integrating deaf children in classrooms rather than institutionalizing them.

In 1981 the State Master appointed a Dogs for the Deaf chairman. Dogs for the Deaf was a non-profit located in Jacksonville; today it is Dogs for Better Lives. One of their dogs demonstrated how he could be a "hearing ear" for those who needed help. The State Grange donated over $5,000 to the non-profit that year alone. Under the first Deaf Activities chairman, the State Grange donated $9,000 to the Applegate Behavior Center, which also had dogs that did demonstrations.

CWA did not really want to give up their deaf activities project, so the next two Deaf Awareness directors were also CWA directors. During those years the CWA bought and donated equipment to help children with hearing impairments and donated $10,000 to Dogs for the Deaf.

In 1992 Deaf Activities became a standard committee with a representative from each district. The committee supported the State Deaf School. A group of 21 toured the school and learned what resources could be loaned to Granges. They also recommended resources available from the National Grange, like Noisy World posters, the Pledge of Allegiance in sign language, a video, and slide show. They bought hearing aids and gave scholarships to deaf children whose parents were Grange members. They encouraged Granges to install or repair their sound system so that members could hear speakers during meetings.

A resolution on newborn hearing screening began at a Youth and Young Adult Conference workshop in 1997. Delegates adopted the resolution, and a House bill was written. Though the bill passed both houses of the Legislature, it was vetoed by the Governor.

Back to the drawing board. An Oregon Newborn Hearing Screening Advisory Committee, chaired by a doctor, was formed. The Governor attended an Awareness Day at the State Capitol. The State Grange Legislative director handed out postcards for delegates to send to their senators and representatives. Finally in 2000, the Governor signed the Newborn Hearing law. In Oregon, hospitals with more than 200 births per year are required by law to perform newborn hearing screenings within the first month of life. Nearly all smaller hospitals and many birthing centers voluntarily provide newborn hearing screenings as part of their standard of care.

As a result of this accomplishment, Oregon's Deaf Awareness Director was named to a National Grange Advisory Committee. The following year Oregon was recognized as a top five deaf activities state at National Grange. Newborn hearing testing became a national campaign.

In 2000 the committee's name was changed from Deaf Activities to Deaf Awareness. The committee donated $5,000 for a dog who was named Granger and $10,000 for a cochlear implant for a member.

In 2007 the committee's name was changed to add Family Health. Deaf Awareness and Family Health covers lots of topics. One Director made it personal and practical by explaining POLST (Physicians Orders for Life Sustaining Treatment) and recommending that conference attendees put a copy of the form along with other health information in an envelope on their refrigerator.

Thirteen Sisters chaired this committee. Tammie Phillips and Kitty Thomas each served six years.

Chairman/Director	Grange	County	Years
Sue Dumolt	Clarkes #261	Clackamas	1981
Doris Wallin	Warren #536	Columbia	1983-84
Irene Homolka	Thurston #853	Lane	1985-88
Doris Reid	Columbia #867	Umatilla	1989-90
Marjorie Miller	Pleasant Valley #537	Tillamook	1991-92
Ruth Steeprow	Lacomb #907	Linn	1992-00
Tammie Phillips	Illinois Valley #370	Josephine	2000-04 2010-12
Kitty Thomas	Milwaukie #268	Clackamas	2004-10
Iva May Van Noy	Mohawk-McKenzie #747	Lane	2012-16
Peggy Jillson	Irving #377	Lane	2016-18
Toni Hoyman	Marys River #685	Benton	2018-21
Lilly Anderson	Willamette #52	Benton	2012-24

COMMUNITY SERVICE COMMITTEE

Granges in Oregon engaged in many forms of community service long before a Community Service Committee was appointed in 1986.

In 1947 Sears Roebuck and the National Grange sponsored a community service contest. In 1958 4,600 Granges throughout the nation entered. Each state's winner was sent on to National Grange for judging. National winners were awarded a total of $60,000 in cash prizes. In 1960 State Master McClure boasted that Oregon's community service winners had placed in the top ten nationally five out of the previous six years. Vale #696 won first prize in the nation in 1960.

In recent years Granges have been encouraged to submit an Annual Community Service Report that records the numbers of hours worked, miles driven, and dollars donated. For example, 57 Granges in 21 counties sent in reports in 1989. Members in those Granges spent 13,393 hours working on projects, drove 6,260 miles, and donated $10,776. Ten years later the numbers increased to 62,564 hours worked, 128,210 miles driven, and $75,860 donated.

Later report forms were simplified to track only the number of hours members worked on Grange-sponsored projects and the number of hours non-members assisted. In 2020, 986 members worked 114,926 hours and 3,426 community members worked 33,821.

The Community Service chair in 1989 told delegates, "We need to establish in the minds of members of our communities that we are not an exclusive farm organization, but a community service organization that promotes the rural quality of life."

Granges are encouraged to make and enter a Community Service Yearbook that illustrates their projects. A yearbook can be a good membership recruiting tool because it shows graphically through photos, newspaper articles, thank you notes, and other documents what the Grange accomplished. Yearbooks are judged at State Session and the first-place winner is sent to National Grange for judging among entries from other states. In 2008 more than 30 Oregon Granges entered yearbooks. Today the top prize is $100 and bragging rights.

In 2001 the Community Service chair started the BOOK project. He ordered agriculturally oriented paperbacks from Scholastic Books. The books were appropriate for first graders. Some of the recipients had never had a book of their own. The first order was for 1,500 books. In four years, the BOOK project purchased 7,034 books that were given to 110 schools.

Since 2004 many Oregon Granges have participated in the Dictionary Project known as Words for Thirds. The first year 14 Granges participated. In 2012, 5,226 Dictionaries were ordered and distributed by Oregon Granges.

Third graders are excited to receive dictionaries from Grange members.

Beginning in 1987, the committee recognized a Volunteer of the Year and in some years identified runners up because there were so many outstanding entries. There are also community service awards for youth and Juniors. Granges are encouraged to nominate a firefighter, law enforcement officer, and teacher of the year in their community.

Nine Sisters and one Brother chaired this committee. Kendell Phillips served a total of nine years.

Chairman/Director	Grange	County	Years
Freda Wolverton	Columbia #867	Umatilla	1986-88
Ellie Aiken	Lookingglass #927	Douglas	1988-94
Genevieve Torgison	Stayton #340	Marion	1994-96
Nina Stables	The Sandy #392	Clackamas	1996-00
Kendell Phillips Kendell & Tammie Phillips	Illinois Valley #370	Josephine	2000-05 2008-12
Clarann Witty	Hurricane Creek #308	Wallowa	2005-08
Patricia Heard	Irving #377	Lane	2012-14

Eva Frost	Warren #536	Columbia	2014-18
Liz Dehne	Walterville #416	Lane	2018-24

VETERANS COMMITTEE

The Veterans Committee became official in 2011 when it was added to the State Grange By-Laws. Prior to that an ad hoc group met at the State Grange office monthly.

Since 2005, members have worn red, white, and blue on the day the State Grange pays tribute to Grange veterans. Each veteran is asked to stand when their service anthem is played. Juniors gave them small flags. In 2012 the Veterans committee set up a "Table of Remembrance."

Sergeant John, a Joys of Living assistance dog, was escorted to the Master's station in 2013 along with his handler. A Veterans Dinner and donations raised $800 for the organization.

On November 11, 2016, Grange members traveled to Albany to march in the Veterans Day Parade, which claims to be the largest west of the Mississippi.

Members of all ages march in the Veterans Day Parade.

The Veterans Committee distributes information to members who are veterans. At the 2018 session, the committee arranged a tour of the United States Coast Guard Astoria Air Station.

Many Granges make and distribute valentines at Veterans' hospitals. Each year the GWA (Grange Workers Activities) Committee sends handmade and donated pillowcases to troops stationed abroad or to a veterans' shelter in the host district. In 2021 more than 200 were sent.

In 2020 delegates passed a resolution to erect a monument on the State Capitol grounds recognizing the service and sacrifice of all Oregon veterans. That project is coming to fruition in time for the State Grange's 150th anniversary.

Four Brothers and one Sister chaired this committee. Jim Clute served five years.

Chairman/Director	Grange	County	Years
Rev. Robert Biggs	Russellville #353	Multnomah	2011
Mark Schnetzky	Tigard #148	Washington	2012-16
Jim Clute	Forest Grove #282	Washington	2016-21
Joanne & David McBride	Hurricane Creek #608	Wallowa	2022-24

INTERIM COMMITTEES

Special committees have been appointed to study a specific question or proposal and report to the delegates at the next State Session.

The first committee to function as an interim committee was appointed in 1876 to create a mutual life insurance company. Between 1882 and 1927 a committee was often appointed to visit the Oregon Agricultural College and report their observations.

OREGON AGRICULTURAL COLLEGE

B. L. Arnold, President of the Corvallis State Agricultural College, attended the 1879 State Session and according to the *Proceedings* "harangued the Grange most eloquently." However, soon after members had concerns about the college's teachings. In 1881 a committee appointed to investigate reported that instruction was failing to connect scientific with practical agriculture. Many graduates were not planning to become farmers. The committee proposed a cadetship in which students would return to the farm to apply what they learned.

In 1882 the State Grange began awarding a medal to the "most outstanding graduate in agriculture." The following year a chair of practical agriculture was created, and a former graduate hired.

The Master of the State Grange in 1886 became an ex-officio member of the Board of Regents along with the Governor, Secretary of State, and State Superintendent of Public Instruction. Clara Waldo, past State Grange Overseer and Lecturer, was the first woman appointed to the Board and served from 1905-1919. Waldo Hall, a graceful and ornate building on the OSU campus, is named after her.

In the 1890s the attitude toward the college changed completely. "There is no better place for our young men and women to be educated than this college." The State Lecturer urged Granges to hold a Farmers' Institute with speakers from the State Agricultural College. During the 1892 Session held in Albany, 225 patrons boarded an Oregon Pacific train to visit the Agricultural College farms. In 1895 the college graduated a class of 50, 13 of whom majored in Agriculture. One was future State Master Austin T. Buxton.

The 31st State Session in 1904 was held in Agricultural Hall. That November, when Oregon hosted the National Grange in Portland, State Master Leedy arranged for a special train to transport 250 delegates and visitors to Corvallis to show off Oregon's Agricultural College. The 1927 State Session was also held on the O.A.C. campus.

The State Grange benefited from its association with the college. Dr. McPherson helped the Legislative Committee prepare bills for the legislature. Lecturers' Schools were held on campus with Extension Service staff demonstrating games, songs, and activities. Extension Service agents were speakers for Agricultural Conferences. In the 1930s a Grange Lecturer's Hour was broadcast every Wednesday from September to spring via KOAC, the Agricultural College broadcast station.

Student Granges organized on campus were O.A.C. Students #611 in 1923, Corvallis Student #870 in 1937, and Mid Valley "O" #960 in 1999.

OAC became Oregon State College in 1937 and Oregon State University in 1961.

OTHER INTERIM COMMITTEES

- Since 1903, interim committees have been appointed periodically to review the By-Laws and propose updates to reflect current practice.
- In 1912 an interim committee investigated forming a cooperative loan association.
- Most interim committees studied an issue, but in 1940 the Farm Labor Committee negotiated a temporary resumption of work 44 hours after they were notified of a stoppage.
- After three hours of debate in 1943, a special committee on the "Japanese problem" was appointed to recommend State Grange policy on the return of Japanese Americans from relocation centers.
- An interim Session Program committee was authorized in 1949 to recommend ways to make Sessions more efficient and shorter.
- In 1950 an Insurance Committee was appointed to study the feasibility of the Oregon State Grange starting its own automobile insurance company.
- In 1952 a County and Local Government Interim Committee recommended that each Master appoint a special committee to report on administrative and taxing agencies such as school, fire, park, port, water, irrigation & drainage, P.U.D., cemetery, sanitary, county court, assessor, budget, relief, and juvenile delinquency agencies.
- An interim Tax Study Committee outlined the pros and cons of different types of taxes: Sales, corporate excise, income, property, personal property, timberland, severance, and natural resources. The committee collected information from other states. They also recommended investigating why the State Liquor Commission had less income in a time of increased consumption.
- In 1958 an interim Committee on Education opposed giving state aid to parochial schools, recommended merit pay for teachers, and the State Master appointing a standing Education committee.

- A Unicameral Legislature interim committee presented both sides of the question and left it to the delegates to decide.
- In 1959 the State Master recommended an interim committee study the feasibility of a Grange Retirement Village, in which individuals would own their own apartments and share eating and recreation facilities.
- The Life Membership Committee recommended taking a poll through the *Grange Bulletin* to determine interest and a fee structure.
- Similar interim committees reported on good roads, state loans, the Oregon retirement pension plan, and Juvenile Camp. Interim committees evaluated moving the State Grange offices from Portland to Salem, proposed that districts rather than counties host State Sessions, and have planned 150th anniversary celebrations.

COOPERATIVES AND AFFILIATE COMPANIES

Despite the rocky start with cooperative buying and selling, delegates agreed in 1876 with a resolution to incorporate the Grange Cooperative Association and canvas each county to sell shares in it. However, by the next Session fewer than 3,000 of the 4,500 shares had been sold. The Agent recommended that the agency be closed "at the earliest practicable moment."

County Councils fared better. In his 1884 Master's Address, R. P. Boise reported that the Linn County Council had increased its co-op business. Grange stores had been established in Josephine County, McMinnville, and Powell's Valley, all doing business in cash, not credit. The *Yamhill County Reporter* in 1900 carried an ad for McMinnville Grange and Farmers Company offering Japanese matting at cost, towels by the dozen, men's pants, shoes, and large sized hats.

A resolution passed in 1915 became the Oregon Cooperative Corporation Act. It recognized co-ops as distinct business entities organized "for the purpose of providing services and profits to its members and not for corporate profit." In 1929, State Master George Palmiter reported that there were 101 cooperative associations in Oregon.

The State Grange Co-operative Exchange was incorporated in 1920 with $5,000 capital stock and plans to sell another $25,000 shares at $10 each. It evolved from the Sherwood Cooperative Exchange for which State Overseer Charles Hays was the Purchasing Agent.

GRANGE SUPPLY COOPERATIVE

In 1934 delegates authorized the Executive Committee to enter into an agreement with the Washington State Grange to buy gasoline and oil and sell it only to members on a cooperative plan. Former State Master Palmiter was hired as a field representative to set up Grange Supply Cooperatives modeled after those in Washington. Palmiter established stations in Klamath Falls, Central Point, Redmond, Hood River, Roseburg, Clackamas, Marshfield in Coos County, and Enterprise in Wallowa County. The stores had a total membership of 870 and an investment in storage facilities and equipment of $12,500. The eight stores purchased 150,000 gallons of gas and fuel oil, and $5,000 worth of tires, batteries, auto accessories.

OREGON GRANGE WHOLESALE

The Oregon Grange Wholesale was established in Portland in 1938. A contract with the Massey-Harris Farm Machinery and Tractor Company resulted in $10,000 worth of machinery and parts being sold in a short period of time. Eight stations grew to eleven with plans for three more. The total number of gallons of gasoline sold was 397,000. The State Grange purchased three buildings at 12th and Salmon in East Portland to house Grange Wholesale and the office of the State Grange Secretary.

The following year, the Grange Wholesale Manager reported total volume grew to $250,000, with huge increases in sales of tires, fertilizer, and machinery. In addition, $10,000 worth of capital certificates at $10 each were sold.

During World War II, Grange Wholesale faced the challenges of rationing, limited supplies, and employees being drafted. However, gross sales continued to be higher each year. The mortgage on the wholesale building was paid off and construction started on a 100 x 200 two-story warehouse. Grange Wholesale ran full-page ads in the *Grange Bulletin*.

Local Grange Co-ops bought in bulk and sold to members at lower prices. Dividend checks shared profits with loyal customers.

After the war, Grange Wholesale opened several retail stores and began building a frozen locker plant and store in Umatilla County. The IRS limited the products that stores could stock to farm supplies and required that co-op dividends be paid at five-year intervals. Delegates approved a change in the membership requirement of cooperative stations to a minimum of 60% Grange members.

In 1948 delegates approved a feasibility study of opening cooperative food and clothing stores for members. The proposal received lots of newspaper coverage. However, the committee reported that "No appreciable savings could be made without a far greater volume than can be expected in a farm community."

In the 1950s the tide turned for Grange Wholesale. They canceled their contract with Massey-Harris when Wholesale was no longer an exclusive distributor in Oregon. By 1953 Wholesale no longer carried any farm machinery, which caused a serious financial loss. Their plan to build a two-story 25,000 square-foot frozen locker in Pendleton was stalled by cost overruns and lack of funds. Wholesale negotiated a bank loan underwritten by an insurance company to complete the project.

A newly hired Wholesale Manger proposed in 1953 having a Wholesale agent in each Grange who would try to order a carload of fertilizer, barbed wire, freezers (30 per car), feed and hay, or fence posts shipped by rail directly to the Grange, thus saving handling and other costs. Neither he nor his idea lasted long.

OREGON GRANGE SUPPLY

Oregon Grange Wholesale became Oregon Grange Supply on August 1, 1955. The primary reason for the change was to give the State Grange control over decision making. The same 35 locally owned and operated retail stores sold merchandise to individual members, and buying pools, each of which paid a membership of $250. The Supply sold $30,000 worth of capital certificates during the re-organization period. The State Grange also purchased the Wholesale building and rented it to Oregon Grange Supply. In the following ten months Oregon Grange Supply sold $900,000 worth of merchandise. The big money makers were Shell petroleum products and the Unico line of farm supplies.

The name changed from Supply back to Wholesale in 1957 when the co-op merged with those in Washington and later two other states. At its peak, Grange Wholesale had 64 stores. It was estimated that the cooperative saved farmers $14,000,000.

For Oregon's 100th anniversary, the State Grange sponsored a "Paint Up" program. Grange Supply provided paint at a low price so that Granges could improve the appearance of the exterior of their halls.

FARMERS UNION CENTRAL EXCHANGE

In 1971, Grange Cooperative Wholesale, with assets of $7,000,000, was sold to Farmers Union Central Exchange in St. Paul, Minnesota. CENEX had several oil wells and a refinery that produced 28,000 barrels a day. The Wholesale's six fertilizer plants and a feed mill became part of CENEX's operation. However, the local Grange supply stores remained independent, and Grange members continued to chair their boards of directors. CENEX sent a representative to State Sessions to present the State Grange with a check for 5% of net sales in Oregon. These checks ranged from $5,400 in 1973 to nearly $20,000 in 1978.

In 1992, CENEX provided a $5,000 grant to the Junior Camp. The camp director developed Camp Co-op with a store and bank to teach campers cooperative buying and selling. CENEX sponsorship of Junior Camp continued until 2003, but then camp was shortened because CENEX cut funds.

INSURANCE COMPANIES

A mutual insurance company is owned by its policyholders. Its sole purpose is to provide coverage for its members, who are given the right to elect its managers and board members. Mutual insurance companies make money by investing in stocks, bonds, or mutual funds. Profits are returned to members as dividends.

LOWER COLUMBIA FIRE RELIEF ASSOCIATION

The association began writing polices in August 1885. By the following State Session, the company had insured member's property valued at $400,000 with no losses. In 1923 the total value of policies in force was $3,500,000 million.

Three men who later became State Masters were early officers and directors of the association. B. G. Leedy served as its President, Jacob Voorhees as Secretary, and William Hilleary as a Director.

In 1932, the Fire Relief Association experienced a 30% increase in losses. The company was able to cover them without having to borrow money. In fact, net profit that year was $3,200. However, the State Master appointed an Interim Insurance Committee to recommend ways to reduce expenses and risks. Many commercial fire companies failed during this period so the fact that the company followed the committee's recommendations was noteworthy. In 1942 coverage in force exceeded $5,000,000. In 1951, Grange Mutual Fire Insurance had 1,000,000 policies issued to Oregon Grange members with premiums totaling $38,000.

GRANGE MUTUAL INSURANCE COMPANY

In December 1955 "Fire" was dropped from the company's name when it began broadening its coverage. GMIC added homeowner and farmowner liability insurance in 1976 and automobile insurance in 1988.

In 1959, the company suffered 92,616 losses, 61% of which were in unprotected areas. State Master Elmer McClure urged Granges to help form fire protection districts. The company helped three fire districts purchase new equipment and gave them five years to pay off the loan.

The company's biggest loss was due to the Columbus Day Storm in 1963. Unlike other companies, their policies did not have a $50 deductible. Their total loss was nearly $500,000. Grange Insurance Association loaned GMIC funds to deal with the crisis.

The company presented the State Grange with a check for ½ of 1% of earned premium income. They provided door prizes at State Sessions like an electric blanket, clock, or travel case. They gave clocks to Granges that added 15 new members.

In 2000 the company spent $80,000 on membership recruitment program, but it did not achieve the desired results. Due to GMIC's financial problems, the company dropped policyholders they consider to be high risk. Grange Mutual filed for bankruptcy in 2002. Oregon Grange membership dropped from 16,099 in 2002 to 9,754 in 2003.

PATRONS' LIFE INSURANCE ASSOCIATION

Patron's Life was organized on October 4, 1899. It also served Grange members in Washington and Idaho. In 1901 the amount the association paid upon the death of a member was limited to $250. Agents were paid a commission of 50 cents per policy. William Hilleary, B. G. Leedy, and C. E. Spence were board members of Patrons' Life.

FARMERS AUTOMOBILE INTER-INSURANCE EXCHANGE

The Exchange was organized in 1928 with $171,000 in assets. By 1941 its assets exceeded $6,000,000. Six Masters of State Granges in the territory served were on its board. At the 1948 Session, State Master Morton Tompkins reported that "Despite an increased accident rate and increased costs, the Farmers Auto Insurance has been able to continue its policy of offering lower rates to its membership." However, he also noted that the State Grange was the only farm organization in Oregon that did not offer to its members auto and casualty insurance written by its own company. He appointed an Interim Insurance Company to study this issue. The Committee concluded that it would cost over $140,000 for the State Grange to start its own auto insurance company.

GRANGE INSURANCE ASSOCIATION

The Washington State Grange formed Grange Insurance Association for its members and was invited to write automobile policies for Oregon members.

In 1953, GIA had 1,800 policies in Oregon. The following year, the company experienced a "highly unsatisfactory" loss ratio in Oregon, but that was true of all leading automobile insurance companies. In 1956, GIA premiums for Oregon members exceeded $400,000. For the first time the company paid a dividend to those who had held coverage since 1950.

In his 1956 Good of the Order Address, State Master Elmer McClure reported that GIA insured 13,000 Oregon members. The company gave 7,777 pins to new members, to those who brought in five or more new members, and to those who attended 20 or more meetings.

GIA contributed $500 in 1959 to the "Paint Up" program the State Grange sponsored for Oregon's Centennial. When the State Grange purchased a larger headquarters building in Portland in 1961, GIA loaned the organization $150,000. After the Columbus Day Storm in 1963, GIA gave Grange Mutual Insurance a rescue loan to cover its 1,100 claims.

Oregon premiums in 1967 exceeded $1,000,000. The following year, premiums increased 14.7% but losses were up 64%. 1970 was the first year GIA missed paying a dividend, but it upheld its agreement to pay the State Grange five cents per member.

When Oregon's no fault insurance law went into effect in 1974, GIA's loss ratio was 125%. The average cost of each of the 35,000 claims was $341.

Delegates in 1965 voted that GIA and Grange Mutual Insurance should consider consolidation. But when GIA proposed a merger in 1981, it was rejected. A conflict dragged on for several years. Meanwhile premiums increased causing some to find cheaper coverage with another company and drop their Grange membership.

Delegates to the 2015 State Session became irate when they learned that GIA would no longer insure Grange halls. Apparently, GIA thought Granges knew of this business decision when most did not.

Today some Oregon members still have GIA coverage. The company awards scholarships to policyholder's children. It pays the Oregon State Grange $1 per member. Since 1987 GIA has covered the expenses for a free Benefits Breakfast held during Session and provides money for State Session door prizes.

GRANGE MUTUAL LIFE

Grange Mutual Life of Nampa, Idaho was founded in 1934 and became licensed to sell policies in Oregon in 1944. The company hired its first Oregon agent in 1947. In the 1950s the company introduced accident, hospital, surgery, and polio policies. They even offered a policy to insure a member's insurability, regardless of age, health, or occupation.

The company made loans to Granges for the renovation, repair, and construction of halls. In 1960, the company paid the Outstanding Young Granger's expenses to State Session and the first-year's premium on a $2,500 life insurance policy. Each year the company presented the State Grange with a check for 1% of the income from policies written for Oregon members.

Grange Mutual Life reported in 1957 that their mortality rate was 32.25%, which meant that fewer than one-third of their insured passed in the previous year. The rate for most companies was 50%. In the 1960s and 1970s, sales increased steadily. However, costs for accident and health claims spiraled, forcing premium increases. The company had its best year in 1972. In 1975 its total assets were $26.5 million. The following year they closed their branch offices and hired Personal Producing Agents and Brokers, who were already licensed by other companies.

Grange Mutual Life became United Heritage Life Insurance Company and United Heritage Property and Casualty. It has offices in Meridian, Idaho. Policyholders do not need to be Grange members.

EPILOGUE

Bill and Mary joined their Community Grange long ago, back when they took their three kids to the Grange hall for the Christmas party. The kids really liked the Santa and the popcorn balls members gave out. With the farm, their jobs, and the kids, Bill and Mary didn't go to Grange meetings or get involved in activities.

Now the two older kids have moved away for jobs and started their own families. They visit a few times a year. Jamie, their youngest son, is taking over the farm. He is growing organic vegetables and selling them through a CSA. He's doing surprisingly well. He got involved in the Grange through the family plan. Until he was 23 years of age, his dues were covered by Bill and Mary's. Jamie was elected to an office. His wife, who's a city girl, is really into baking from scratch, canning, and quilting. She plans to enter some of the State GWA contests at the next State Session.

Bill retired and Mary has cut back her hours so when they were asked to help with a dinner, they were happy to volunteer. They had so much fun that night. The event raised lots of money for the Grange. Soon they were helping with other projects.

Mary had lots of ideas for what the Grange could be doing in the community. She suggested a recycling project, stuff that the garbage company won't take but various groups can use. Why not adopt a needy family at Christmas; give them gifts, help them decorate, and show that their neighbors care? How about putting in a booth at the county fair to show what this Grange is doing? If they spruced up the hall and grounds, they could rent it more often.

All these ideas led to Mary being elected Grange President. She appointed committees and organized a work party. At first Edna, the oldest member, was quite critical. “This is not the way we’ve always done things in this Grange.” Then Mary couldn’t believe it, but Dick made a motion that the Grange close or consolidate with another. He said that when Edna passes, this Grange will not go on. So why bother. Fortunately, his motion was voted down.

Several of the new renters became members. So did some who came to hear talks on gardening. Attendance at meetings picked up. Edna’s attitude improved. She liked what she saw happening.

The life of this hypothetic Grange continues. Sometimes the children or grandchildren of members step up and carry on. Other times an existing member who hasn’t contributed much realizes what the loss of a Grange would mean to their community. And sometimes it’s a community member who sees potential that others have lost sight of.

It isn’t possible to predict how long the Grange will continue in Oregon. But its purpose, aims, and structure have withstood the test of time.

APPENDIX: SUBORDINATE/ COMMUNITY GRANGES

Between 1872 and 2000, 962 Granges were organized in Oregon. Thirty five did not survive a full year. However, 22 remained active for 100 or more years.

This list shows the year Granges were organized and when they were declared dormant, surrendered their Charter, or consolidated with another Grange. The 163 Granges that are currently active are bolded. Some of them have been reorganized. For example, Eagle Valley #656 has been active continuously since 1925 while Elkhorn #908 became dormant sometime after 1945 and was reorganized in 2010.

Some names are listed more than once with different numbers, like Pine Valley. These two Granges may or may not have met in the same hall or community.

Grange	Organized	Dormant	Reorganized
Baker County			
Baker City #152	1874	1886	
Dixie #843	1936	1963	

Durkee #653	1924	2005	
Durkee Progressive #519	1914	1917	
Eagle Valley #656	**1925**		
Eldorado #153	1874	1879	
Elkhorn #908	**1945**		**2010**
Hereford #665	1925	1960	
Keating #823	1935	2005	
Mahogany #188	1876	?	
McEwen #651	1924	1951	
Missouri Flat #612	**1923**		**2007**
Muddy Creek #648	1924	1928	
New Bridge #789	**1931**		
Pine Valley #452	1911	1930	
Pine Valley #815	**1934**		
Pleasant View #517	1914	1925	
Powder River #169	1974	1976-77	
Richland #491	1912	1915	
Sparta #763	1930	1934	
Sparta #764	1934	1954	
Stewart #805	1932	1946	
The Home #904	1944	1951	
Unity #660	1925	1997	
Wingville #150	1874	1888	
Wingville # 850	1924	2004	

Benton County

Alsea #77	1874	1876-77	
Bellfountain #277	1896	1914	
Corvallis #242	1890	1922	

Corvallis Student #870	1937	1942	
Fairmount #252	**1891**		
Hope #269	**1894**		
King's Valley #66	1874	1892	
Kings Valley #278	1896	1904	
Laurel #69	1874	1876-77	
Luckimute #643	1924	1942	
Marys River #549	1916	1919	
Marys River #685	**1927**		
Mid Valley "O" #960	1999	2002	
Monroe #239	1890	1893	
Mountain View #429	1910	1989	
O. A. C. Students #611	1923	1942	
Orleans #50	1874	1876-77	
Philomath #13	1873	1893	
Soap Creek #14	1873	1902	
South Benton #756	1930	1969	
Summit #432	**1910**		**1920**
Toledo #168	1874	1876-77	
Union #154	1874	1876-77	
Willamette #52	**1874**		

Clackamas County

Abernethy #346	**1904**		
Bakers Bridge #552	1916	1920	
Barlow #262	1893	1898	
Beavercreek #115	1874	1877	
Beavercreek #276	**1895**		
Boise #256	1892	1896	

Boring-Damascus #260	**1893**		**1901**
Brightwood #869	1937	1940	
Brightwood #926	1948	1974	
Butte Creek #82	1874	1904	
Canby #135	1874	1876-77	
Carver Mt #961	2000	2009	
Cascade #120	1874	1878	
Central #276	1895		
Clackamas #298	1901	1914	
Clarkes #261	**1893**		**1926**
Colton Foothills #831	1935	2014	
Damascus #41	1874	1874	
Damascus #260	1893		
Eagle Creek #2	1873	1877	
Eagle Creek #297	**1901**		
Electric #336	1903	1905	
Elliott #514	1914	1916	
Excelsior #16	1973	1876-77	
Frogpond #111	**1874**		
Garfield #317	**1902**		
George #622	1924	1949	
Harding #122	**1874**		**1886**
Highland #70	1874	1876-77	
Highland #261	1893	1921	
Highland #875	1937	2005	
Highland Grove #136	1874	1879	
Holcomb-Outlook #833	1873	1999	
Ladd Hill #757	1930	1956	
Maple Lane 296	1901	1966	
Maplewood #662	**1925**		

Marquam #850	1936	1941	
Marshfield #1	1872	1984	
Milwaukie #200	1885	1887	
Milwaukie #268	**1894**		
Molalla #40	1873	2006	
Molalla #310	**1902**		
Monitor #716	1929	1950	
Mountain View #142	1874	1878	
Mount Zion #121	1874	1893	
Mulino #40	1873	2006	
Necanicum #565	1917	1919	
Needy #81	1874	1876-77	
Oregon Pioneer #1	1938	1972	
Oswego #175	1874	1974	
Redland #796	**1931**		
Rosemont #838	1935	2001	
Spring Water #108	1874	1876-77	
Springwater #263	**1893**		
Sunflower #333	1903	1907	
Sunnyside #842	**1936**		
Teasel Creek #255	1891	1899	
The Sandy #392	**1909**		
Tualatin #111	1874		
Twentieth Century #341	1903	1920	
Upper Molalla #83	1874	1877	
Viola #185	1875	1878	
Warner #117	**1874**		**1882**
Willamette #888	1939	1985	
Wilsonville #600	1922	1934	

Clatsop County

Brownsmead #822	**1934**	
Clatsop #156	1874	1877
Elsie #430	1910	1913
Jewell #431	1910	1914
Jewell #876	1937	2003
Knappa #382	1908	1914
Logan #412	1910	1919
Necanicum #806	1932	1984
Nehalem Valley #804	1932	1972
Netel #410	**1910**	
Olney #793	**1931**	
Pacific #413	**1910**	
Walluski #566	1917	1935
Wickiup #722	**1929**	
Young's River #172	1874	1887

Columbia County

Armstrong #456	1911	1923
Beaver Homes #518	**1914**	
Beaver Valley #186	1875	
Beaver Valley #306	**1901**	
Canaan #871	1937	1954
Cedar Grove #320	1902	1918
Chapman #788	1931	2001
Clatskanie #182	1875	1876-77
Clatskanie #321	1902	1994
Columbia City #177	1875	1877

Deer Island #334	1903	1937	
Deer Island #947	**1980**		
Everart #572	1918	1919	
Fern Hill #592	**1920**		
Fishhawk #337	1903	1904	
Goble #329	1903	1923	
Marshland #901	1944	2002	
Mayger #332	1903	1905	
Milton #322	1902	1907	
Natal #302	**1901**		
North Union #176	1874	1876-77	
Quincy #327	**1903**		
Rainier #326	1903	1905	
Scappoose #144	1874	1876-77	
Scappoose #303	1901	1911	
South Scappoose #844	1936	1988	
Vail #294	1901	1912	
Vernonia #305	**1901**		
Warren #536	**1915**		**1926**
Winema #652	1924	1970	
Yankton #301	**1901**		

Coos County

Allegany #762	1930	1937	
Arago #288	1898	1900	
Arago #580	1919	1926	
Bandon #398	1909	1917	
Bandon #702	**1928**		**2014**
Bridge #730	**1929**		

Broadbent #729	1929	2004
Catching Inlet #690	1927	1942
Coos Bay #397	1909	1915
Coos River #45	1874	1876-77
Coos River #701	1928	1942
Coquille #290	1898	1899
Coquille #396	1909	1993
Coquille City #167	1874	1876-77
Fairview #739	1929	1965
Gravel Ford #304	1901	1914
Gravelford #859	1936	1942
Greendell #834	1935	1954
Greenacres #834	1954	2022
Hall's Prairie #164	1874	1880
Lakeside #589	1920	1922
Laurel #180	1875	1878
Maple #171	1874	1876-77
McKinley #582	1919	2002
Myrtle #289	1898	2016
North Bayside #691	**1927**	
North Coquille #173	1874	1976-77
Remote #318	1902	1905
Sumner #865	1936	1988
Willowdale #319	1902	1904

Crook County

Culver #486	1912	1914
Grandview #485	1912	1913
Grizzle Butte #640	1924	1948

Held #636	1924	1933	
Lamonta #483	1912	1914	
Lone Pine #803	1932	1946	
Lookout Mt #741	1929	2016	
Ochoco #635	1924	1957	
Pickle Island #384	1908	1912	
Post #638	1924	1952	
Powell Butte #383	1908	1912	
Powell Butte #629	1924	2001	
Prineville #404	1909	1912	
Suplee #732	1929	1961	

Curry County

Arch Rock #849	1936	1941	
Chetco #765	**1930**		
Flora #299	1901	1901	
Flora's Creek #191	1882		
Lower Rogue #768	1930	1934	
Most Western #711	1928	1937	
Ophir #767	1930	2020	
Rogue River #190	1881	1887	
Sixes #856	**1936**		**2006**
Westmost #711	1928	1937	
Westmost #884	1938	1970	

Deschutes County

Alfalfa #678	1926	1964	
Cloverdale #623	1924	1938	
Eastern Star #482	1912	2009	

High Desert #482	1912	2018	
Little Deschutes #939	**1954**		
Pine Forest #632	**1924**		
Plain View #624	1924	1958	
Pleasant Ridge #630	1924	1941	
Redmond #812	**1933**		
Terrebonne #663	**1925**		
Tumalo #631	1924	1973	

Doug

Ash Valley #957	1995	2008	
Azalea #448	1911	1917	
Azalea #786	**1931**		
Brockway #461	1911	1913	
Camas Valley #300	1901	1903	
Camas Valley #521	**1914**		**1932**
Canyonville #109	1874	1891	
Cleveland #435	1910	1916	
Coles Valley #248	1890	1892	
Coles Valley #439	1911	1915	
Coles Valley #727	1929	1936	
Cow Creek Valley #187	1875	1878	
Days Creek #467	1911	1913	
Drain #458	1911	1942	
Edenbower #509	1914	1916	
Elk Creek #458	1911	1942	
Elk Head #887	1939	1960	
Elkhorn #149	1874	1877	
Evergreen #460	1911	2016	

Fair Oaks #684	1927	2012	
Fred Wetherly #852	1936	1990	
Garden Valley #487	1912	1916	
Glendale #530	1915	1924	
Glide #462	1911	1957	
Gunter #919	1947	1975	
Hayhurst #902	1944	1948	
Kellogg #466	1911	1916	
Kellogg #811	**1933**		
Lookingglass #927	**1949**		
Loon Lake #721	1929	1966	
Lower Umpqua #858	1936	1939	
Melrose #434	1910	2011	
Mount Scott #151	1874	1876-77	
Mowitza #457	1911	1917	
Myrtle #59	1874	1892	
Myrtle #557	1917	1920	
Myrtle Creek #442	**1911**		**1938**
Nonpareil #889	1939	1943	
North Douglas #890	1939	1941	
North Douglas #936	1953	2004	
North Umpqua #949	1988	1994	
Oak Creek #473	1911	1913	
Oakland #86	1874	1876-77	
Oakland #724	1929		
Olalla #913	1946	1948	
Pass Creek #573	1918	1920	
Progressive #480	1912	1919	
Rescue #420	1910	1944	
Rice Valley #905	1944	1944	

Riddle #715	1929	1957	
Riversdale #731	**1929**		
Roseburg #59	1980	1992	
Smith River #585	**1920**		
South Deer Creek #440	1911	1992	
South Umpqua #777	1931	1940	
South Umpqua #914	1946	1963	
Sunnydale #877	**1938**		
Sutherlin #527	1915	1916	
Sutherlin Comm #724	**1929**		**1930**
Tenmile #749	1930	1940	
Umpqua #28	1873	1878	
Umpqua Valley #852	1936	1990	
Union No 2 #51	1874	1881	
Wilbur #114	1874	1876-77	
Wilbur #447	1911	1936	
Winchester Bay #906	1944	2011	
Winston #559	1917	1919	
Yoncalla #78	1874	1893	
Yoncalla #451	1911	1912	
Yoncalla #529	1915	1920	

Gilliam County

Blalock #205	1887	1891
Buckhorn #479	1912	1934
Butte Creek #224	1889	1894
Condon #225	1889	1894
Condon #446	1911	1918
Cottonwood #618	1923	1926
Ida #217	1889	1890

Igo #315	1902	1970
Juniper #444	1911	1912
Kohler #599	1921	1925
Lonerock #251	1890	1895
Lonerock #449	1910	1918
Lonerock #740	1929	1963
Mayville #203	1887	1912
Mikkalo #704	1928	1989
Shuttler Flat #209	1888	1890
Snowshoe #257	1892	1894
Willows #672	1926	2011

Grant County

Canyon City #161	1874	1891
Daniel Clark #162	1874	1890
Fern Creek #607	1922	1930
Fox Valley #614	1923	1943
Hamilton #616	1923	1928
Kemberly #627	1924	1927
Long Creek #615	1923	1927
Long Creek #836	1935	1940
Monument #617	1923	1926
Monument #742	1929	2004
Mount Vernon #163	1874	1878
Mount Vernon #659	**1925**	
North Fork #604	1922	1930
Ritter #626	1924	1962
Rosebud #735	1929	1965
Silvies #787	1931	1947
South Fork #761	1930	1936

Strawberry #661	1925	2016

Harney County

Crane Creek #874	1937	1947
Crow Camp #494	1913	1916
Diamond #750	1930	1936
Drewsey #507	1914	1915
Drewsey #738	1929	1993
French Glen #774	1931	1931
Poison Creek #776	1931	2004
Ryegrass #463	1911	1931
Silber Creek #499	1913	1919
Sunset #472	1911	1916
Valley View #459	1911	1916
Van #510	1914	1915
Waverly #468	1911	1914

Hood River County

Dee #553	1916	1919
East Hood River #250	1890	1892
Odell #508	1914	1961
Parkdale #500	**1913**	
Pine Grove #356	**1905**	
Rockford #501	**1913**	

Jackson County

Agate #525	1915	1919
Applegate #138	1874	1876-77

Applegate #488	1912	1913	
Ashland #87	1874	1876-77	
Bellview #759	**1930**		
Butte Falls #928	1949	1973	
Central Point #124	1874	1876-77	
Central Point #373	1907	1911	
Central Point #698	**1928**		
Eagle Point #123	1874	1876-77	
Eagle Point #664	**1925**		
Enterprise #489	**1912**		
Forty-Nine #700	1928	1943	
Gold Hill #534	1915	2013	
Griffin Creek #848	1936	2010	
Harmony Point #137	1874	1891	
Jacksonville #88	1874	1891	
Jacksonville #700	1928	1943	
Lake Creek #541	1915	1918	
Lake Creek #697	**1928**	**1925**	
Live Oak #655			
Phoenix #104	1874	1876-77	
Phoenix #779	**1931**		
Roxy Ann #646	1924	1928	
Roxy Ann #792	**1931**		**2017**
Sams Valley #113	1874	1891	
Sams Valley #666	1925	1992	
Shady Cove #931	1950	1999	
Talent #699	1928	1952	
Upper Applegate #839	1935	2012	
Upper Rogue #825			
Valley View #564	**1935**	1917	

Wagner #240	1890	1910	
Willow Spring #477	1912	1918	

Jefferson County

Ash Butte #802	**1932**		
Black Butte #620	1923	1937	
Blizzard Ridge #555	1916	1918	
Crooked River Ranch #955	1993	2010	
Gateway #548	1916	1918	
Gateway #932	1951	1954	
Haystack #495	1913	2004	
Lower Bridge #544	1916	1918	
Mud Springs #619	1923	2007	
Opal City #495	1913	2004	
Opal City #925	1948	1950	
Paulina #734	1929	1957	

Josephine County

Applegate Valley #839	2011	2017	
Deer Creek #371	**1907**		
Dimmick #376	1908	1911	
Fruitdale #379	**1908**		
Grave Creek #782	1931	1941	
Illinois Valley #370	**1907**		**1930**
Josephine #179	1874	1888	
Kerbyville #178	1875	1876-77	
Merlin #471	1911	1931	
Merlin #933	1952	1982	

Missouri Flat #857	1936	1942	
Monument #241	1890	1892	
Morris Hill #385	1908	1910	
Mt. Saxton #945	1963	1969	
Mt. Sexton #484	1912	1924	
Murphy #470	1911	1919	
Murphy #790	1931	1934	
North Pacific #911	**1945**		
Provolt #912	1946	2004	
Redwood #760	**1930**		**2022**
Rogue River Valley #459	1911	2013	
Shan Creek #794	1950	1990	
Sunny Valley #916	**1946**		
Unity #474	1911	1914	
Washington #181	1875	1892	
Wilderville #372	1907	1913	
Williams #399	**1909**		**1917**

Klamath County

Agency Lake #944	1963	1966
Altamont #873	1937	1943
Beatty #736	1929	1931
Bly #771	1931	1967
Bonanza #772	1931	1941
Fort Klamath #775	1931	1962
Four Leaf Clover #405	1909	1911
Henley #708	1928	1960
Hildebrand #706	1928	1944
Keno #719	1929	1934

Klamath Falls #402	1909	1912	
Langell Valley#709	1928	1933	
Langell Valley #883	1938	1942	
Langell Valley #915	1946	1957	
Lost River #846	1936	1999	
Malin #707	1928	1963	
Merrill #403	1909	1912	
Merrill #717	1929	1969	
Midland #781	**1931**		
New Bly #958	1996	2003	
Poe Valley #710	1928	1995	
Shasta View #830	1935	2006	
Williamson River #714	1928	1940	
Winema #948	1980	2000	

Lake County

Alpha #571	1918	1922	
Dry Creek #593	1920	1924	
East Side #583	1919	2002	
Fort Rock #758	**1930**		
Hot Springs #183	1875	1881	
Summer Lake #754	1930	1966	
Thomas Creek #581	**1919**		**1927**
Valley Falls #930	1950	2002	
Vernon #481	1919	1926	
Warner Valley #712	1915	1935	
Westside #598	1921	1926	
Westside #854	**1936**		

Lane County

Ada #570	**1917**		
Alvadore #538	1915	2002	
Central #360	**1906**		**1930**
Charity #76	1874	1894	
Chesher #236	1890	1891	
Coast Fork #243	1890	1913	
Cottage Grove #75	1874	1876-77	
Cottage Grove #443	1911	1913	
Coburg West Point #535	**1915**		
Coyote #55	1874	1876-77	
Creston #548	1913	1918	
Creswell #64	1874	1882	
Creswell #496	**1913**		
Crow #450	**1911**		**1921**
Deadwood #602	1922	1930	
Deer Horn #567	1917	1919	
Dorena #835	**1935**		
Elmira #523	**1915**		
Eugene City #56	1874	1876-77	
Fall Creek #146	1874	1876-77	
Fir #316	1902	1905	
Fir Butte #118	1874	1876-77	
Four Oaks #528	1915	2010	
Franklin #155	1874	1899	
Franklin #478	1912	1919	
Franklin #751	1930	2006	
Glenada #594	1920	1932	

Goldson #868	**1936**		
Goshen #101	1874	1894	
Goshen #561	**1917**		
Grand Prairie #26	1873	1899	
Hayes #266	1893	1895	
Hebron #845	1936	2001	
High Prairie #943	1962	1970	
Indian Creek #569	1918	1924	
Irving #377	**1908**		
Jasper #532	**1915**		**1932**
Junction City #43	1874	1876-77	
Junction City #433	1910	1925	
Junction City #744	**1930**		
London #937	**1954**		
Long Tom #688	**1936**		
Lorane #54	**1874**		
Lowell #531	1915	1919	
Lowell #745	**1930**		
Lynx Hollow #291	1898	1899	
Main River #550	1916	1966	
Maple Creek #551	1916	1950	
Mapleton #584	**1920**		
McKenzie #107	1874	1876-77	
McKenzie River #878	1938	1943	
Mohawk #147	1874	1895	
Mohawk #411	1910	1924	
Mohawk Valley #922	**1948**		
Mohawk-McKenzie #747	**1930**		
Mount Holly #204	1887	1893	
North Fork #492	1912	2011	

Oakridge #900	1941	1942	
Oakridge #952	1992	1999	
Pleasant Grove #139	1874	1876-77	
Pleasant Hill #65	1874	1878	
Pleasant Hill #284	1897	1915	
Royale #265	1893	1898	
Santa Clara #542	1916	1922	
Santa Clara #746	**1930**		
Silk Creek #880	1938	1940	
Siuslaw #54	1973		
Siuslaw #694	1924	1932	
Spencer's Butte #126	1874	1880	
Spencer Creek #365	1907	1911	
Spencer Creek #855	**1936**		
Springfield #12	1873	1888	
Springfield #378	1908	1925	
Thurston #308	1902	1903	
Thurston #853	**1936**		
Trent #539	1915	1919	
Triangle #533	**1915**		
Union #47	1874	1889	
Walterville #416	**1910**		**1932**
Walton #238	1890	1891	
White Oaks #531	1915	1919	
Willakenzie #498	1913	2010	

Lincoln County

Bay View #862	1936	1942
Big Elk #506		
Big Elk #560	1933	1979

Big Elk #954	1993	1994	
Eddyville #428	1910	1925	
Elk City #515	1914	2004	
Five Rivers #423	1910	1927	
Lincoln #395	1909	1998	
Mt. Dell #424	1910	1951	
Nashville #903	1944	1958	
North Lincoln #861	1936	2012	
Reed Creek #851	1936	1962	
Salmon River #516	**1914**		**1937**
Siletz Valley #558	**1917**		**1923**
Sunnyridge #898	**1941**		
Taft #575	1919	1928	
Tidewater #621	1923	1925	
Tidewater #810	1933	1971	
Toledo #168	1910	1995	
Waldport #425	1910	1919	
Yachats #422	1910	1914	
Yachats #809	1933	1983	
Yaquina Head #934	1952	1998	

Linn County

Acme #165	1880	1881	
Ash Swale #364	1907	1920	
Banner #165	1874	1876-77	
Banner #387	1909	1912	
Beaver #44	1874	1876-77	
Berlin #814	1934	1940	
Brownsville #20	1873	1876-77	

Calipooia #414	1910	1942
Callamette #543	1916	1981
Center #97	1874	1876-77
Charity #103	1874	2018
Corinthian #8	1873	1877
Crowfoot #314	1902	2007
Diamond Hill #821	1934	1936
Evening Star #924	1948	1956
Fox Valley #374	1907	1919
Grand Prairie #10	1873	1969
Halsey #264	1893	1904
Happy Home #46	1874	1882
Harmony #23	1873	1927
Harrisburg #11	1873	1901
Holley #325	1903	2004
Hope #24	1873	1876-77
Jordan Valley #42	1874	1912
Knox Butte #22	1873	1904
Lacomb #417	1910	1912
Lacomb #824	1935	1936
Lacomb #907	**1945**	
Lake Creek #818	1934	2007
Lebanon #21	1873	1885
Morning Star #311	**1902**	
Oak Plain #6	1873	1929
Orient #58	1874	1876-77
Peoria #116	1874	1880
Peoria #415	1910	1914
Richardsons Gap #783	1931	1940
Riverside #259	1893	1896

Rock Hill #193	1883	1889	
Sand Ridge #57	1874	1941	
Santiam #37	1873	1906	
Santiam Valley #828	**1935**		
Scio #33	1873	1880	
Scio #923	1948	2003	
Shedd #9	1873	1876-77	
Sodaville #85	1874	1885	
Sodaville #313	1902	1906	
South Brownsville #19	1873	1876-77	
Springbank #409	1910	1921	
Sweet Home #381	1908	1920	
Sweet Home #816	1934	1935	
Syracuse #53	1874	1877	
Tangent #7	1873	1920	
Western Star #309	1902	2017	

Malheur County

Arcadia #524	1915	1919	
Arock #755	1930	2012	
Big Bend #386	1908	1916	
Big Bend #686	1927	1951	
Big Bend #946	1964	2003	
Boulevard #389	**1909**		**1925**
Brogan #886	1904	1964	
Chalk Butte #899	1941	1957	
Crescent #547	1916	1919	
El Dorado #817	1934	1968	
Harper Westfall #725	1929	1936	

I. O. N. #837	1935	1942
Jamieson #882	1938	1940
Jordan Valley #896	1940	1953
Juntura #891	1939	1947
Kingman #863	1936	1960
Malheur #170	1874	1876-77
Nyssa #438	1911	1917
Ontario Heights #917	1947	1990
Oregon Slope #713	1928	1973
Oregon Trail #687	1936	2001
Owyhee #437	1911	1919
Park Grove #522	1914	1918
Ridge View #893	1939	1952
Rivers Bend #408	1910	1915
Riverside #895	1940	1942
Ruby #892	1939	1949
Snake River #819	1934	1940
Utopian #390	1909	1912
Vale #696	1928	2023
Wild Rose #807	1933	1941
Willowcreek #879	1914	1983
Willow River #520	1914	1919

Marion County

Abiqua #133	1874	1876-77
Ankeny #540	1915	1968
Aumsville #436	1910	1919
Brooks #349	1904	1912
Butteville #74	1874	1950

Capitol #959	1998	2002
Chehulpan #68	1874	1891
Chemawa #785	1931	1945
Crowfoot #314	1902	2007
Evergreen #512	1914	1917
Fairfield #720	**1929**	
Fairview #141	1874	1876-77
Gervais #140	1874	1876-77
Gervais #375	1908	1915
Hollywood #513	1914	1916
Howell Prairie #80	1874	1892
Hubbard #132	1874	1876-77
Keizer #785	1931	2017
Liberty #292	1899	1901
Lyons #828	1935	
Macleay #293	**1900**	
Monitor #286	1897	1902
Mount Horeb #556	1917	1920
Mount Vernon #134	1874	1876-77
North Howell #274	1895	2014
Red Hill #778	1931	1951
Roberts #829	1935	1962
Rock Point #48	1874	1884
Round Prairie #106	1874	1886
Salem #17	1873	1949
Scotts Mills #791	1931	1933
Scotts Mills #938	**1954**	
Silverton #748	**1930**	
Silverton Hills #743	1929	1966
Stayton #340	1903	2001

Surprise #233	1889	1947
Turner #18	1873	1894
Union #563	1917	1923
Union Hill #728	**1929**	
Woodburn #79	**1874**	
Waldo Hills #275	1895	1898
Waldo Hills #918	1947	1974

Morrow County

Blue Mountain #235	1890	1893
Dry Fork #673	1926	1930
Eight Mile Center #210	1888	1890
Fair View #216	1889	1894
Greenfield #579	**1919**	
Irrigon #641	1924	1942
Irrigon #935	1952	1967
Lena #813	1934	1942
Lexington #726	1929	2018
Rhea Creek #669	1925	1982
South Springs #215	1888	1891
Victory #211	1888	1890

Multnomah County

Achme #166	1874	1880
Columbia #267	**1893**	
Evening Star #27	1873	1976
Fairview #344	1904	1960
Friendly #897	1940	1993
Gresham #270	**1894**	

Lents #352	1905	1996	
Multnomah #71	**1874**	**1910**	**1913**
Parkrose #921	1947	1951	
Peninsula #307	1901	1903	
Pleasant Valley #348	**1904**		
Powell's Valley #84	1874	1887	
Rockwood #323	**1902**		
Russellville #353	**1905**		
Sauvies Island #143	1874	1876-77	
Sauvies Island #840	**1935**		
Skyline #894	**1940**		
St. Johns Comm #950	1990	2009	
Troutdale #951	1990	1998	
Western Star #145	1874	1898	
Willamette #119	1874	1876-77	
Woodlawn #350	1904	1919	

Polk County

Ballston #249	1890	1892
Brush College #586	1920	1989
Buell #637	**1924**	
Buena Vista #4	1873	1876-77
Buena Vista #628	1924	1928
Dallas #39	1873	1876-77
Dallas #61	1874	1890
Dallas #247	1890	1904
Dallas #358	1906	1910
Dallas #769	1930	1940
Falls City #847	1936	1948

Garretson #60	1874	1876-77
Highland #287	1897	1904
McCoy #465	1911	1919
McCoy #634	1924	1937
Mill Creek #91	1874	1894
Monmouth #5	1873	1876-77
Monmouth #258	1893	1904
Monmouth #288	1898	1900
Monmouth #476	1911	1972
Mono #25	1873	1920
Oak Grove #198	**1885**	
Oak Point #3	1873	1885
Oak View #226	1889	1892
Perrydale #30	1873	1876-77
Pleasant Valley #201	1885	1891
Rickreall #671	**1926**	
Riverside #493	1913	1915
Salt Creek #197	1885	1905
Spring Valley #62	1874	1889
Spring Valley #464	1911	1914
Sunnyside #312	1902	1905
Suver #253	1891	1904
Suver #633	1924	1933
West Salem #885	1938	1955

Sherman County

Bigelow Springs #208	1888	1895
Bigelow #454	1911	1916
Harland View #682	1926	1979

Kent #688	1927	1951	
Klondike #689	1927	1951	
Locust Grove #505	1914	1917	
Rufus #506	1914	1916	
Rufus #826	1935	2006	
Shearer #676	1926	1934	
Sherman #237	1890	1986	
Wheat #227	1889	1894	

Tillamook County

Bay View #280	1896	1899	
Beaver #400	1909	1912	
Cloverdale #355	1905	1967	
Fairview #273	**1895**	**2011**	**2013**
Fidelity #174	1874	1876-77	
Kilichis #800	1932	2003	
Miami Cove #909	1945	1995	
Nestucca #503	1913	2001	
Oretown #354	1905	2001	
Pleasant Valley #537	1915	2007	
Sandlake #546	**1916**		**1936**
South Prairie #281	1896	1901	
South Prairie #808	1933	1984	
White Clover #279	1896	1927	
White Clover #784	**1931**		

Umatilla County

Alta #96	1874	1876-77	
Butter Creek #184	1875		

Camas Prairie #668	1925	1946
Cold Spring #213	1888	1895
Cold Spring #801	1932	2006
Columbia #577	1919	1920
Columbia #867	**1936**	
Cottonwood #245	1890	1892
Echo #798	1932	1941
Eureka #214	1888	1891
Ferndale #441	1911	1914
Fork City #681	1926	1935
Fruitvale #335	1903	1905
Fruitvale #658	1925	1951
Helix #223	1889	1948
Hermiston #576	1919	1920
Holdman #692	1927	1935
Hudson Bay #361	1906	1981
Juniper #212	1888	1892
Meadowville #94	1874	1876-77
Midway #95	1874	1876-77
Milton #29	1873	1878
Myrick #753	1930	1968
Pendleton #93	1874	1876-77
Stanfield #502	1913	1916
Stanfield #657	1925	2017
State Line #693	1928	2005
Tillacum #799	1932	2005
Tum-a-Tum #343	1904	1909
Umatilla #609	1923	1926
Union #244	1890	1892
Vansycle #221	1889	1889

Vansycle #703	1928	1935	
Walla Walla River #342	1903	1906	
Westland #827	1935	1962	
Weston #34	1873	1876-77	
Weston #246	1890	1892	
Weston Mountain #670	1926	1938	
Wild Horse #35	1873	1876-77	
Wild Horse #797	1932	1979	
White Eagle #683	**1927**		
White Owl #798	1932	1941	

Union County

Blue Mountain #345	1904	1991	
Catherine Creek #841	1935	1964	
Cove #128	1874	1876-77	
Cricket Flat #606	1922	1971	
Crystal #347	1904	1911	
Fair View #131	1874	1876-77	
Fort Union #952	**1993**		
Ladd Canyon #695	1928	1931	
LaGrande #127	1874	1880	
Meadowbrook #680	1926	1929	
Medical Springs #427	1910	2001	
Mt. Fannie #388	1909	2005	
Pleasant Grove #475	**1911**		**2006**
Riverside #406	1910	1916	
Rockwall #679	**1926**		**2009**
Summerville #130	1874	1876-77	
Telocaset #578	1919	1929	

Union #129	1874	1876-77	
Union #647	1924	1927	
Wolf Creek #596	**1921**		

Wallowa County

Alder Slope #645	1924	1941	
Eden #832	1935	1943	
Flora #419	1910	1913	
Flora #649	1924	1927	
Grouse Flat #929	1949	1950	
Hurricane Creek #608	**1923**		
Imnaha #677	1926	2006	
Liberty #613	**1923**		
North End #820	**1934**		
Paradise #421	1910	1912	
Pine Grove #644	1924	1945	
Pioneer #401	1909	1914	
Promise #601	1922	1963	
South Fork #605	**1922**		
Trout Creek #610	1923	1942	
Wallowa #603	1922	1931	
Wallowa #881	1938	2003	

Wasco County

Antelope #723	1929	1932	
Barlow Gate #157	**1874**		**1928**
Chenowith #591	1920	2008	
Cherry Park #667	**1925**		**2004**
Douglas Hollow #222	1889	1893	

Eight Mile #587	1920	1950	
Endeavor #380	1908	1911	
Fairfield #219	1889	1891	
Farmers #231	1889	1890	
Frankton #357	1905	1912	
Friend #597	1921	1940	
Grass Valley #229	1889	1894	
Harmony #254	1891	1893	
Highland #206	1888	1896	
Liberty #218	1889	1891	
Lone Pine #752	1930	1976	
Lone Star #160	1874	1879	
Lower Calipooia #445	1911	1922	
Milbrae #228	1889	1900	
Mill Creek #590	1920	2001	
Mosier #234	**1889**		**1930**
Mt. Hood #220	1889	1894	
Mt. Hood #369	1907	1912	
Mountain View #366	1907	1910	
Nasene #230	1889	1890	
Ocheco #159	1874	1876-77	
Odell #368	1907	1909	
Olalla #367	1907	1908	
Pinecrest #504	1913	1931	
Prineville #158	1874	1876-77	
Ramsey Park #352	**1905**		
Shady Brook #654	1925	1934	
Summit #232	1889	1896	
Three Mile #588	1920	1929	
Tywaser #363	1907	1915	

Wapanitia #189	1877	1878
Wasco #38	1873	1876-77
Wasco #207	1888	1896

Washington County

Aloha #773	**1931**	
Banks #625	1924	1931
Beaverton #100	1874	1885
Beaverton #324	1902	1999
Bethany #418	1910	1920
Butte #148	1874	1927
Cornelius #63	1874	1876-77
Columbia #89	1874	1876-77
Dixie Mountain #860	**1936**	
Fanno Creek #962	2000	2002
Farmington #110	1874	1888
Fidelity #283	1896	1904
Forest Grove #67	1874	1876-77
Forest Grove #282	**1896**	
Gales #282	1896	
Green Mountain #295	1901	1943
Greenville #49	1874	1876-77
Hillsboro #73	**1874**	
Kinton #582	**1917**	
Leedy #339	**1903**	
Lewis and Clark #328	1903	1910
Phoenix #202	1887	1876-77
Phoenix #285	1897	1899
Riverside #526	1915	1950

Rock Creek #481	1912	1914
Rock Creek #795	1931	1936
Scholls #338	**1903**	
Sherwood #272	1895	2007
Sunset #941	1958	2003
Tigard #148	**1874**	
Wapato #90	1874	1885
Wapato #490	1912	1916
Washington #99	1874	1885
Washington #313	**1902**	
West Union #72	1874	1885
Winona #271	**1895**	

Wheeler County

Clarno #674	1926	2002
Lost Valley #554	1916	1922
Mitchell #737	1929	1931
Service Creek #675	1926	1933
Spray #568	1914	1954
Spray #940	**1954**	
Twickenham #574	1918	1922
Twickenham #733	1929	1933
Winlock #497	1913	1935

Yamhill County

Amity #102	1874	1889
Carleton #391	1909	1949
Chehalem #92	1874	1876-77
Chehalem Center #780	1931	1962

Cove Orchard #545	1916	1977	
Dayton #330	1903	1909	
Fernwood #770	**1930**	**2016**	**2019**
Fort Hill #639	1924	1977	
Hopewell #910	1945	1946	
Lafayette #32	1873	1880	
McMinnville #31	**1873**		
Moores Valley #362	1907	1930	
Newberg #331	1903	1905	
North Yamhill #33	1873	1880	
North Yamhill #393	1909	1920	
Sheridan #98	1874	1876-77	
Sheridan #394	1909	1913	
Sheridan #595	1921	1945	
Sunny Crest #642	1924	1937	
Unionvale #407	1910	1918	
Unity #112	1874	1876-77	
Unity-Dundee #920	1947	1949	
Walnut #455	1911	1914	
Webfoot #718	1929	1962	
West Chehalem #125	1874	1876-77	
Wheatland #872	1939	1962	
Whitson #511	1914	1933	
Willamette #105	1874	1876-77	
Willamina #199	1885	1887	
Willamina #639	1924	1977	
Yamhill #545	1916	1977	
Yamhill #956	1993	1993	

ABOUT THE AUTHOR

Marilyn is a 65+-year Grange member. She joined the Junior Grange the week of her fifth birthday, held most offices, and entered contests ranging from canning to public speaking. When she joined the adult organization, members elected her Lecturer. She loved planning programs for 24 meetings a year. Then work moved her out of state to teach speech, represent an educational publisher, and write training manuals and online help for software companies. When she retired and returned to Oregon, she immediately had a calendar filled with activities. She is a life member of North Bayside Grange and President of Winona in Tualatin.

Made in United States
Troutdale, OR
07/31/2024

21675319R00206